ENGLISH-ARABIC
ARABIC-ENGLISH
CONCISE ROMANIZED DICTIONARY

For the Spoken Arabic of Egypt and Syria

THE EDITORS OF HIPPOCRENE BOOKS

DI053748

HIPPOCRENE BOOKS, INC.
New York

Fourth printing, 2001.
Copyright© 1999 Hippocrene Books.
This dictionary is based on the *English-Arabic
Conversational Dictionary* by Richard Jaschke.

For information, address:
HIPPOCRENE BOOKS, INC.
171 Madison Avenue
New York, NY 10016

ISBN 0-7818-0686-0

Printed in the United States of America.

CONTENTS

PRONUNCIATION GUIDE

The Vowels

a	short *a* like in English *fat*
â	long *a* like in English *far*
ai	like in English *aisle*, or *y* in *my*
au	like *ou* in *out*
e	short *e* like in English *end*; the final *e* is not silent, but pronounced as the *e* in English *tenement*
ê	long like in the *a* in English *fame*
i	short *i* as in English *till*
î	long *i* like in English *fatigue*
o	short *o* like in English *not*
ô	long *o* like in English *no*
u	short *u* like in English *full*
û	long *u* like in English *moon*

The Consonants

b	like in English *ball*
d	like in English *day*
D	an emphatic *d* formed by placing the tongue against the lower palate instead of against the teeth
f	like in English *fire*

g	like in English *gift*
h	like in English *house*
H	an emphatic *h* pronounced with a strong expulsion of air from the chest
j	like in English *just*
k	like in English *key*
kh	like the guttural *ch* in the Scottish pronunciation of *loch* but more from the throat
l	like in English *lily*
m	like in English *mat*
n	like in English *noon*
q	*k*-sound produced in the throat somewhat behind the *c* in English *cool*. **In the greater part of Syria and in some parts of Egypt, as in Cairo, it is silent at the beginning of the word.** In the middle of a word, it appears as a pause, or as a strong breathing.
r	rolled *r*
R	an exaggerated gargling, uvular *u*-sound formed by pressing the tongue against the lower palate
s	like in English *seven*
S	emphatic *s*-sound formed by placing the tongue against the lower palate instead of against the teeth
t	like in English *today*

T	emphatic *t*-sound formed by placing the tongue against the lower palate instead of against the teeth
w	like in English *will*
y	like in English *year*
z	like in English *zeal*
'	a very strong guttural sound produced by compression of the throat and expulsion of the breath
,	shows the place where a slight pause must be made, or where at least the word must be suddenly interrupted

Each letter must be distinctly sounded, for example the *th* in 'istHi' as *t-h*, not as the *th* in 'mathematics.' Exceptions to this rule are *kh* and *sh*, because they represent one letter/sound only.

ABBREVIATIONS

acc.	accusative
adj.	adjective
adv.	adverb
anat.	anatomic
coll.	collective noun
conj.	conjunction
def.	definite
Egyp.	Egyptian Arabic
f.	feminine
geogr.	geographic
imp.	imperative
indic.	indicative
intrans.	intransitive
lit.	literally
loc.	local
m.	masculine
med.	medical
mot.	motoring
mus.	music
n.	noun
pl.	plural
prep.	preposition
pron.	pronoun
rel.	religious
s.b.	somebody
s.th.	something

sg.	singular
subj.	subject
suff.	suffix
Syr.	Syrian Arabic
trans.	transitive verb
v.	verb

ENGLISH-ARABIC DICTIONARY

Both the Syrian and Egyptian dialects are given, the latter in italics. Where there is no Arabic in italics or the entry is not identified, the Syrian and Egyptian are alike.

A

a.m. qabl iD-Duhr

abdomen baTn

ability ahlîyi *ahlîya*

able ahl la … *ahl li…*; qâdir la … *qâdir li …*

ablution wuDû' *tawaDDi;* **to perform religious ~s** twaDDa *itwaDDa*

abolish abTal

about (around) Hawalai' *Hawâli;* (near to) taqrîban, takhmîn, Haraki (the latter Syr. only); (concerning) bi-khuSûS; **~ ten pieces** Harakit 'ashra qiTa' *yîgi 'ashara qiTa'*

above fauq *fôk,* fauq min fôk *min;* **~ all** qabl il-kull; **from ~** min fauk *min fôk*

abroad fî blâd ajnabîyi *fî bilâd barra*

absence Raibi *Rêba;* **during my ~** b-Raibti *bi-Rêbeti, fî Riyâbi*

absent (adj.) Râyib *Râ'ib;* **to ~ oneself from** ibta'ad 'an *itbâ'ad 'an*

abundance ziyâdi *ziyâda*

7

abundant zâyid *zâ'id*
abuse (v.) shatam
academy kulliyi *kulliya*
accelerate asra'
accent lafZi *lafZa*
accept qibil
accident Hâdis
accompany râfaq *rafaq*
according b-maujib *bi-mûgib*, Hasab
account Hisâb
accusation tuhma pl. tuham
accuse s.b. taham
accustomed - **to get ~ to** t'auwad 'ala *it'awad 'ala*
ache (n.) waja' *waga'*, (v.) wiji' *wigi'*; **my head ~s**
      râsi byûja'ni *râsi btûga'ni*
acid HâmiD
acknowledge i'taraf; **~ment** i'tirâf
acre feddân
action 'amal pl. a'mâl
adapter wuSla muhaaya'a
add jama' *gama'*
addition - **in ~ to this** fauq haida, Rair zâlik *Rêr zâlik*
address 'unwân
adjust sauwa
administration idâre *idâra*
admission fee dukhûlîyi *temen id-dukhûl*
adorn zaiyan *zaiyin*
adult kabîr *kibîr*

advantage fâida
advertisement i'lân
advice mashwara
advise shâwar *shâwir*
affair amr pl. 'umûr
afraid khâyif *khâ'if*; **to be ~ of** khâf min; **I am ~ we
     will be late** bkhâf nit'akh'khar *bakhâf
     nit'akh'khar*
Africa afriqya, ifriqya
after (time) ba'd; (behind) khalf, khalf min, wara
     (with pron. suff. waraa-); (according to)
     bi-Hasb b-maujib *bi-mûjib*
afternoon ba'd iD-Duhr *ba'd iD-Duhr*
afterwards ba'dên
again 'ad, tâni marra *tâni marra*
against Didd, 'ala
age (of human beings) 'umr; (century, generation) jîl
     gîl pl. ijyâl *igyâl*
agency wakâle *wikâla*
agent wakîl pl. wukala
ago qabl; **long ~** qabl min zamân *qabla min zemân*
agree on s.th. ittafaq 'ala
agriculture zarâ'a
aid (n.) musâ'ada
air base qâ'ide jauwiye *qâ'ida gauwiya*
air-conditioning mukayif hawâ', takyîf
air hawa; **take a breath of fresh ~** shamm il-hawa
airmail barîd jauwi *barîd gauwi*

airplane Taiyâra *Tâ'ira*
airport maTâr
alarm indâr
alcohol alkuhûl
Aleppo Halab
Alexandria iskindiriya
alike mutashâbih *mutshâbeh*
alive Hai, Taiyib
all kull, jamî' *gamî'*; (everything) il-kull, kullo
allergic Hassâsi
allergy Hassâsiye *Hassâsiya*
allow samaH; ~ **me** ismaH-li; **~ed** jâyiz *gâ'iz*
almond lauz *lôz*
almost illa qalîl *illa shuwwaiye*
alms iHsân
alone wâHid; **I ~, you (m.) ~** waHdi, waHdak, etc.;
       leave me ~ khallîni
alphabet abjadiya *abgadiya*
also kazâlik *kazâlik*, kamân *kemân*, *bard*
alter Raiyar, baddal *baddil*
although wa'in *win, wen*; **~ it is very difficult for**
       me ma' inno Sa'b ktîr 'alai'yi *ma' inno Sa'b*
       ketîr 'alêye
altitude irtifa'
altogether sawa
always dâyman *dâ'iman*
ambassador safîr
amber kahrubâ *kahramân*

ambulance sayyârit il-is'âf
American amrîkâni
amiable laTîf
ammunition zakhîra *mûnet 'askar*
among bain *bên*
amount mablaR pl. mbâliR *mebâliR*
amulet Hirz *taHwîTa*
anchor Hadîd
ancient qadîm pl. qudm
and wa, wi
anesthetic binj *bing*
angel malak *melek* pl. mlâyiki *melâ'ika*
anger RaDab
angle zâwiyi *zâwya*
angry (with s.b.) zilân min, zilân 'ala *za'lân min,*
            za'lân 'ala
animal Haiwân *Hêwân* pl. Haiwânât *Hewânât*; **wild**
            ~ waHsh pl. wuHûsh
ankle ka'b pl. k'âb; **I have sprained my** ~
            infa'kashit ijri *itfa'raket rigli*
annihilate 'adam
announce a'lan
annoy kaddar
annoyed zilân *za'lân*
another âkhar f. ukhra pl. ukhar; Rair *Rêr*
answer jawâb *gawâb* pl. ijwibi *agwiba;*
            (v.) jawâb *gâwib*, radd jawâb *raddê*
            gawâb

anterior muqaddam, auwal

anthem nashîd; **national ~** nashîd waTani

antibiotics antibiyôtîk

antiquities antîkât

ant(s) (coll.) naml

any aHad, Hada *Hadd*

anything ashma kân *ayy Hâga*

apostle rasûl pl. rusul

appear - it ~s mbaiyin haik *il-bai'yin kide*

appendix (anat.) zâyida dûdiya zâ'ida dôdiya; (of a
           book) zail *dêl*

appetite qâblî'yi *nafs shahîya*; **I have no ~** mâ-li
           qâblî'yi *mâ-lish nafs*

appetizer muqabbil *mushahi*

apple(s) (coll.) tiffâH

application Talab

apply (ask) Talab

appointment (time and place) mî'âd; (assignment)
           ta'yîn; (command) amr

approach (to draw near) qarrab; (imp.) qarriib *qarrab*

approval istiHsân *istiSwâb*

approve istaHsan *istaHsin*, istaSwab

apricot(s) (coll.) mishmish

April nisân *abrîl*

apron fûTa, wazri maryula

Arab 'arabi pl. 'arab

Arabic 'arabi; **what is this called in ~?** shû ism
           haida bil-'arabi? *ismo ê bil 'arabi?*

arch qanTara pl. qanâTir
architect muhandis
area mintaqa *mantiqa*
argue iHtajj *iHtagg*; **I cannot ~ with you** mâ aqder
    ahâjjak *mâ aqder ahâggek*
arm îd pl. iyâdi *eyâdi*
armpit bâT *ibâT*
army 'asker pl. 'asâkir; jaish *gêsh* pl. juyûsh *giyûsh*
around Hawalai *Hauwalê*
arrange rattab *rattib*
arrest (n.) Habs; (v.) waqqaf
arrival wuSûl
arrive wiSil
arrogant mutekabbir *mutkabber*
arrow sahm
art fann pl. fnûn *funûn*; (skill) San'a
artichoke arDeshôke *kharshûf*
artificial maSnû'
artisan Sanâ'i pl. Sanâ'iyi *Sanâ'iye*
artist fannân pl. fannânîn
as (like, similar) mitl *zai*; (since) Hais *Hês*, b-Hais
    bi-Hês; **~ big, ~ much as as** qadd, bit-
    tamâm; **~ far as** la-Hadd *li-Hadd*; **~ for**
    min yamm, min jihit *min gihet*; **~ if** ka-in
    ke-in; **~ long as** mâ dâm; **~ soon ~** auwil'ma
    Hâlan (Syr. only)
ascend Tili'
ashamed - to be ~ istaHa; **be ~!** istHi! *istaHi!*

ashes rimâd

ashtray manfaDa *Taffâya*

Asia âsiya

ask sa'al; ~ **for** sa'al 'an *sa'al'ala*; (demand) Talab;
　　　how **much do you ~ for it?** kaddaish
　　　baddak fî haida? *kâm terîd 'ala shân di?*;
　　　you ~ too much biTlub zyâdi *betiTlub
　　　ziyâde*

asleep nayim *na'im*; **to fall ~** Rifi

aspect manzar pl. menâzir

assist sâ'ad *sâ'id*

asthma dâ rabwi

astonished - to be ~ t'ajjab *it'aggib*

Aswan aswân

asylum malja' *malga'*

at (in) fî; (near, by) 'ind *'and*; (with) ma', ma'a;
　　　~ **home** fil-bait *fil-bêt*; ~ **three o'clock**
　　　is-sâ'a tlâti *is-sâ'a telâte*; ~ **once** Hâlan

atmosphere falak *felek, gau*

atomic bomb qunbulat zarriyat *qunbula zarriya*

atonement kaffâra

attack - to ~ s.b. hajam 'ala *hagam 'ala*

attention intibâH; **to pay ~ to** dâr bâlo 'ala *khalla
　　　bâlo 'ala*

attentive mitnabbih, muntabih

attest (v.) Saddaq 'ala

auction mazâd

August âb *aRosstos*

aunt (on the father's side) 'ammi *'amma*; (on the
      mother's side) khâli *khâla*
author mu'allif
authorities hukûmi, hkûmi *hukûma*
autumn kharîf
aversion kirha
awake (adj.) fâ'iq
awkward simij *Ralîz*

B

baby raDî' pl. raDâ'i
bachelor a'zab *'âzib*
back (part of the body) Dahr; **to come, go ~** riji' *rigi'*
backgammon Taula
backside kafal
backwards la-wara *li-wara*, la-khalf *li-khalf*
bacteria jurtûma *gurtûma* pl. jarâtim *garâtim*
bad radi pl. irdyi *ardiye*
bag shanTa pl. shonaT
baggage amti'a
bail - one who stands ~ kafîl *kefîl*, Dâmin
baker khibbâz *khabbâz*
balance mîzân
balcony mamsha, balkûn *balakôn*
bald 'azlaT f. zalTa
ball kura *kora*
banana(s) (coll.) mauz *môz*

band (ribbon) shirîT *sherîT*; (of musicians) naubi *nôbe*
bandage Dimâdi *Dimâda*
bank bank pl. bunûk
bankrupt miflis *mufellis*
bar bâr
barber Hillâq *Hallâq*
barefoot Hâfi, Hifyân (the latter Syr. only)
bargain (n.) musâwama; (v.) sâwama
bark (v.) 'awa
barley sha'îr
barn ambar *shûne*
barrel barmîl pl. barâmîl
basket selli *salla* pl. silâl
bath Hammâm, Himmâm (the latter Syr. only); **~tub** Haud *HôD*
bathe (take a bath) tRassal *itRassal*, tHammam *istaHamma*
battle qitâl
bay jûn *gûn*
be kân; **how are you** (m.)? kîf Hâlak? *ezaiyak?*
beach shâTi
beak minqar
beam (of light) shi'a pl. ashi'a
bean (French ~s) lûbyi *lûbyia*; (haricot ~s) faSûlya; (dry broad ~s) fûl
bear (suffer, stand) iHtamal
bear dubb
beard daqn, liHyi *liHya*

beast waHsh pl. wuHûsh

beat Darab

beautiful kwaiyis *kuwaiyis* jamîl *gamîl*

beauty jamâl *gamâl*

because la'in *li'in*, b-Hais *bi-Hês*

become Sâr

bed farshi *serîr*, **to go to ~** nâm

Bedouin badawi *bedawi* pl. badu

beef laHm baqar

beer bîra

bee(s) (coll.) naHl

beetle jîz *gîz*, khunfusa pl. khanâfis

beets shmandar, shamandar *bangar*

before (of place) quddâm; (of time) qabl, min qabl;
        (conj.) min qabl, qabl mâ *qable mâ*

beg shaHad *shaHat*

beggar shiH'Hâd *shaH'Hât*, sâ'il

begin (intrans.) ibtada

behave salak

behavior taSarruf

behind (prep.) wara min, khalf min; (adv.) min wara,
        min khalf

belief îmân; (opinion) Zann, fikr

believe Saddaq; (think, suppose) Zann, iftakar; (in
        God, etc.) âman bi…; **~ me** Saddiqni
        Saddakni

bell jaras *garas*; **ring the ~!** duqq il-jaras! *duqq
        il-garas!*

belly baTn

belong khaSS; generally expressed by the prep. la *li*
       only; **this ~s to me** haida ili

below taHt

bend (trans.) lawa

benefit (profit) naf'

benevolent khaiyir

beside jamb *gamb*

best il-aHsan

bet (n.) rahn; (v.) râhan

better aHsan, aHsin (the latter Syr. only)

between bain *bên*

beverage sharâb pl. sharbât

beyond fauq *fôq*

bible ktâb il-mqaddas *kitâb il-muqaddas*

bicycle darrâje *'agala*

big kebîr

bilingual bi-luRatên

bill Hsâb *Hisâb*

bind (tie) rabaT

bird Tair *Têr* pl. Tiyûr, Tyûr (the latter Syr. only)

birth mîlâd

birthday 'îd mîlâd; ~ **party** Haflit 'îd mîlâd

bit - a little ~ shwaiyi *shuwaiye*; ~ **by** ~ bit-tâbi' *bi-*
       tadrîg

bite (of insects) 'add

bitter murr

black aswad *iswid* f. sauda *sôda*; ~ **market** sûq sauda
       sûq sôda

18

bladder masâni *mesâna*

blade (of a knife) naSli *naSla* pl. niSâl

blame (n.) laum *lôm*; (v.) lâm

blanket Hirâm, Hrâm pl. aHrima

blasphemy kufr

blaze laHîb

bleed - **it is ~ing** Tili' id-damm *kharr id-damm*

bless bârak *bârik*; **God ~ you** allah ybârik fîk *allah
          yebârik fîk*

blessed mubârak, mabrûk

blind a'ma pl. 'imyân, *'imi*

blister baqbûqa *buqbêqa*

blond ashqar f. shaqra pl. shuqr

blood damm; **~ money** diyi *diya*; **~ transfusion** naql
          damm

blow (a stroke) Darb *Darba*

blow - **~ one's nose** tmakh'khaT *itmakh'khaT*; **~ up a
          photo** takbîr sûra

blue azraq f. zarqa pl. zurq

blunt tilfân *talfân*, *mutallim*

blush iHmarr

boar khanzîr berri, Hallûf

boat qârib; **~man** falayki

body beden, jism *gism*

bog na'S *baTîHa*

boil (trans.) salaq; **~ed** maslûq; (intrans.) Rili

bold jasûr *gasûr*, shaji' *shagi'*

bolt (door) daqqâra

bomb qunbula pl. qanâbîl

bone 'aDm pl. 'iDam
book ktâb *kitâb* pl. kutb *kutub*; **~seller** kutubi, kutbi;
     ~store maktabi *maktaba*
boot Hizâ' 'âlî sâq pl. aHzîya 'âlî sâq
border Hadd pl. Hudûd
bored of zi'lân min *za'lân min*
born maulûd
borrow from ista'âr min
both ittnain *il-etnên*
bother 'azâb
bottle qannîni *qizâza* pl. qanâni *qizâzât*
bottom (foundation, basis) asâs
bowl sulTâniyi *sulTâniye*
box 'ulbi *'ilba* pl. 'ulab *'ilab*
boy walad pl. ûlâd
boycott muqâTa'a
bracelet suwâri *iswîra* pl. asâwîr
braces Hammâl pl. Hammâlât
brain dimâr *mukh'kh*
brake farmala
bran nakhâli *nakhale*
branch (a big one) 'imd *far'*; (a thin one) shilH *RuSn*
brass nuHâs aSfar
brave shaji' *shagi'*
breach (opening) khurq
bread khubz *êsh*
breadth 'ard *'urd*
break (v.) kasar, kassar

breakfast fuTûr
breast Sidr
breath nafas *nefes*; **~ing** tanaffus
bribe (n.) bartTîl, rishwi *rashwa*; (v.) barTal; **to
            receive a ~** tabarTal
brick kirmîd
bride 'arûsa pl. 'arâyis *'arâ'is*
bridegroom 'arîs pl. 'irsân
bridge jisr *qanTara* pl. jusur *qanâTir*, *kubri*
bright (shining) lamî' *naiyir*
bring jâb *gâb*; **to ~ in** fauwaT *dakh'khal*; **to ~ out**
            Taila', Talla'
broad 'arîd
broadcast izâ'a
broken maksûr
broker samsâr *simsâr* pl. semasra *samasra*
bronze nuHâs aSfar *naHâs aSfar*
brook moi *moiye*
broom miknsi *maknasa*
broth marqit laHm *maraqat laHm*
brother akh pl. ikhwi *ikhwe*, ikhwân; **~-in-law** Sihr
            pl. aShâr
brown (of the human complexion) asmar (f.) samra
bruise (n.) raDDa
brush firshâyi *furshe*
bucket saTl
buckle (n.) bukli pl. bukal *abzîm* pl. *abâzîm*
buffalo jamûs *gâmûs* pl. jawâmîs *gawâmîs*

bug(s) (coll.) baqq

build 'ammar *bana*

building 'amâr pl. 'amârât, bina *bine, bunya* pl. ibnyi
abniye

bull taur *tôr* pl. tîrân

bulletin board lauH i'lânât *lôh i'lânât*

bunch (of grapes, etc.) 'anqûd; (of flowers) bâqa

burden Himl

burdensome tqîl *teqîl*

burglar sâriq

burn (trans.) Haraq; (intrans.) sha'al *wala'*; (become
consumed by fire) iHtaraq *itHaraq*

burst (intrans.) infazar, faqa'

bury dafan

bus buS *ôtôbîs*; ~ **station** maHaTTet buSât
maHaTTat ôtôbîs; ~ **stop** mauqef buSât
mauqef otobîs

bush 'ullaiqa *'ullêqa*

business shuRl pl. ishRâl; **how is ~?** kîf il-ishRâl?
ezai il-ishRâl?; **that is my ~** haida kâri *di
maSlaHti*; **you have no ~ here** mâ ilak
shuRl haun *mâlak shuRl hene*

busy mashRûl

but amma, *lâkin*, lâken (the latter Syr. only); (except)
illa, Rair *Rêr*; (only) bass *bess*

butcher liH'Hâm *laH'Hâm*

butter zibdi *zibde*

butterfly(ies) (coll.) farâsh

button zirr *zurâr* pl. zrâr
buy (v.) ishtara
by (near) 'ind *'and*, jamb *gamb*; (through) bi, min,
  bi-wâsTa; ~ **God** wallâh *wallâhi*; ~ **your life**
  wiHyâak *waHyâtak*

C

cab taksi
cabbage malfûf *korumb*
cabinet (furniture) dûlâb pl. dawalîb
cable silk
cactus Subbair *Subbêr*, *Sabbâra*
café qahwi *qahwa* pl. qahâwi
cage qafas
Cairo il-qâhira, maSr
cake tôrta *ka'ka*
calamity balîyi *belîye*
calculate Hasab, Hâsab *Hâsib*
calculation Hsâb *Hisâb*
calendar taqwîm *natîga*
calf (animal) 'ijl *'igl*; (of the leg) baTTa *sammâna*
call (v.) ittaSSal; **what is this ~ed** in Arabic? kîf
    bîsammûh di bil-'arabi? shû ismo haida
    bil-'arabi? *ismê di bil-'arabi ê?*
call - phone ~ (n.) mukâlame tilîfûniye *mukâlama*
    tilîfûniya
calm (n.) hudû

camel jamal *gamal* pl. jimâl *gimâl*; ~ **driver** jammâl
      gammâl
camera kamîra
camp mkhayyam *mukhayyam*
can (n.) 'ulbi *'ilba* pl. 'ulab *'ilab*, ~ **opener** fataHat
      'ulab *fataHat 'ilab*
can (v.) qidir; **I cannot** mâ byimkinni *mâ yimkinîsh*
canal qanâ', tir'a
cancel alRa
cancer saraTân
candle sham'a
cane qaSab
cannon madfa' *medfa'* pl. mdâfi' *medâfi'*
cap Tâqiye *Tâqiya*
cape râs
caper ûbâr, qubbâr
capital (town) 'âSimi *'âSima*; (money) rismâl *rasmâl*
captain qubTân
captive yasîr pl. yusara
car sayyâra *'arabiya*
caravan karwân *qâfila*
card waraqi *waraqe*
care - **to take ~ of** dâr il-bâl 'ala *khalla il-bâl 'ala*;
      take ~! dîr bâlak! *khalli bâlak!*, û'a!,
      twaqqa! *itwaqqa!*; (threatening) îyâk!; **~ful**
      mutnabbih
cargo shuHna
carpenter nijjâr *naggâr*

carpet sijjâdi *saggâda*
carriage 'arabâyi *'arabiya*
carrier 'ittâl *shaiyâl*
carrot(s) (coll.) jazar *gazar*
carry Hamal
cart karra *karro*
case (cause in court) da'wa pl. da'âwi; (state, condition) Hâl pl. aHwâl
cash kâsh
castle (fortress) qal'a; (palace) sarâya
cat quTT
catalogue qâ'ime, fihrist
cataract shillâl *shallâl*
catch misik; **~ a disease** in'ada *misik maraD*
caterpillar dûd
Catholic kâtûlîki pl. kwâtli *katâlka*
cauliflower qarnabîT
cause (n.) sabab pl. asbâb; (v.) sabbab
cautious mutnabbih
cave (cavern) maRâra pl. maRâyir
cease (v.) inqata'
cedar arzi *erza* pl. arz *erz*
ceiling saqf *suqf*
celebrate iHtafal
celebration iHtifâl; (of marriage) faraH
celery krafs *karafs*
cellar qabu *qabwa*
cemetery tirbi *turba*, *maqbara* pl. *maqâbir*

censorship murâqaba

center waSt *wuSt*, markaz *merkaz* pl. marâkiz
      merâkiz

century qarn pl. qurûn

certain (sure) mu'akkad, akîd *ekîd*; (designated,
      fixed) mu'aiyan, muqaddar

certainly bala shakk, SaHîH, mu'akkad, akîd, halbatt

certificate shihâdi *shihâda* pl. shihâdât

certify Saddaq 'ala

chain silsila

chair kursi pl. krâsi *karâsi*

chance Sudfi *Sudfa*; **by ~** biS-Sudfi *biS-Sudfa*

change (alteration, n.) tiRyîr *taRyîr*; (small money)
      fakka; (v.) Raiyar, baddal *baddil*

changeable mutRaiyir

chapel zâwyi *zâwiya*

charity iHsân

chase (to drive away) dash'shar *Tarad*

chaste 'afîf

chat (v.) tHâdas *itHâdit*

cheap rakhîS *rikhîS*

cheat (n.) Rish'sh; (v.) Rash'sh

check shêk

cheek khadd pl. khudûd

cheese jibn *gibn*

chess shaTranj *shaTrang*

chest (large box) Sandûq pl. Sanâdîq

chest (part of the body) Sidr

chestnut kastani *abu farwe*
chew 'alak *madaG*
chicken farrûj *farrûg* pl. frârîj *farârîg*
chickpea(s) (coll.) HummuS
chief ra'îs
child walad pl. ûlâd; (small ~) Tifl pl. aTfâl
chin daqn
choice ikhtiyâr
cholera hawa il-aSfar
choose ikhtâr
Christian naSrâni pl. naSâra; mesîHi
Christmas 'îd il-mîlâd
church knîsi *kenîsa* pl. knâyis *kenâyis*
cigarette sigâra pl. sagâ'ir
cinnamon qurfi *qirfa*
circle dâyri *dâ'ira* pl. dawâyir *dawâ'ir*
circumcise Tah'har, khatan
circumcision khiTân, tiThîr *taThîr*, Tuhûr
circumstance Hâl, zarf pl. zrûf *zurûf*
cistern maSna' *Sahrîg*
citadel qal'a
citizen muwâTin
city medîna pl. mudun
civil war Harb ahliye *Harb ahliya*
claim (n.) da'wa, iddi'â; (v.) idda'
class (social) Tabaqa; (school) Saff pl. Sufûf
clean (adj.) naDîf pl. nDîf. (v.) naDDaf
clear Sâfi; (indisputable, distinct) wâDiH, zâhir

clerk kâtib *mistakhdim*

clever mâhir, Hâziq, shâTir

climate manâkh *hawa*

climb Tili'

clipped (cut off) maqSûS, maHlûq

clock sâ'a

close (near to) qarîb min, jamb min *gamb min*;
         (shut, v.) Ralaq; (finish) khatam

cloth nasîj *nasîg* qumâsh

clothes libs pl. libâs kiswi *kiswa*

cloud Raim *Rêm* pl. Ryûm *Riyûm*

clove qurunful

clumsy Rashîm pl. Rushm

coach 'arabâyi, 'arabîyi *'arabîya*; **~man** 'arabaji,
         'arbaji *'arbagi*

coal faHm

coast shâTi *shaTT*, sâhil; **~al** sâhili

coat mi'Taf

cock dîk pl. diyûk

cockroach SarSûr pl. SarâSîr

coconut jauz hindi *gôz hindi*

code (law) qanûn pl. qanâwîn

coffee qahwi *qahwa*; (unground coffee) binn *bunn*;
         ~house maqha

coffin tâbût

coin sikki *sikka*

cold (catarrh) rash-H; (adj.) bârid, **to catch a ~** akhad
         bard *khad bard*;

cold (n.) bard; **it is ~** id-dinyi bard *id-dinya bard*;
    to be ~ birdân *bardân*
colic qûlanj *maRas*
collar qabbi *yâqa*
collect jama' *gama'*
college jâmi'a *gâmi'a*
color laun *lôn*
column 'amûd pl. 'awâmid
comb (n.) mushT *mishT*
combat (n.) muqâtali *muqâtala*
come ija *gâ, gi*; **to ~ in** fât *khash*; **to ~ up** Tili'
comfort (ease, n.) kêf, irtiyâh, râha; (consolation)
    tasliyi, tislâyi *ta'zîye*
comfortable muraiyih
command (n.) amr pl. awâmir; (v.) amar
commerce tijâra *tigâra*
common (usual) 'âdi; **in ~** bil-ishtirâk, sawîyatan; **~ly**
    Râliban
company (commercial) shirki *shirka*
compass bûSla
compassion shafâqa
complain about itshaka min, tshakka min *itshakka
    min, shaka*
complaint shakwa, shkâyi *shikâya*
complete (adj.) kâmil; (v.) akmal, kammal
compose (put together) rakkab *rakkib*
conceal khabba
computer kumbûter

concern (v.) khaSS; **as far as … is ~ed** bi-khuSûs…,
min yamm…, min jihit *min gihet*

concert konsêr *Haflit mûsîqa*

conclude (finish) kammal

condemn Hakam 'ala

condition (state) Hâl, Hâli *Hâla*; (stipulation) sharT
pl. shrûT *shurûT*; **under the ~ that**
bi-sharT in

conduct (guidance) Hidâye; **a safe ~** amân

confess qarr, i'taraf

confirm akkad, sabbat

congratulate hanna

congratulations mabrûk

conquer istaula 'ala

conscience dimmi *dimma*

consciousness - lose ~ faqad il-wa'i

consent to s.th. (v.) riDi bi, qibil

considerable 'azîm

constipation imsâk

consul qunSul

consulate qunsulâto *qonsolâto*

consultation mashwara *mushâwara*

contagious byi'di *bi'di*

contaminated mitlauwis

contemptuous Haqîr

content with mabsûT min, râDi bi

contents maudû' *môdû'*

continent qarra

continue kammal *kammil*

contraband tahrîb
contraceptive wasl min' il-Haml
contract kuntrâtu
contradict Dâdad *khalif*
contrary Didd
conversation Hâdis *mukâlama*
cook (v.) Tabakh; **~ed** maTbûkh
cool bârid
copper nuHâs *naHâs*
Copt, Coptic qibTi pl. iqbâT
copy nuskha
coral mirjân *morjân*
cord Habl, marsa
cork fillîn *filli*
corn durra
corner rukn pl. arkân
corpse maiyit, jîfi *gîfi*
corpulent jasîim *gasîm*
correct SaHîH, maDbûT *mazbûT*
correspondence mukatâbi *mukâtaba*
cost (price) qîmi; (expenses) maSrûf; (v.) kallaf
        kallif; **what does it ~?** bi-kâm
        bi-qaddaish
cotton quTn
cough (n.) sa'li *sa'la*
council majlis *meglis*
count (v.) 'add
country blâd *bilâd* pl. bildân *buldân*
couple jauz *gôz*

courage shajâ'a *shagâ'a*
courageous shâji'*shâgi'*
court maHkami *maHkama*
courtyard Haush *Hôsh*
cousin (son of father's brother) ibn il-'amm;
(daughter of father's brother) bint il-'amm;
(son of father's sister) ibn il-'ammi *ibn il'-amma*; (daughter of father's sister) bint il'-ammi *bint il-'amma*; (son of mother's brother) ibn il-khâl; (daughter of mother's brother) bint il-khâl; (son of mother's sister) ibn il-khâli *ibn il-khâla*; (daughter of mother's sister) bint il-khâli *bint il-khâla*
cover (n.) RaTa; (for the bed) liHaâf pl. luHûf;
(v.) RaTTa
cow baqara
coward jabân *gabân*
crab saraTân pl. sarâTîn
crack (n.) shaqq
cradle mahd
craft (trade) San'a; (skilled ~) Hirfa pl. Hiraf
cramp tashannuj *tashannug*
crawl dabdab
cream qishTa
create khalaq
creation khalq
credit krêdito
crescent hilâl

cress jirjîr *gargîr*
cricket SarSûr
crime jinâyi *ginâya*
crippled mukarsaH *mukassaH*
crocodile timsâH pl. tmâsîH *temâsîH*
crooked a'waj *'awag* f. 'auja *'ôga* pl. 'ûj *'ôg*
crop (produce) Rille *Ralla*
cross (v.) 'abar
crow qâq pl. qîqân
crowd zaHmi *zaHma*
crown tâj *tâg* pl. tîjân *tîgân*
crucifix Salîb pl. Sulbân
cruel qâsi, zâlim
crutch 'ukkkâzi *'ukkkâza* pl. 'akâkîz
cry (n.) SiyâH; (v.) biki *baka*
crystal billôr
cube ka'b
cucumber(s) (coll.) khiyâr
culture saqâfa
cunning (n.) Hîli *Hîla* pl. Hiyal; (adj.) khabîs *makkar*
cup finjân *fingân* pl. finâjîn *finâgîn*
cupboard khizâni *dûlâb* pl. khazâyin *dewâlîb*
cupola qubbi *qubba*
cure (n.) shifa; (v.) shafa, 'alaj *'alig*
curse (n.) la'ni *la'na*; (v.) sabb; **God ~ you** allah
          yil'anak; **~ed** mal'ûn
curtain birdâyi *sitâra*
cushion (of a sofa) masnid pl. msânid *mesânid*

custom 'âdi *'âda* pl. 'âdât, 'awâyid *'awâ'id*

customs jumruk *gumruk*

cut (v.) qaTa', qaSS

cutlet barzûla *kastalêta*

cypress sarwi *sarwa* pl. sarw

D

daily yaumi *yômi*

dairy products muntajât Halîb *muntagât laban*

dam sadd; **the Aswan High** ~ is-sadd il-'âli

damage (n.) Darar; (v.) Darr

Damascus dimashq

Damietta dumyât

damp (adj.) ruTib *riTib*; **~ness** ruTûbi *ruTûba*

dance (n.) raqS; (v.) raqaS; **~r** raqqâS

danger khaTar, mukhâTara

dare tajâsar *itgâsar*

dark (of color) Ramîq; (obscure, dusk) 'itm *Dilim*;
        it has grown ~ Sâr 'atm *id-dunya Dilmet*

date (time) târîkh

date (fresh fruit) balaH *beleH*; (dried fruit) tamr

daughter bint pl. bnât *banât*; **~-in-law** zaujit il-ibn
        zôgit il-ibn

dawn fajr *fagr*

day yaum *yôm* pl. iyâm; (in opposition to night) nhâr
        nehâr; ~ **after tomorrow** ba'd bukra *ba'de*
        bukra; **the** ~ **before yesterday** auwil

imbâriH *auwal imbâriH, auwal ams*; **~light**
Dau *nûr*

dead maiyit

dead-end alley zuqâq

deaf aTrash

dealer bîyâ' *baiyâ'*

dear maHbûb, 'azîz; **my ~** yâ 'aini, Habîbi

death maut *môt*

debt dain *dên* pl. dyûn *diyûn*

deceit Rish'sh

deceive Rash'sh

December qânûn il-auwal *dessember*

decide Hakam

decision Hukm pl. aHkâm

declaration taSrîH

decorate zaiyan *zaiyin*

deep Ramîq *RawîT*

defend Hâma 'an, dafa' 'an

degree daraji *darage* pl. darajât *daragât*

delay (n.) ta'khîra; (v.) akh'khar

delta id-delta

deluge Tûfân

demand (n.) Talab; (v.) Talab

democracy dîmûqrâTiya

denial inkâr

dentist Tabîb asnân

department qism pl. aqsâm

departure raHîl, safar

deposit rahn
dervish darwîsh *derwîsh* pl. darâwîsh
descend nizil
descent nizûl
describe waSaf
description waSf, Sifa; **detailed ~** waSf tafsîli
desert SaHrâ' pl. SaHâra
deserve istaHaqq
desire (n.) shahwa pl. shahawât; (v.) Ririb
desk ktâbe *maktab*
desolation waHshi *waHsha*
desperate mai'ûs
dessert Hilw
destiny naSîb, maktûb
destroy rauwaH, kharrab
detail tafsîl pl. tafsîlât; **in ~** bit-tafsîl; **~ed** tafsîli
detective bûlîs khafîya *bolîs sirri*
devil iblîs, shîTân *shêTân*
dew *nidi nida*
dialect lahja *lahga*
diamond almâs
diarrhea isHâl
dictionary qâmûS
die (cube) ka'b
die (v.) mât
difference (between two things) farq; (opposition)
       khilâf *ikhtilâf*
different Rair *tâni*

difficult Sa'b; **~y** Su'ûbi *Su'ûba*
dig Hafar, bakhash
digestion haDm
diligence ijtihâd *ightihâd*, shaTâra
diligent mujtahid *mugtahid* shâTir
dining room ûdit sufra *ôdit sufra*
dinner 'asha
diploma shahâda
direct (v.) dall; **~ me to a doctor** dillni 'ala Tabîb
            dillini 'ala Tabîb
direction ittijâh *ittigâh*, naHye *naHya*, Saub
directly Hâlan, râsan, mubâsharatan
director mudîr
dirt wasakh, wakhm; **~y** wusikh *wisikh*
disability ta'auwuq *'agz*
disabled mu'auwaq *'âgiz*
disagree takhâlaf *ikhtalaf*
disappear Râb *ikhtafa*
disaster muSîbi *muSîba*
discount (n.) khaSm
discover kashaf, iktashaf; **~y** iktishâf
discuss bâhas *itbâhis*, nâqish; **~ion** munâqsha
disgusted with qirif min, istaqraf min
dish SaHn *sulTânîya*; (meal) SaHn pl. SuHûn
disk qurS pl. iqrâS
dismiss 'azal *Tarad*
distance bu'd
distant b'îd *be'îd*

distinct wâdiH, zâHir
distinguished sharîf
distrustful muthim
ditch khandaq pl. khanâdiq
dive RaTas
divide qasam, qassam
divine ilâhi
diving suit badlit RaTs
division qism pl. aqsâm, tiqsîm *taqsîm*
divorce (n.) Talâq; (v.) Tallaq (with acc.); **~d**
        miTTallaq
do 'imil *'amal*; **how ~ you ~?** kîf Hâlak? *ezai'yak?*
doctor (med.) Tabîb pl. aTib'ba
dog kalb *kelb* pl. klâb *kilâb*
doll 'arûsa
dolphin dilfîn *dolfîn*
dome qubbi *qubba*
done (cooked) mustwi *mustewi*
donkey Himâr, Hmâr *Humâr* pl. Hamîr
door bâb pl. ibwâb, bwâb; **~man** bauwâb
dot nuqTa pl. nuqaT
double (adj.) muDâ'af, mijwiz *migwiz*
doubt (n.) shakk; **no ~** bala shakk, min dûn shakk;
        (v.) shakk, shakkak; **~ful** mashkûk
dough 'ajîn *'aggin*
dove(s) (coll.) Hamâm
down la-taHt *taHt*; **~hill** bin-nâzil; **~ward** nâzil;
        ~wards min fauq la-taHt *min fôq li-taHt*

dowry mahr, dûta

doze (drowse) Rifi

drag (trans.) saHab, jarr *garr*

draw (to pull) saHab, shadd; (with a pencil) rasam

dream (n.) Hulm *Hilm* pl. aHlâm; (v.) Halam *Hilim*

dress (ladies' ~) fuStân pl. faSâTîn; (v.) labbas *labbis*

dried munash'shaf, nâshif

drink (n.) shirb *shurb*, sharâb pl. sharbât; (v.) shirib

drive sâq; **~ a nail in the wall** daqq mismâr bil-HaiT *daqq musmâr bil-HêT*; **~r** sa'iq sauwâq; **~'s license** rukhSat sewâqa *rokhSit siwâqa*

drown Rarraq; **to be ~ed** Ririq *itRarraq*

drowsy na'sân

drum Tabl, dirbekki *darabukka*

drunk sikrân *sakrân*

Druse durzi pl. drûz *durûz*

dry (adj.) yâbis, nâshif; (v., trans.) nash'shaf *nash'shif*; (v., intrans.) yibis, nishif

duck(s) (coll.) baTT

due wâjib *wâgib*

dull 'ikir

dumb akhras

durable mâkin, daiyân *gâmid*

dust (n.) trâb *turâb*

duty (obligation) wâjib *wâgib*, wâjbi *wâjiba* pl. wâjbât *wâgibât*; (tax) rasm *resm* pl. rusûm

dyed maSbûR

E

each kull

eagle nisr *'uqab* pl. nsûra *'aqîba*

ear udn, daini *widn* pl. dainât *ûidân*

earlier qabl

early bakkîr *bedri*; ~ **in the morning** bakkîr iS-SubH
badri iS-SubH; **it is yet (much) too** ~ ba'd
bakkîr (ktîr) *lissa bedri (ketîr)*

earn kisib

earnest jadd *gadd*; **in** ~ min jadd, 'an jadd *'an gadd*

earrings Halaq; **a pair of** ~ jauz Halaq *gôz Halaq*

earth (planet) arD; (mould, dust) trâb *turâb*

earthquake zalzali *zilzâl*

easily bi-suhûli *bi-suhûla*

east sharq

Easter 'îd il-fiSiH

eastern sharqi

easy sahil *sahl*

eat akal *kal*

echo Sada

ecology muHâfaZa 'ala l-bî'a

economize waffar, Sammad

economy iqtiSâd

edge Haffi *Haffa*, Taraf pl. aTrâf

edible mâkûl, mittâkil *mitâkil*

edition Tab'

editor muHarrir

educate rabba *addib*

educated ribyân, mrabba *murabbi*
education tirbyi, tirbâyi *tarbîya*
eel Hinklîz ti'bân samak
efficient fa"âl, muntij *muntig*
egg(s) (coll.) baiD *bêD*; **soft boiled ~** brisht *birisht*;
        hard boiled ~ maslûq Taiyib; **fried ~**
        mishwi *mashwi*
Egypt maSr
Egyptian maSri
eight tmânyi, tmâni *temanya, temen*
eight hundred tmanmîyi *tumnemîya*
eighteen tminTa'sh *temantâsher*
eighth tâmin f. tâmni *tamna*
eighty tmânîn *temânîn*
either (each) kull; **~ ... or ...** yâ ... yâ...; *weyâ ...*
        weyâ..., yimma ... yimma..., *yâmâ ...*
        yâmâ..., *weyâmâ ... weyâmâ ...*
elbow kû' *kô'* pl. kî'ân
elections intikhâbât
electric kahrabi
electricity kahraba
elephant fîl pl. ifyâl
elevator miS'ad *asansêr*
eleven Hd'ash *Hdâsher*
else Rair *Rêr*; **~where** Rair maTrah *maTrah tâni*
embarrassment tabashlul *istiha*
embassy safâra
embrace (v., hug) 'anaq

embroider Tarraz; **~y** taTrîz

emerald zumurrud

emergency Hâla iDTirâriya; **~ brake** farmalat
    Tawâri; **~ landing** hubûT Tawâri

emigrate Hâjar *Hâgar*

employee mistakhdem

employer makhdûm

empty (adj.) fâriR, fâdi; (v.) farraR

enamel mîna

enclose aHât (surround); aDâf ila (join)

end nihâyi *nihâya*; **at the ~** fin-nihâyi *fin-nihâya*,
    bil-âkhir; **at the ~ of** bi-âkhir il-…; **~less** illi
    mâlo nihâyi *elli mâlôsh nihâya*; (v., intrans.)
    khalaS *khilis*; (v., trans.) khallaS

enemy 'adu pl. a'âdi

engaged makhtûb

engine âli *âla*

engineer muhandis *muhandes*

English inglîzi pl. inglîz

enjoy s.th. itmatta' bi

enough Hâji, bass *bess*, kfâyi *kfâya*; **to have had ~**
    shibi'

enter dakhal, khash'sh

entertainment tasliya

entire kull, kâmil; **~ly** bil-kullîyi *bil-kullîya*

entrance dukhûl

enumerate 'add, Hasab

envelope Zarf pl. Zurûf

envious Hasûd
envy Hasad
equal mûsâwi
erase maHa
errand mishwâr *mushwâr* pl. mshâwîr *meshâwîr*
error RalaT
escalator sullam mutaHarrik *sillim mutaHarrik*
escape (v.) Harab
espionage tajassus *tagassus*
estate (property) mulk pl. imlâk, emlâk
esteem (n.) i'tibâr, iHtirâm; (v.) i'tabar, iHtaram
estimate (n.) Hisâb; (v.) tamman *tammin*
eternal (without beginning) azali; (without end)
          abadi; (in general) dâyim *dâ'im*
eucalyptus kâfûr
Europe urubba
even (level, adj.) sahl; (also, adv.) Hatta; ~ **if** wa'in
          wen
evening masa *misa*; **good ~** masa masal khair *misal*
          khêr; **in the ~** il-masa, 'ashîyi *il-'ishe*
event wâqi'a *waq'a* pl. waqâyi' *waqâ'i*; Hâdisi
          Hadsa pl. Hawâdis
eventually ittifâqan
every kull; ~**body** kullmîn, kull wâhid *kulli wâHid*
evident zâher *bâyin*; ~**ly** iz-zâher *zâhiran*
evil (misfortune) muSîbi *muSîba*; (wickedness) sharr;
          (adj.) radi
exact (adj.) maDbûT, mazbûT; ~**ly** tamâm

exaggerate bâlaR, 'azzam

exaggeration mubâlaRa

examination faHs, imtiHân

examine faHas, imtaHan

example matal *mesel* pl. imtâl *emsâl*; **for** ~ masalan
  meselen

excellence (goodness) faDl

excellence (when addressing s.b.) sa'adtak (m.)
  sa'adtik (f.)

except (prep.) illa, min'ada; (conj.) ~ **that** Rair in
  Rêr in

exception istisnâ

excess baggage 'afsh zâyid *'afsh zâ'id*

excessive zâyid *zâ'id*

exchange (place, n.) bursa; (v.) baddal *baddil*, Raiyar

exchange rate si'r

excuse (apolopgy, n.) ma'zira; (pretext) 'uzr; **to** ~
  oneself i'tazar; ~ **me** lâ twâkhidna *mâ
  ti'âkhiznîsh*

execute (put to death) qatal; (accomplish) kammal

exhaust (n.) mâsurat il-'adim *shakmân*

exhibition ma'raD

exist wijid *wigid*, inwajad *itwagad*; ~**ence** wujûd
  wugûd

exit (n.) khurûj *khurûg*; **where is the** ~**?** mnain
  il-khurûj? *fên il-khurûg?* wain il-bâb?
  fên il-bâb?

expect istanZar *intaZar*, naZar, istanna

expense kilfi *kulfa*; maSrûf pl. maSârif

expensive bîkallif *bîkellif*, Râli

experience tijribi *tagriba*; **~d** mujarrib *mugarrib*;
        shâTir

expert khabîr pl. khubarâ

explain fassar

explanation tafsîr

explode infajar *infagar*

exports (n.) taSdîrât

express (by language, v.) lafaz; **~ train** qaTr sari'
        quTâr il-eksebriss

external barrâni; **~ly** min khârij *min khârig*

extinguish Tafa

extract (draw out, v.) qala'; (select) intakhab

extraordinary fauq il-'âdi *fôq il-'âde*

extreme âkhir, Râyi; **~ly** lil-Râyi

eye 'ain *ên* pl. 'uyûn; **~brow** Hâjib *Hâgib* pl. Hwâjib
        Hwâgib; **~lid** jifn *gifn* pl. jifûn *gifûn;*
        ~witness shâhid 'ain *shâhid 'ên*

F

fabric nasîj *nasîg*

face (n.) wish *wagh*

fact wâqe' *Haqîqa*

factory ma'mal *fabrîka*

faint (v.) Rushi 'alaih *Rumia 'alêh*

fair (blond) ashqar f. shaqra pl. shuqr

---

fair (frank, just) ʿâdil
fairy tale Hkâyi *Hikâya*
faith îmân; **~ful** amîn
fall (n.) waqʿa; (v.) waqaʿ
false (counterfeit) mazRûl, falsu; (of persons) kizzâb
     kaddâb, khâyin *khâʾin*
familiar maʿlûf, maʿrûf
family ahl, ahl il-bait *ahl il-bêt*, ʿâyli *ʿêla* pl. ʿiyâl
fan mirwaHa *marwaHa* pl. marâwiH
fanatic mitʿaSSeb
far bʿîd *baʿîd*; **~ off** bʿîd *baʿîd*; **how ~ is it from here
     to...?** qaddaish bʿîd min haun la...? *qaddi ê
     il-mesâfe min hene li...?*; **how ~ is it to
     walk?** qaddaish bil mâshi? *qaddi ê bil-
     mâshi?*; **is it ~?** baʿdo bʿîd? *lissa baʿîd?*;
     ~ too little qalîl ktîr *qalîl ketîr*; **~ too much**
     ziyâdi bi-ktîr *ziyâde bi-ketîr*
fare ujret iT-Tarîq *ugra*
farm mazraʿa pl. mazâriʿ
farthest abʿad
fashion mûda
fast (abstinence, n.) Siyâm, Saum *Sôm*; **~ month**
     (ninth month of the Muslim year) ramaDân
fast (adj.) sariʿ; (adv.) qawâm
fat (n.) dihn, saman *semen*; (adj.) midhin; (of living
     beings) samîn
fatal (deadly) qatîl; (destined) muqaddar
fate naSîb

father ab pl. âbâ'; **~-in-law** Hamu
fatigue ta'b *ta'ab*
fault zamb pl. zunûb; khaTa, khaTtîyi *khatîya khaTâya*; **~y** maRlûT
favor ma'rûf, faDl
favorite (adj.) mufaDDal
fear (n.) khauf *khôf*; (s.b. or s.th. v.) khâf min
feast 'îd, 'aîd pl. i'yâd
feather rîshi *rîsha* pl. riyâsh
February shbâT *febrâ'ir*
fee ujra *ugra*
feed Ta''am, 'aiyash, 'allaq la *'allaq li*
feel Hass, istaHass; **I do not ~ well** Hâsis mâ-li *mâ-lish kêf*
felt labbâd *libd*
female (adj.) mu'annas
fence Ha'iT
fennel shumre *Habba sôdâ*
ferry ma'diye
festival mahrajân *mahragân*
fetch jâb *gâb*
fever Humma, sukhûni *sukhûna*
few qalîl; **a ~** ba'D, kam *kâm*
fidelity amâni, wafa
field Haqli pl. Huqûl, RaiT *RêT*
fifteen khamsTa'sh *khamstâsher*
fifth khâmis f. khâmsi *khamsa*
fifty khamsîn

fig(s) (coll.) tîn
fight (n.) qitâl; (v.) qatal, tqâtal *itqâtil*
figure (aspect, form) hai'a, qâmi *qâma*; (number) 'adad
fill (v.) malla *mala*; **~ed with** ... milyân bi ... *malyân bi...*; **have one's ~** shibi'
final nihâ'i, akhîr
find laqa; **how do you ~ this?** kîf bitshûf haida? *ezai bitshûf di?*
fine (n.) jaza naqdi *geza naqdi*
fine (adj.) rafî' *rufai'ya'*, raqîq
finger iSba' *Subâ'* pl. aSâbî'; **fore~** sabbâbi *shâhid*; **middle ~** Tawîl, wasTâni *wusTâni*; **little ~** khanSar; **~nail** Zufr *Dufr, Difr* pl. aZfâr *Dawaafir*
finish (trans.) kammal, khallaS; (intrans.) tamm
fire nâr; (incendiary) Harîq *Harîqa*; **~place** ujâq *mauqid*
firm (solid) mâkin
first auwal, aulâni *auwalâni* f. aulânîyi *auwalâniya*
fish (coll.) samek *samak*; **~ing** Said is-samek *Sêd is-semek*
fit (to be suitable) mnâsib *munâsib*; **this coat does not ~ me** hal mi'Taf mâ byiji 'alaiyi *il-mi'Taf da mâ beyigîsh 'alêye*
five khamsi *khamsa*
five hundred khamsmîyi *khumsemîya*
flag 'alam
flame lahîb

flash (n.) barq; **~light** flâsh
flat (level) munbasiT
flatter (v.) mallaq; **~y** tamlîq
flea BarRût pl. brâRît *berârît*
flee harab, fall
fleet 'amâra
flesh laHm
flight Tayarân *Tairân*, rihla
floor (story) Tabaqa *dôr*
floor (of a room) arD
flour (n.) TaHîn *daqîq*
flower zahra pl. zhûr *zuhûr*
flu bard
flute shabbâbi *nai*
fly(ies) (coll.) dibbân *dubbân*
fly (v.) Târ
foam raRwi *raRwa*
fog Dabâb; **~gy** muRaiyim
follow taba', liHiq
food Ta'âm *akl*; **cooked ~** Tabkh, Tabîkh
foolish majnûn *magnûn* pl. mjânîn *megânîn*
foot ijr, rijl *rigl* pl. irjul *argul*; **my feet are swollen**
            ijraiyi wârmîn *riglêye warmîn*; **I sprained**
            my ~ infakashit ijri *itfaraket rigli*; **~ball**
            kurat il-qadam
for (conj.) fa'inn; (in favor of, prep.) min shân *'ala*
            shân, la *li*; (in place of) 'iwaD, bdâl *bidâl*;
            ~ what reason li-ai sabab *li-aiyi sabab*

forbidden mamnû'

force (strength) qûwi *qûwa*; **by ~** bil-Rasb; (v.) ajbar

forehead jibîn *gibîn*, jibîni *gibîna*, *gubha*

foreign ajnabi *agnabi* pl. ajânib *agânib*, khawâga pl.
        khawâgât

forget nisi

forgive sâmaH

fork furtai'ki, shauki *shôka* pl. shuwak

form qâlib pl. qwâlib *qawâlib*

former Sâbiq; **~ly** Sâbiqan

fortress qal'a

fortune (luck) Hazz; (wealth) Rina

forty arb'în *arba'în*

forward la-quddâm *li-quddâm*

found (v.) assas *assis*, **~ation** asâs

fountain naufara *nôfara*, *fasqiya*

four arb'a *arba'*

four hundred arb'amîyi *rub'êmîya*

fourteen arbaTa'sh *arba'tâsher*

fourth râbi' f. râb'a *rab'a*; (fourth part) rub' pl. erbâ'

fox ta'lab pl. ta'âlib

fraction kasr pl. ksûr *kusûr*

fragrance rîHa

frame birwâz pl. barâwîz

frank Sadîq

free Hurr; **~dom** Hurrîyi *Hurrîya*

French frinsâwi *feransâwi*

fresh Tari

Friday yaum ij-jum'a *yôm il-gum'a*
fried maqli
friend SâHib pl. iSHâb, SHâb *aSHâb*
fright khauf *khôf*
frog Difda' *Dufda'* pl. Dafâdi'
from min
front wish *muqaddam*; **in ~ of** quddâm, min quddâm
frontier Hadd pl. Hudûd
fruit fâkiha pl. fuâki *fewâkih*
fry qala
fuel wuqûd
fugitive Hirbân *Harbân*
full milyân *malyân*; (with food) shab'ân
funeral dafn, jinâzi *genâze*, mash'had
fur farwi *kurk*
furious RaDbân
furnished mafrûsh; **a ~ apartment** shaqqa mafrûsha
future mustaqbal *mustaqbil*; **in the ~** bil-mustaqbal

G

gag nukta pl. nukat
gain (n.) makseb, kasb; (v.) kisib
galore bi-wafra
gambling qumâr
game la'b *li'b*
garage garâsh
garbage zibâla; **~ man** zabbâl

garden (orchard) bustân pl. bsâtîn *besâtîn*; (flower ~)
    jnaini *genêne*; **~er** janainâti *ganâ'ini*

garlic tûm *tôm*

gas kâz *Râz*, *gâz*; **~ station** maHattit banzîn

gate bauwâbi *bauwâba*

gather (v.) jama' *gama'*; **~ing** (of people) maukib pl.
    mwâkib *mewâkib*

gazelle Razâli *Razâla*

gender jins *gins*

general (adj.) 'umûmi; **in ~** 'umûman, Râliban

generous karîm, khaiyir

gentleman saiyid, sîd

genuine khâliS, SaHîH

geography jigrâfiya *gogrâfiya*

German almâni pl. almân

get (arrive) wiSil; (become) Sâr; (fetch) jâb *gâb*;
    (find) shâf; (obtain) nâl; (receive) laqa

ghost(s) (coll.) jinn *ginn*

giddiness daukha *dôkha*

giddy daukhan *dôkhan*

gift 'aTîyi *'aTa*, hadîyi *hedîya* pl. hadâya

gilt mudah'hab

ginger zinjfîl *ganzabîl*

giraffe zarâfi *zarâfa*

girl bint pl. bnât *banât*

give 'ata, 'ada; **~ back** radd; **~ in** sallam

Giza gîzeh

glad masrûr, firHân *farHân*

glass qizâz; **drinking** ~ kubbâyi *kubbâya*

glasses naDâra (sg.)

glory iftikhâr, fakhr

gloves quffâz

glue (n.) Riri; (v.) Rarra

go râh; ~ **down** (sun) Rarab; ~ **for a walk** shamm
il-hawa; **what is ~ing on?** shû Sâyir?
il-khabar ê?

goat ma'zi *mi'za* pl. ma'z

God allâh; ~! yallah!, yâ rabb!, yâ laTîf!; **~father** shibîn

gold dahab *diheb*; **~smith** SâyiR *Sâ'iR*

golf la'b iS-Sûlajân *la'b iS-Sôlagân*

good (adj.) Taiyib, mlîH *melîH*; (n.) khair *khêr*; ~
Friday il-jum'al Hazîni *ig-gum'al Hazîna*;
~s baDâ'a; mâl pl. amwâl

goose (coll.) wazz *wizz*

gout nuqrus

government Hukûmi *Hukûma*

gradually bit-tidrîj *bit-tedrîg*

grain Habbi *Habba*

granddaughter Hafîda

grandfather idd *gidd*

grandmother sitt

grandson Hafîd

grape(s) (coll.) 'ainab *'ênab*

grass Hashîsh, 'ishb

gratis bi-lâsh *ba-lâsh*, ba-lâ taman *bi-lâ temen*,
majjânan *maggânan*

grave qabr pl. qubûr
gravity tiql
gravy marqit laHm *maraqat laHm*
gray rimâDi *rumâDi*
grease duhn *shaHm*
great kebîr, kbîr (the latter Syr. only)
greedy Tamî' *Tammâ'*
Greek yunâni pl. yunân
green akhDar f. khaDra
greet s.b. sallim 'ala; ~ **all your family from me**
          sallim-li ktîr 'ala jamî' ahl baitak *sallim-li
          ketîr 'ala gemî' ahle bêtak*
grief asaf, Ramm
grieve Ramm
grind TaHan, TaH'Han
grocery store dukkân ma'kûlât
groom sâyis *sâ'is*
gross (unrefined) khishin
ground arD pl. arâDi; (foundation) asâs
grow (intrans.) kibir; (trans.) rabba
guarantee (n.) kfâli *Damân*; (v.) tkaffal 'an *itkaffal
          'an*, Daman li
guardian waSi
guess (v.) Hazar
guest Daif *Dêf* pl. Diyûf
guide dâlûl *dalîl* pl. dwâlîl *dulala*
guilty miznib; **not** ~ bala zamb
guitar gîtâra

gulf jûn *gûn*
gun bârûdi *bunduqiya* pl. bwârîd *banâdiqa*
gut (intestine) miSrân pl. maSârîn
gutter (n.) mizrâb
gypsum jefsîn *gibs*
gypsy(ies) (coll.) nawar

H

haberdasher khurdâji *khurdâgi*
hair sha'r; **I want my ~ cut** baddi quss sha'ri *'âyiz*
     aquSS sha'ri; **~dresser** kuwafêr
half nuSS
hall qâ'a
ham jambûn *gambûn*
hammer shâkûsh *miTraqa*
hand yad, îd pl. iyâdi *ayâdi*; **~brake** farmalit yad;
    ~bag shanTa; **~writing** ktâbet yad *khaTT*
handkerchief maHrami *mendîl* pl. mHârim *menâdîl*
handicapped muq'ad
handle (of a basket, knife) maqbaD pl. maqâbiD; (of
    a door) saqqâTa *suqqâTa*
happen waqa' *wiqi'*, Hadas *Hasal*, Sâr
happiness sa'd, bakht, Hazz
happy sa'îd, mis'ad
harbor mîna pl. miyan
hard qâsi, shedîd; **~ for s.b.** Sa'b 'ala; **~ly** bi-Su'ûbe;
    ~ship Su'ûbe

harem Harîm

harm (n.) Darar; (v.) Darr; **there is no** ~ mâfi Darar *mâfîsh Darar*, mâ bîsâyil *mâ yiDurrish*

harp 'ûd

harvest (~ing, cutting, n.) HaSîdi *HaSîda*; (time, crop) mausim *môsem* pl. mwâsim *mewâsim*

haste (n.) 'ajal *'agel*

hat qubba'a *bornêTa*

hate (n.) buRD; (v.) baRaD; **~d** mamqût

haughtiness kibriya

haughty mutkabbir *mutakabbir*

have (possess) malak; **I** ~ ili *li*, **you have** ilak *lak*, etc.; **I** ~ **to do** 'alaiyi *'alêye*

hawk bâr

hay hashîsh

hazard (danger) khaTar; **~ous** mukhûf

he hû *hûwa, hûwe*

head (n.) râs pl. ru'ûs; (chief) ra'îs *re'îs*, raiyis

headache waja' râs *waga' râs*

heal (trans.) shafa; (intrans.) shifi, SaHH

health SaH'Ha, salâmi *salâma*; **~y** sâlim, SiH'Hi; **to be ~y** ta'âfa

hear simi'; ~ **from** simi' an

heart qalb pl. qulûb; ~ **attack** nauba qalbiya

heat (n.) Harr, shaub *shôb*; (v., trans.) sakh'khan; (intrans.) sakhan

heaven sama pl. samawât

heavy taqîl pl. tiqâl

Hebrew 'ibrâni
hedgehog qunfud
heel ka'b
height 'ulûw
heir wâris pl. warâsi
Heliopolis maSr gedîda
hell jahannam *gahannam*
hello âlô
help (n.) musâ'adi *musâ'ada*; ~! madad!, (v.) sâ'ad
       sâ'id
hen jâji *farkha*
herd (n.) qâTî'
here haun *hene*; ~ **take!** khôd *khod*
heritage irs, mîrâs, wirti *wirâsa*
hide (trans.) khabba; (intrans.) itkhabba
high 'âli
highway Tarîq 'âm
hijack khaTaf; ~**er** khaTTâf
hill tall *tell* pl. tlâl *tulûl*
hippopotamus Hsân il-baHr *Husân il-baHr*, faras
       il-nahr
hire (v.) istakra, istaja *istagar*
history târîkh
hoarse mabHûH
hold (grasp, v.) misik; (contain) sâ'; (last, to be
       strong) Dâyan, misik
hole Hufra pl. Hufar
holidays fusaH *agâza*

hollow (adj.) farîR, fâDi

holy muqaddas

home (country) waTan; (house) bait *bêt*; **at ~** fil-bait *fil-bêt*; (whither?) lil-bait lil-bêt

honest amîn *emîn*, mustaqîm

honey 'asal

honor (n.) sharaf; (v.) karram, iHtaram; **~able** mukarram

hope (n.) amal; (v.) ammal, t'ammal *it'ammal*; **I ~, let us ~** insh allah

horizon ufq *ufuq*

horn (animal) qarn pl. qurûn; (mot.) kilâks

horse faras pl. afrâs, (coll.) khail *khêl*; **~shoe** na'l

hospital mustashfa

hospitality Diyâfa

host muDîf

hostage rahîna pl. rahâyin

hot sukhn

hotel hôtello *ôtîl*, *fonduq*

hour sâ'a pl. sâ'ât

house bait *bêt* biyût, dâr; **~boat** qarab b-khaimi *qârib b-khêma*

how kîf *kêf*, *ezai*; **~ much** qaddaish *qaddi ê*, kâm; **~ever** ma'a zâlik

huge 'azîm

human (not divine) bashari; (not animal) insâni; **~ity** insânîyi *insânîya*

humble mitwâDi

humility tawâDu'
hundred mîyi *mîya*
hunger jû' *gû'*
hungry jû'ân *gi'ân, gî'ân*
hunt (v.) Saiyad, iSTâd; **~ing** Said *Sêd*
hurricane zauba'a shedîda
hurry (v. or n.) 'ajal *'agal*
hurt (injured) maDrûr; **it ~s** yûja' *yûga'*
husband jauz *gôz*
hush iskut! *uskut!*
hut khuSS *'ish'sha*
hyena Dab' pl. Dibâ'
hygiene SiH'Ha
hymn (rel.) tartîl
hypocrisy nifâq, munâfaqa
hypocrite munâfiq

I

I ana
ice talj *talg*; **~ cream** bûZa *gelâti*
idea fikr pl. afkâr
identification card bitâqat hawiyat *kart taHqîq*
          esh-shakhSiya
idiot mahbûl *'abîT*
idol Sanam pl. aSnâm
if (with indic.) iza; (with subj.) lau *lô*; **~ not** mâ, lau
          mâ *lô'lâ in*

ignorant jahil *gahil*

ill marîD, Da'îf, D'îf *'ayân*; **~ness** maraD pl. imrâD

illiterate ummi

imitate qallad *qallid*

imitation tiqlîd rkhîS *taqlîd rikhîS*

immoral fâHish, dinis

immortal dâyim *dâ'im*

impartial mâlo RaraD *mâlosh RaraD*; **~ly** bala RaraD

impatient qalîl is-Sabr

impolite khishin

important muhimm

impose on s.b. Rash'sh

impossible mush mumkin, muHâl, mustaHîl

imprison sajan *sagan*, Habas

improve (trans.) SaH'HaH; (intrans.) tHassan
      itHassan; **~ment** tisHîH *tasHîH*, tislîH
      taslîH

impure nijis *nigis*

in (at a place) fî; (within) jûwa *gûwa*; (whither?) la
      li, fî

incapable 'âjiz 'an *'âgiz 'an*

inclined to do s.th. ili khâTir ktîr … *lîye khâTir
      ketîr…;* **I do not feel ~** mâ ili khâTir abadan
      mâ fîsh khâTir ebeden

included mashmûl

income irâd, dakhl

increase (n.) izdiyâd; (v., trans.) kattar; (intrans.)
      keber

incredible lâ tuSaddaq
indecent fâHish, razîl
indeed (in truth) bil-Haqîqa; (yes) aina 'am
indemnify s.b. 'auwaD 'ala *'auwaD li*
independence istiqlâl
independent mustaqill
indigo nîl
indigestion talabbuk fil-mi'di *talabbuk fil-mi'da*;
          (~ resulting from overeating) tukhmi *tukhma*
infant Tifl
infectious mu'di
infinite illi mâlo nihâyi *elli mâlôsh nihâya*
inflammation iltihâb
inflation intifâkh *nafkh*
inform khabbar *khabbir*, akhbar; **~ation** ma'lûmât
inhabitant sâkin pl. sukkân; **~s** ahâli
inject Haqan; **~ion** Huqna pl. Huqan
injure jaraH *garaH*; **to be ~d** itjaraH *itgaraH*
injury jarH *garH* pl. jirâ *girâH*
inn manzil *menzil* pl. mnâzil *menâzil*; lukanda
          lokanda
inner jûwâni *gûwâni*
innocent ba-la zamb
innumerable lâ yu'add, lâ yuHSa
inquire istakhbar 'an, faHaS
inscription ktîbi *kitâba*
insects Hasharât
inside (n.) bâTin; (adv.) jûwa *gûwa*

insight into iTTilâ' 'ala, wuqûf 'ala; **to get an ~**
    waqaf 'ala
inspector mufattesh
instance for ~ masalan *meselen*
instead 'iwaD, bdâl *bidâl*
instrument âli *âla*
insult (v.) 'azzar *shatam*
intend qaSad
intention qaSd, nîyi *nîya*, maqSûd; **I have the ~**
    of … nîyti in … *nîyeti in* …
interest (concern) naf', SâliH pl. SawâliH; (premium)
    fâyiz *fâ'iz*, faraD; **I have no ~ in this affair**
    mâ ili SâliH bi-hashî *mâ lîsh SâliH bi-shê di*;
    ~ing muhimm; (v.) raRRab fî
interpreter mutarjim *mutargim*
intestines maSârîn
into la *li*, fî
introduce (a person) qaddam, 'arraf
introduction (book) muqaddama; (personal) taqdîm
invent ikhta'ra'; **~ion** ikhtirâ'
invest qallad
investigate faHaS
investigation faHS
invite da'
invitation da'wa
invoice Hsâb *Hisâb*
iron (metal) Hadîd; (adj.) min Hadîd
iron (household ~) makwa, mikwa; (v.) kawa

irrigate saqa; **~d** misqi *masqi*
irrigation siqâyi *siqâya*
island jazîri *gezîra* pl. jazâyir *gezâ'ir*
itch (n.) jarab *garab*
ivory sinn il-fîl

J

jacket jâkêt
jail sijn *sign*
jam (preserve) mirabba; **traffic ~** zahmit il-muwâSlât
janitor bauwâb
January qânûn it-tâni *yanâyir*
jasmine yâsimîn, fill *full*
jaundice rîqân
jealous Raiyûr
Jerusalem il-quds
Jew, Jewish yahûdi pl. yahûd
jewel jauhar *gôhar* pl. jawâhir *gawâhir*; **~er** jauharji
          gôhargi
job shuRl
join waSal; **~ed** mawSûl
joke (n.) nukta pl. nukat; (v.) mazaH *hazzar*
Jordan il-urdun
journal jurnâl *gurnâl*
journey safar
joy surûr, faraH
judge qâDi

jug brîq *ebrîq*
juice zûm *'aSîr*
July tammûz *yûlie, lûliye*
jump (n.) naTTa; (v.) fazzi *fezze*
junction waSl
June Hazîrân *yûniye*
jurisdiction Hukm
just (at this moment) hallaq *dil-waqt*
just (adj,) minSif, 'âdil; **~ice** 'adl, inSâf

K

keep (retain) Hafaz *HafaD*; (hold) misik; **~ far from**
       ibta'ad 'an, tabâ'ad 'an *itbâ'ad 'an*
key miftâH *muftâH* pl. mfâtîH *mefâtîH*
kidnap khataf, **~per** khaTTâf
kidney (food) kilwi *kilwa* pl. kalâwi; (anat.) kilya
kill qatal; (slaughter) dabaH
kind (sort, class) nau' *nô'* pl. inwâ'
kind (adj.) laTîf, anîs, âdemi, *zarîf*; **~ness** faDl
       pl.afDâl, ma'rûf; **to have the ~ness**
       tfaDDal *itfaDDal*; **have the ~ness!**
       TfaDDalu! *itfaDDalu!* **we thank you for**
       your ~ness nishkur afDâlak
king malik pl. mulûk; **~dom** mamlaki *memlaka*
kiss (n.) bausi *bôsa*, bûsi *bûsa*; (v.) qabbal *bâs*,
       bauwas
kitchen maTbakh

knee rikbi *rukba* pl. rikbât *rukab*

kneel raka'

knife sikkîn, sikkîni *sikkîna* pl. skâkîn *sekâkîn*

knit Hayyak

knock (beat) khabaT; (~at the door) Daqq il-bâb

knot (n.) 'uqdi *'uqda*; (tie) 'aqad

know 'irif; **do you ~ English?** bta'rif inglîzi?
     beta'raf ingelîzi?; **I ~ nothing about it** mâ
     'indi khabar 'anno *mâ 'andîsh khabar
     'anno*; **is it ~n to you that ...** ma'lûmkon in
     ma'lûmkum in ...

knowledge ma'rifi *ma'rifa* pl. ma'ârif; 'ilm pl. 'ulûm

knuckle (foot) ka'b; (hand) burjuma *burguma* pl.
     barâjim *barâgim*

Koran il-qur'ân

L

label waraqe *waraqa*

labor union niqâbat 'ummâl

laboratory ma'mal

lace rubâT pl. rubâTât

ladder sullam *sellim* pl. slâlîm *selâlîm*

lady sitt

lake buHaira *buHêra*

lamb Hamal; (meat) laHm kharûf

lame (adj.) a'raj *a'rag*; **~ness** 'arj *'arg*

lament nâH

lamp miSbâH

land (surface, real estate) arD pl. arâDi; (continent,
　　　shore) barr; **arable ~** Haqli; (v.) Tili'

landlord SâHib il-bait *SâHib il-bêt*

landscape manZar Tabî'i

lane zuqâq pl. zuqâqât

language (speech, words) kalâm *kelâm*; (of a people)
　　　lisân pl. ilsini *alsina*; luRa pl. luRât

lap (n.) HuDn

large kebîr, 'arîD

last (adj.) âkhir; **~ night** mbârHa fil-lail *embâreH
　　　fil-lêl*; **~ year** sint il-mâdyi, sint il-ma'Dit
　　　is-sana elli fâtet, 'âm il-auwil *'âm il-auwal*;
　　　at ~ bin-nihâyi *nehaito*

last (v.) dâm; **~ long** Tauwal, Râb; **how long will it
　　　~?** qaddaish baddo yTauwil *qaddê yeTauwil,
　　　qadde yerîb*

latch saqqâTa *suqqâTa*

late wakhri; **to be ~** t'akh'khar *it'akh'khar*; **it is
　　　already ~** Sâr wakhri, fât il-waqt; **~r** ba'dên;
　　　at the ~st at 8 o'clock 'al-ktîr is-sâ'a tmânyi
　　　'al-ktîr is-sâ'a temanye; **~ly** akhîran

laugh (v.) DiHik; **~ at** DiHik 'ala

laundry Rasîl

laurel shajrit il-Râr *shagarat il-Râr*

law qanûn pl. qawânîn; **~suit** qadiya, da'wa pl.
　　　da'âwi

lawyer muHâmi

lay (put) waDa'; ~ **down** naiyam *naiyim*
lazy kislân *kaslân, kasûl*, tembel
laziness kasal
lead (metal) rSâS *ruSâS*
lead (v.) qâd, wadda; **where does this road ~ to?**
     la-wain bitwwaddi had-darb? *'ala fên*
     yiwaddi id-darb di?
leaf waraqa, warqa pl. ûrâq *aurâq*
leak (n.) wakf; (v.) wakaf *nazz*
lean (adj.) naHîf, rafî' *rufaiy'ya'*
learn t'allam *it'allim*; (hear) simi', istakhbar
lease (n.) ijra *ugra*
least il-aqall; **at ~** bil-aqall, aqall mâ yekûn, bil-qalîli
     'ala l-aqall
leather jild *gild*; (adj., of ~) min jild *min gild*
leave (n.) izn, istîzân; **to take ~** ista'zan *ista'zin*;
     (v., trans.) tarak, khalla, dash'shar *saiyib*;
     (intrans.) insaraf, râH; **the mail ~s Cairo at**
     6 o'clock il-busTa bitsâfir min il-qâhira
     is-sâ'a sitti *il-busTa bitsâfir min il-qâhira*
     is-sâ'a sitte
Lebanon il-lubnân
left shmâl *shemâl*; **on the ~ hand** 'ala îdak ish-shmâl
     'ala îdak esh-shemâl
leg rijl *rigl*
legal shar'i
lemon(s) (coll.) laimûn *lâmûn*
lemonade laimûnâDa *lêmûnâta*

lend sallif, sallaf

length Tûl

lentil(s) (coll.) 'ads, 'ades

less than aqall min

lesson dars pl. durûs

let (permit) khalla; **~ alone**, **~ go** dahsshar *saiyib*, tarak

letter (character) Harf pl. Hurûf; (a note) maktûb *gawâb* pl. mkâtib *gawâbât*

lettuce khass

level mustawâ

liar kizzâb *keddâb*

liberal karîm *sakhi*; **~ity** karam, sakhawi *sakhawa*

library maktabi *maktaba*

lice (coll.) qaml

license plate numrit ôtombîl *nimrit ôtombîl*

licorice sûs

lid RaTa

lie (n.) kizbi *kidba*; (v.) kizib *kidib*

lie down (v., rest extended, of persons) nâm

lie (v.) **the book ~s on the table** il-ktâb 'aT-Tauli, il-ktâb maHTûT aT-Tauli *il-kitâb 'aT-Tarabêza*

life 'umr, hayât; **in my whole ~** kull iyâm 'umri *Tûl 'umri*; **~less** jâmid *gâmid*

light (n.) Dau *nûr*; **it is ~** fi Dau *fîh nûr*; **switch on the ~** ish'al iD-Dau *iftaH an-nûr*; **turn off the ~** iTfi iD-Dau *iTfi in-nûr*; **~bulb** lamba;

~**house** manâra; ~**ning** barq; **it was ~ning**
    baraqit *baraqet*
light (bright, of color) fâtiH; (not heavy) khafîf;
    (easy) sahil *sahl*
like (adj.) mitl *zai*; ~**wise** kazâlik *kezâlik*
like (v.) Habb; **I ~ this better than ...** haida bHibbo
    aktar min ... *di baHibbo aktar min...;* **I ~**
    that very much ana ktîr mabsûT min haida
    ana mabsûT ketîr min di; **I would ~ to know**
    ... ana bHibb ktîr a'rif *ana baHibb ketîr*
    a'raf; **I don't ~ that** mâ baddi haida, mâ
    brîd haida *mâ aHibbish di;* **as you ~** mitl mâ
    bitrîd *zai mâ terîd*
liking - **that is to my ~** haida 'ala khâTri *di 'ala*
    khâTri
limb 'aDu pl. a'Da
lime kils *gîr*
line (stroke, stripe) khaTT; (in a book) saTr pl. suTûr;
    (row) Saff pl. Sufûf; **to range in a ~** Saff,
    Saffaf
linen (n.) kittân; (adj.) min kittân
lining (of clothes) baTâni *baTâna;* **with ~** mubaTTan
lion asad
lip shiffi *shiffa* pl. shifâf *shafâ'if;* ~**stick** aHmar
    shafâyif *aHmar shafâ'if*
liquid mâyi'
listen tsamma' *ista'ma';* ~ **to me** isma'ni
literal Harfi; ~**ly** Harfîyan

little zRîr *zuRaiyar* pl. zRâr *zuRaiyerîn, zuRâr*

live 'âsh; (dwell) qa'ad, sakan; for the present tense,
the participle is generally used: **I ~ …** ana
sâkin…; **have you ~d there a long time?**
qa'adt ktîr haunîk? *qa'adt ketîr henâk?* **~ly**
nishiT

liver kibdi *kibda*

lizard Hirdaun *Hardûn*

load (n.) Hamli *Hamla*; (v.) Hammal *Hammil*; **~ed**
maHmûl

loaf raRîf *riRîf* pl. irRifi *arRifa*

loan qarD

lobster karkand

local call mukâlama maHalliya

lock (n.) Râl pl. Râlât, *kâlûn*; (v.) sakkar *sakk*; (with a
padlock) qafal; **~ed** musakkar, maqfûl

locksmith Hiddâd *Haddâd*

locust jarad *garad*

loneliness waHdânîyi *waHdânîya*, waHdi *waHda*

long (adj.) Tawîl pl. Tuwâl; **~ time** zamân Tawîl
zemân Tawîl, zamân ktîr *zemân ketîr*; **to be
or last ~** Tauwal; **don't be ~** lâ Ttauwil *mâ
TiTauwalsh*; **for a ~ time** min zamân *min
zemân*; **~ before** qabl min zamân *qabla min
zemân*; **as ~ as** qaddmâ *qaddi mâ*, mâ dâm;
~er than (measure) aTwal min; (time) aktar
min; **I can't wait any ~er** mâ biqdir istanzir
aktar *mâ aRdarsh astanna aktar*; **how much**

~er will it last? qaddaish bîTauwil ba'd?
qaddi ê biTauwal lissa?

long for (v.) ishtâq la *ishtâq li*

longing shauq *shôq*

long-distance call mukâlama khârîjiya *mukâlama khârîgiya*

look (n.) naZar pl. anZâr; (appearance, aspect) hai'a *shôfa*

look (v.) shâf; **~ after s.b.** dâr il-bâl 'ala *khalla il-bâl 'ala*; **~ for** dauwar 'ala, fattash *fattish* 'ala; **what are you ~ing for?** 'ala aish bitfattish? *itfattish 'ala ê?;* **~ out!** û'a!, Dahrak!

lose Daiya'; (at a game, etc.) khisir; **I lost ...** ana khisrân ... *ana khasrân...;* **to ~ one's way** Da' *tâh*

loss khasâra *khusâra*

lost Dâyi'

lot (luck, chance) naSîb; (share) qism pl. aqsâm; **by ~** bil-qur'a

lot a ~ ktîr *ketîr*; **a ~ of people** ktîr min in-nâs *ketîr min in-nâs*

loud 'âli; **~ly** bil- âli

loudspeaker mukabbir pl. mukabbirât

love (n.) maHabbi *maHabba*, Hubb; (amorousness) 'ishq, hawa, Rarâm; **in ~ with** muRram fî; (v.) Habb; **~r** muHibb

low wâTi; (mean) razîl khabîs; **~er** tiHtâni *taHtâni*

luck (good ~) Hazz, HaDD; (chance) naSîb; **~y** sa'îd

luggage amti'a, 'afsh; ~ **control** teftîsh il-'afsh; ~
    porter 'ittâl *shaiyâl*
lukewarm fâTir
lunch fuTûr, Rada
lung rîa
lute 'ûD

M

machine mâkina, âla
mad majnûn *magnûn*
madam madâm
magazine majalla *magalla*
maid shaRRâla
mail barîd; ~**box** sandûq busTa
make 'imil; ~ **me** …! a'mil-li …! *i'mil-li …!*
make-up mâkiyâj *ziwâq*
malaria malarya
male dakar pl. dukûra
man rijjâl *râgil* pl. rjâl *rigâla*
manage dâr, dabbar; ~**r** mudîr
mango (coll) manga
mankind insân pl. nâs, bashar
manners good ~ edeb
many ktîr *ketîr*; ~ **people** nâs ktîr *nâs ketîr*; **how** ~
    qaddaish *qaddi ê*, kâm
map kharTa
marble rukhâm
March adâr *mârs*

mark (n.) 'alâmi *'alâma*

market sûq pl. iswâq; **~place** sâHa

Maronite mârûni, mûrâni pl. mwârni *muwârna*

marriage ziwâj *zewâg*, jêzi *gawâz*

married mutjauwiz *mitgauwiz*

marrow mukh'kh

marry (trans.) zauwaj *zauwig*; (intrans.) tjauwaz
          itgauwiz

martyr shahîd pl. shuhadâ

mass qaddâs pl. qadâdîs

master m'allim *me'allim*

mat HaSîri *HaSîra* pl. HuSr

match (n.) shiH'HâTa, shaH'HaiTa *kibrît*

match (v.) waffaq; **~ing** miwaffaq

matter - **what's the ~ with you?** shû bâk? *mâlak?*; **it
          does not ~** haida mâ hû shî *di mush Hâga*,
          mâ bîsâyil *mâ 'alêsh*

mattress farshi, firâsh pl. furûsh *martaba* pl. *marâtib*

may qidir; **~ one here...?** biyiqdir il-wâHid haun...?
          biqdir il-wâHid hene...?; **where ~ that be?**
          wain baddo ykûn? *fên buddi yekûn?*

May îyâr, nûwâr *mâyo*

mayor raiyis il-baladîyi *re'îs il-beledîya*

meadow marj *merg* pl. mrûj *murûg*

meal akli *akla*

mean (imagine, v.) Zann; (signify) **what does that ~?**
          shû ma'nâh?, shû ma'nâto?; **that ~s** ya'ni
          ma'nâh ê?

mean (adj.) razîl pl. arâzîl

mean in the ~ time fî nafs il-waqt

meaning ma'na pl. ma'âni

means (n.) wâsTa pl. wasâyiT *wasâ'iT*; (income) mâl
pl. amwâl; **by ~ of** b-wâsTit *bi-wâsiTat*; **by
all ~** Hais kân, bi-kull il-iHwâl; **~ of
transportation** wasâyil il-muwâslât
wasâ'il il-muwâslât

measles dashîshi *deshîsha*

measure (n.) qyâs *qiyâs*; (v.) qâs

meat (coll.) laHm; (single piece) laHmi *laHma*; **a
piece of ~** shaqfit laHm *hiTTet laHm*; **boiled
~** laHm maslûq; **roast ~** laHm miqli, rôsto;
fresh ~ laHm Tari; **fat ~** laHm midhin;
~balls kufta, kofta; **lean, boneless ~**
laHm Sabb

mechanic makinisti

medical Tibbi

medicine (science) Tibb; (drug) dawa pl. idwyi *adwiya*

meet lâqa, iltaqa *qâbil*; (each other) talâqa *itqâbil*;
~ing ijtimâ'*igtimâ'*; **~ing place** makân
il-ijtimâ' *makân l- igtimâ'*

melody laHn pl. alHân

melon(s) (coll.) baTTîkh aSfar shamâm

melt dâb

member 'aDw pl. a'Dâ; **~ship** 'uDwiya; **~ship card**
kart 'uDwiya

menace (n.) tihdîd; (v.) haddad, khauwaf

mention (n.) zikr; (v.) zakar, jâb sîrit *gâb sîret*

merchandise baDâ'a *buDâ'a*

---

merchant tâjir *tâgir* pl. tujjâr *tuggâr*

merciful - **the ~** (God) ir-raHmân

mercury zaibaq *zêbaq*

mercy raHmi *raHma*; **to ask for ~** istarHam

merry farHân

messenger raSûl, barîd

metal ma'din pl. ma'âdin

microphone mikrofôn

midday Duhr

middle (n.) wasT *wusT*; (adj.) wasTâni *wusTâni*; **in the ~** fî wasT *fî wusT*

midnight nuSS lail *nuSS il-lêl*

midwife dâyi *dâya*, qabla

mild (character) laTîf; (taste) Rair Harîf *Rêr Harîf*

mile mîl pl. amyâl; **~age** 'addâd il-amyâl

milk Halîb *laban*

mill TâHûn (f.) TawâHîn

million milyûn pl. mlâyîn *melâyîn*

minaret mâdni *mâdna* pl. meâdin

mind (n.) bâl; **to be ~ful** khad bâlu, khalla bâlu

mind (v.) i'tana; **never ~** lâ ba's, mâ bîsâyil *mâ yidûrrish*

minister wazîr pl. wuzarâ

ministry (governmental) wazâra, wizâra; **~ of Finance** wazâret il-mâliya; **~ of the Interior** wazâret id-dâkhiliya; **~ of Justice** wazâret il-'adlîye *wazâret il-Huqûq*; **Foreign ~** wazâret il-khârijiya *wazâret il-khârigiya*

minute daqîqa daqâyik *daqâ'iq*

miracle 'ajîbi *agîba*

misfortune muSîbi *muSîba*

miss (lose, lack) faqad; **I ~ed the bus** fâtni l- buS
   fâtni l- ôtôbîs; **~ing** nâqiS; **one of the bags**
   of my luggage is ~ing nâqiS wâHid mnish-
   shonaT *nâqiS wâHid min esh-shonaT*

mistake RalaT, RalTa; **to make a ~** RiliT fî; **did you**
   not make a ~? manak Riltân? *mantish*
   RalTân?; **you made a ~** RliTT *RiliTT*;
   excuse me, it was my ~ lâ twâkhidni kân
   RalaT minni *mâ ti-âkhiznîsh kân RalaT*
   minni; **you are ~n** inta Riltân *inta Raltân*;
   by ~ bil-RalaT

mistrust tuhmi *tuhma*

misunderstanding sû tafâhum

mix (v., trans.) khalaT; **~ed** makhlûT

moderate (adj.) mu'tadil

modest basîT

moment daqîqa, laHza

monastery dair *dêr* pl. idyuri, dyûra *diyûr*

Monday yaum ittnain *yôm il-etnên, l-etnên*

money maSâri, fulûs *flûs*; **small ~** fakka; **~ changer**
   Sirrâf *Sarrâf*

monk râhib pl. ruHbân

monkey qird pl. qurûd

monster masîkh

month shahr pl. ish'hur, sh'hûr; **~ ly** shahri

moon qamar; **full ~** badr; **new ~** hilâl; **eclipse of the**
   ~ khusûf il-qamar

more kamân *kemân*; **~ than** aktar min; **the ~ ... the ~**
   ... kullma ... kullma, qaddma ... qaddma;
   once ~ tâni marra

morning SubH, SabaH; **good ~** SabaH il-khair *SbâH*
   il-khêr; **in the ~** iS-SubH; **this ~** il-yaum
   'ala bukra *in-naharda iS-SubH*; **tomorrow ~**
   bukra 'ala SubH *bukra is-SubH*

mortgage (n.) rahn

mosque jâmi' *gâmi'* pl. jawâmi' *gawâmi'*; (small
   one) masjid *masgid* pl. msâjid *msâgid*

mosquito(s) (coll.) nâmûs

mosquito net nâmûsîyi *nâmûsîyia*

most aktar; **~ people** aktar in-nâs *aktar in-nâs*

mother umm pl. ummhât *ummahât*; waldi *walda*; **~-
   in-law** Hamât

mother-of-pearl Sadaf, Safad

motor muHarrik; **~boat**; qârib bi-muharrik; **~cycle**
   darrâja bukhârîya, môtôsîkl

mount Tili'; (get on a horse) rikib

mountain jabal *gebel* pl. jibâl *gibâl*

mourning maHzana; **~ woman** (hired female
   mourner) niddâbi *naddâba*

mouse fâr pl. *firân*

mouth tumm, timm *fumm*; (of animals) bûz; **~wash**
   RarRara

move (v., trans.) Harrak, (intrans.) tHarrak *itHarrak*;
   (**~ house**) naqal '*azzil*

movie film pl. aflâm; **~ theater** sinima

Mr. is-saiyid

Mrs. is-saiyida

much ktîr *ketîr*; **too ~** ktîr *ketîr*, ziyâdi *ziyâda*; **very ~** ktîr khâliS *ketîr khâliS*, ktîr jiddan *ktîr giddan*; **~ more** aktar biktîr *aktar biketîr*; **far too ~** ziyâdi biktîr *ziyâda biketîr*; **~ money** maSâri ktîr *fulûs ketîr*

mud tîn, waHl; **~guard** rafraf

muezzin mu'ezzin *mu'eddin*

multiply Darab

municipality baladîyi *beledîya*

murder (n.) qatl; (v.) qatal; **~ed** qatîl; **~er** qâtil

muscle(s) (coll.) 'aDal

museum matHaf pl. matâHif

mushroom fuTr

music mûsîqa; **~ian** 'âzif

musk misk

Muslim muslim pl. muslimîn

must (v.) generally rendered by 'lâzim' (necessary) or 'wâjib 'ala *wâgib 'ala*' with following prefix tense: **I ~ start now** lâzim sâfir hallaq *lâzim asâfir dil waqt*; **you ~ do** that wâjib 'alaik innak ta'mil haida *wâgib 'alêk ti'mil di*; **you ~ not do that** mâ lâzim ta'mil haik *mush lâzim ti'mil kide*

mustard khardal *mustarda*

mutton laHm Ranam, laHm Dâni

myself ana nafsi

mystic Sûfi

N

nail (metal) mismâr pl. msâmir *mesâmir*; (finger)
      Difr *Dufr* pl. aDâfir *Dawâfir*

naked 'iryân *'aryân*

name (n.) ism pl. asmâ, asâmi; **in the ~ of God**
      bismillâh; (v.) samma

namely ya'ni

narrow (adj) Daiyik

nasty (dirty) wakhim; (infamous) qabîH

nation umma; **~al** waTani, ahli; **~ality** jinsiya *ginsiya*

native country blâd *bilâd*, waTan

natural Tabî'i

nature Tabî'a

near jamb min *gamb min*; **~er than** aqrab min

nearly quraiyib

neat sarîf, nâzik

necessary lâzim, Darûri

necessity luzûm

neck 'unq, raqbi *raqaba*, nuqra; **~lace** 'iqd *'uqd*,
      Tauq *Tôq*

need (n.) 'âzi *'âza*; (v.) 'âz, i'tâz, iHtâj *iHtâg*

needle ibri *ibra* pl. ibar

negligent mutRaffil *muRaffal*

negotiate dabbar

neighbor jâr *gâr* pl. jîrân *gîrân*; **~hood** DawâHi

neither ~ ... **nor** lâ ... ulâ *lâ ... walâ*; ~ **one nor the
      other** lâ haida ulâ haida *lâ di walâ di*; ~ **so
      nor so** lâ haik ulâ haik *lâ kide walâ kide*

nephew (son of the brother) ibn il-akh; (son of the
    sister) ibn il-ukht

nerve(s) (coll.) a'Sâb

nest 'ish'sh, wikr

net (n.) shabaki *shabaka*

net (adj.) Sâfi

network (n.) shabaki *shabaka*

never abadan

new jdîd *gedîd* pl. jdâd *gudâd*, judud *gudud*

New Year râs is-sini *râs is-sana*; **happy ~** (to sg.m.)
    kull sini winta sâlim, kull 'âm winta Taiyib
    kull sana winta Taiyib, kull sana winta
    bkhêr; (to pl.) kull sini wintu sâlmîn, kull
    'âm wintu Taiyibîn, kull sini wintu bkhair
    kull 'âm wintu Taiybîn, kull sana wintu
    Taiyibîn, kull sana wintu bkhêr

news khabar pl. akhbâr; **what is the ~?** shû fî jdîd?
    ê fîh gedîd?

nice kwaiyis *kuwaiyis*, zarîf

niece (daughter of the brother) bint il-akh; (daughter
    of the sister) bint il-ukht

night lail *lêl* laili *lêla* pl. iyâli *leyâli*; **in the ~,**
    at ~-time bil-lail *bil-lêl*; **it has become ~**
    Sâr lail *Sâr lêl*; **to pass the ~** nizil, bât

nightingale bulbul

Nile in-nîl; **~ Valley** wâdi in-nîl

nine tis'a

nine hundred tis'mîyi *tus'emîya*

nineteen tisaTa'sh *tis'atâsher*

ninety tis'în

ninth tâsi' f. *tâs'a*

no lâ; **have you ~ …?** mâfi 'indak…? *mâfîsh '
  andak …?*; **~ one** mâ Hada *mâ Haddish*;
  ~ doubt bala shakk; **~ ceremony** min dûn
  tiklîf

noble sharîf

nobody mâ Hada *mâ Haddish*

noise Raushi *dausha*

noiseless bil-wâTi

nominate 'aiyan *'aiyin*; **to be ~d** t'aiyan *it'aiyin*,
  tsamma *itsamma*

non-smoking Rair mudakh'khin *Rêr mudakh'khin*

none mâ Hadda *mâ Haddish*

nonsense kalâm fâreR, hals; **to speak ~** takallam
  ba-la ma'na

noon Duhr

north shmâl *shemâl*; **~ern** shmâli *shemâli*; **~ wind**
  hawa shmâli, hawa smâwi *hawa baHri*

nose minkhar pl. manâkhîr *anf* pl. *unûf*

not mâ mush, mish; **~ at all** abadan, qat'an

nothing mâ shi, mâshi *mush Hâga*; **for ~** bi-lâsh
  ba-lâsh; **as good as ~** ka-inno mâshi *ke-inno
  mush Hâga*; **that is ~** mâ hû shi *mush Hâga*,
  mâ bîsâyil *mâ 'alêsh*

notwithstanding faDlan 'an

November tishrîn it-tâni *nôvember*

now hal-waqt *dil-waqt*; ~ **then!** yalla!
number (n.) 'adad, numro; (v.) 'add
nun râhibi *râhiba* pl. râhbât
nurse (in hospital) mumarriDa; (for childcare) dâdâ
        pl. dadawât
nut jauz *gôz*
nutmeg jauzit iT-Tîb *gôz it-Tîb*

O

oar miqdâf pl. maqâdîf
oasis wâHa
oath yamîn *yemîn*; **to take the** ~ Halaf yamîn *Hilif*
        yemîn
obelisk msalli *mesalla*
obey Tâwa'
objection - there is no ~ mâ fîsh mâni'
oblige RaSab; ~**d** majbûr *magbûr*
obscene fâHish, dinis
observe lâHaz *lâHiz*
obstacle mâni' pl. mawâni'
obstinacy 'inâd
obstinate mu'ânid, 'anid
obstruct sadd
obtain nâl, HaSal 'ala *itHaSal 'ala*, HaSSal
occasion furSa pl. furaS
occident maRrib; ~**al** maRribi
occupied (seat, bathroom, phone) mashRûl;
        (territory) muHtall

occur Sâr *gara*
ocean baHr il-muhîT
October tishrîn il-auwal *oktôber*
odd (number) fard; (strange) Rarîb
odor rîHa
of min
off! rûH
offense ihâni *ahâna*
offer (n.) dafa'; (v.) qaddam *qaddim*; (to bid for)
    dafa' fî; **what can I ~ you?** shû biqdir
    qaddimlak? *aqaddimlak ê?;* **I ~ you ... for it**
    bidfa'lak ... fîh *badfa'lak ... fîh*
office (place) maktab
officer zâbiT pl. zubbâT
official rasmi
often ktîr *ketîr*, amrâr ktîri *imrâr ketîra*
oil (food) zait *zêt*; (petrol) bitrûl *betrôl*, naft
ointment marham pl. marâhim, duhûn
old (not young) kbîr *kebîr*; (not new) qadîm
    pl. qudm; (ancient) 'atîq pl. 'itiq;
    (not fresh) bâyit *bâ'it*; (elderly) 'ajûz *'agûz*;
    ~ man shaikh *shêkh*; **~ woman** 'ajûza
    'agûza; **~ age** shaikhûkha *shêkhûkha*;
    how ~ are you? qaddaish 'umrak?
    ê 'umrak?
oleander difl
olive(s) (coll.) zaitûn *zêtûn*
olive oil zait zaitûn *zêt zêtûn*
olive tree zaitûni *zaitûna*

on fauq *fôq*, 'ala (contracted with the following
    article: 'ala il-kursi = 'al kursi ~ **the chair**)

once marra, fil-qadîm, fil-mâDi (the latter two more
    formerly); (one single time) marra waHdi
    marra waHda; **all at ~** bil-marra

one wâHid f. waHdi *waHda*; ~ **after the other** wara
    ba'dhon *wara ba'duhum*; ~ **another** (we,
    you, they ~ another) ba'dina, ba'dkon
    ba'dukum ba'dhon *ba'duhum*; ~ **by ~**
    wâhidan wâhidan, fardan fardan

onion(s) (coll.) basal

only (single, adj.) wâHid; (but, adv.) faqaT, lâkin

open (adj.) maftûH; (v.) fataH; **to be ~** infataH
    itfataH; ~ **... for me!** iftaHli ...!; **the ~ land**
    fil-barrîyi *fil-khâla*

operator 'âmil tilîfûn

opinion Zunn *Zann*, fikr; **what is your ~?** shû
    fikrak? *fikrak ê?*, shû râyak? *râyak ê?*

opponent khaSm pl. ikhSâm

oppose khalaf

opposite qibâl

oppression zulm

or yâ, yimma, willa *wala*

orange(s) (coll.) burdqân *bortuqân*

orchestra jamâ'at mûsîqa *gamâ'at mûsîqa*

order (arrangement, n.) tirtîb *tartîb*; (command)
    amr pl. awâmir; (~for goods) tûSyi *tauSîya*;
    (religious ~) rahbâni *rahbâna*; (command, v.)

amar; (~ goods) waSSa; **to put into** ~ rattab
rattib

order - in ~ **to** li-ajl *lagl*, min shân ta *min shân*, *'ala
shân*, Hatta, tâ

ordinary 'âdi, i'tiyâdi

organ (mus.) urgun

organ (anat.) 'uDw pl. a'Dâ'

oriental sharqi

origin aSl; **~al** aSli; **~ally** min il-aSl

ornamentation naqsh

orphan yatîm pl. îtâm

ostrich na'âmi *na'âma*

other âkhar f. ukhra pl. ukhar; **the ~ day** haidâk il-
yaum *in-nahâr dok-hâ*

otherwise willa

ought - he ~ to be here kân lâzim inno ykûn haun
kân lâzim yekûn hene

out (where?) barra; (whither?) la-barra *barra*

outer (external) barrâni

outside khârij *khârig*; **from ~** min barra

outskirts DawâHi

oven furn

over fauq *fôq*, fauq min *fôq min*, 'ala; **put it ~ it**
HuTTo fauq minno *HuTTo fôq minno*; **~ five
hours** aktar min khams sâ'ât *aktar min
khamas sâ'ât*; **to be ~** (remain) biqi, fiDil; **to
be ~** (have finished) tamm

overcome Ralab

owe - **how much do I ~ you?** qaddaish ilak 'alaiyi?,
qaddaish ilak 'indi? *kâm lâk 'alêye?, kam
lâk 'andi?;* **you still ~ me s.th.** ba'do ili
ma'ak shî, ba'do ili 'indak shî *lissa lîye
ma'ak shê, lissa lîye 'andak shê*
owl(s) (coll.) bûm
owner mâlik, SâHib
ox taur *tôr* pl. tîrân
oxygen oksîjên

P

p.m. ba'd iD-Duhr *ba'd id-Duhr*
pace mashi, mashyi
pack (v.) Hazam, Dabb *Sarr*
package Tard pl. Turûd
padlock qufl *qifl*
page (book) SaHfa pl. SuHuf
pain waja' *waga'*; **~ful** alîm, bîwajji' *biwaggi'*;
~killer musakkin
paint (n.) laun *lôn*; (v.) rasam; **~er** rassâm; **~ing**
lauHa *lôHa*
pair jauz *gôz*
palate Hulqûm
Palestine filasTîn
Palestinian filasTîni
palm tree(s) (coll.) nakhl
pants banTalôn

paper waraq; **sheet of** ~ waraqa pl. ûrâq *aurâq*
parachute miZallat hubûT
paradise janni *ganna*
paralyzed mashlûl
parasite Tufaili *Tufêli*
parasol shamsiyi *shamsiya*
parcel Tard pl. Turûd
pardon - **I beg your** ~ na'am?
parents il-wâldain *il-wâlidên*
park (v.) rakan il- sayyâra *rakan il-'arabiya*
park (n.) montaza
parrot babâRa, babRâl *babaRân*
parsley baqdûnis
part (n.) juz' *guz'* pl. ajzâ' *agzâ'*
partial juz'i *guz'i*
partisan (follower) tâbi' pl. taba'a
partner sharîk pl. shuraka; ~**ship** shirka, mushâraka
partridge Hajal *Hagal*
party (political) Hizb pl. aHzâb; (company) jamâ'a
        gemâ'a; (social gathering) Hafla pl. Hafalât;
        (soirée) sahra; (v.) iHtafal
pass (n.) mamarr; (cross, v.) 'abar; (go by) marr
passage (~way) mamarr
passenger râkib pl. rukkâb
passion (affection, love) hawa; (desire) shahwa pl.
        shahawât
past (n.) mâDi; (pron. loc.) wara; (pron. time) ba'd
paste (v.) laSaq

patch ruq'a pl. ruqa'; **~ed** muraqqa'
patent (invention) ikhtirâ'
paternal abawi
patience Sabr
patient (adj.) Sabûr
patient (n.) marîD pl. marDa
patriarch (rel.) baTrak pl. baTârki *baTârika*
patrol dauriya
pattern naqsh; (cloth) rasm
pavement blâT *balâT*
pay (n.) ijra *ugra*; (v.) dafa'; **how much do I have to
         ~?** qaddaish lâzim idfa'? *qadde 'aiz minni?*
         qaddaish 'alaiyi? *kâm 'alêye?*; **I want to ~**
         baddi idfa' *'âyiz adfa'*; **I have paid** dafa't
         ana; **I shall ~ on receipt** bidfa' waqt
         it-tislîm *adfa' waqt it-teslîm*; **to whom do I
         have to ~ that?** la-mîn baddi idfa' haida?
         limîn adfa'di?; **~ment** dafa'
pay phone tilîfûn 'âm
pea(s) (coll.) bâzella *bisilla*
peace salâm, SulH; **~ful** salmi
peach(es) (coll.) durrâq *khôkh*
peacock Tâwûs
pear(s) (coll.) njâS *kummitra*
pearl(s) (coll.) lûlu
peasant fallâH *fellâH* pl. fallaHîn *fellaHîn*
pebble baHSa *HaSwa*
pedestrian mâshi

peel (n.) qishr; (v.) qash'shar

pen qalam pl. aqlâm

pension ma'âsh

people (persons) nâs; (nation) sha'b pl. shu'ûb;
     many ~ nâs ktîr *nâs ketîr*

pepper (n.) filfil

percent bil-mîyi *bil-mîye*

perfect (adj.) kâmil

performance (theater) Hafla

perfume 'iTr

perhaps belki, rubbama

peril khaTar; **~ous** mukhauwif

permission izn, rukhsa; **with your ~** bi-iznak, bil-
     izn; **have you received ~** akhatt izn?; **to ask
     for ~** ista'zan *istazin*

person shakhS pl. ashkhâS; **~al** shakhSi, zâti, khâSS

perspire 'iriq; **I am perspiring a lot** ana 'irqân ktîr
     ana 'arqân ketîr

perspiration 'araq

petition Talab

petrol banzîn

petroleum naft

Pharaoh fir'aun *far'ôn*

pharaoni *fara'ôni*; **relics of the ~ period** *asâr
     fara'ôniya*

pharmacy Saidaliya; (~ open 24 hours) Saidaliya
     lailiya *Saidaliya lêliya*

philosopher failasûf *flâsfi* pl. fêlasûf *felâsifa*

philosophy falsafa
photograph (n.) Sûra pl. Suwar; (v.) Sauwar; **~er**
    musauwir
physician Tabîb pl. aTibba
piastre qirsh pl. qurûsh
pick (gather) qaTaf; **~ out** intakhab, **~ up** (lift) qâm;
    ~ it up! qîmo! *shîlo!*
pickles turshe *turshi*
pickpocket (n.) nash'shâl
picture Sûra pl. Suwar
piece qaT'a pl. qiTa'
pig khansîr
pigeon(s) (coll.) Hamâm
pilgrim Hâjj *Hâgg* pl. Hujjâj *Huggâg*; **~age** Hajj *Hagg*
pill Habbi *Habba*
pillar 'amûd pl. 'awâmîd
pillow wisâda
pilot Tayyâr
pin dabbûs pl. dababîs
pincers kimmâshi *kammâsha*
pine Snaubar *Sanôbar*
pink wardi
pious taqi pl. itqya, mutdaiyin
pipe (tobacco) qasabi *qasaba*
pistachio(s) (coll.) fustuq
pity (n.) shafaqa, raHmi raHma; (v.) riHim; **what
    a ~!** Harâm! *yâ khasâra!*
place maHall pl. maHallât; (large open ~) mîdân *mêdân*

plain (ground level; smooth) sahl, sahli pl. suhûl;
      (clear) zâhir, Sâfi

plan khiTTa

planet kaukab *kôkab*

plant (n.) nabât; (v.) Raras

plaster (cataplasm) lazqa; (for walls) Tîn

plastic blâstîk; **made of** ~ min blâstîk

plate SaHn pl. SuHûn

platform raSîf

play (n.) la'b *li'b*; (v.) li'ib

plea Hijji *Hugga*

plead (a cause) Hâma 'an

pleasant maqbûl, laTîf

please (v.) 'ajab *'agab*; **that ~s me very much** haida
      bya'jibni ktîr *di bi'gibni ketîr*; **(in order) to**
      ~ you min shân khâTrak *'ala shân khâTrak*;
      as you ~ 'ala kêfak, 'ala khâTrak, bkhâTrak;
      ~d masrûr; **to be ~d** insarr, firiH, inbasaT

please (to a male, speaker offering s.th.) tfaDDal
      itfaDDal; (to a female, speaker) tfaDDali
      itfaDDali; ~ **enter** tfaDDal fût *itfaddal*
      khush'sh (to male, speaker requesting s.th.)
      min faDlak; (to a female, speaker requesting
      s.th.) min faDlik

pleasure Hazz; **with the greatest ~** bi-mazîd is-surûr
      bi-mezîd is-surûr; 'ar-râs wil'ain *'ar-râs*
      wal-'ên

pledge rahn

plenty ktîr *ketîr*

plough (n.) sikki *miHrât*; (v.) Harat, falaH

plum(s) (coll.) khaukh *berqûq*

plumber samkari

plunder (n.) nahîb; (v.) nahab, salab

p.m. ba'd iD-Duhr *ba'd id-Duhr*

pocket jaib *gêb*; **to put in the ~** HaTT bi-jaib *HaTT bi-gêb*; **to have one's ~ picked** *itnashal*

pod qishr

poem shi'r pl. ish'âr

poet sha'îr pl. shu'ara; **~ry** shi'r

point (dot) nuqta pl. nuqat; (sharp end) râs pl. ru'ûs; **~ed** murauwas *masnûn*

poison (n.) samm, simm; (v.) sammam; **~ous** musimm, sammi

pole (stick) qaDîb pl. quDbân

pole (geogr.) quTb

police shurTa *bolîs*; **~ station** markaz ish-shurTa *markaz il-bolîs*; **~ officer** zâbit bôlis

polish (n.) jila *gila*; (v.) jala *gala*

polite laTîf

politics syâsi *siyâsa*

polluted mitlais

pollution talaus

pomegranate(s) (coll.) rummân

pond birka

pool birka

poor (without money) faqîr pl. fuqara; (miserable) maskîn *meskîn* pl. msâkîn *mesâkîn*

pope bâbâ
poplar Haur *Hôr*
popular mash'hûr
population sukkân
porcelain Sîni
pork laHm khanzîr
port mîna pl. mawâni
Port Said bûr sa'îd
portion qism pl. aqsâm
portrait Sûra pl. Suwar
position mauDi'
possession mulk
possible mimkin *mumkin*
post office busTa, maktab busTa
post office box Sandûq busTa, Sandûq il-barîd
postage ijrit busTa *ugrat busTa*; ~ **stamp** Tâbi'
    il-barîd pl. Tawâbi' il-barîd
postcard tazkaret busTa
pot tanjara *tangara* pl. tnâjir *tenâgir*
potato(es) (coll.) buTâTa *baTâTis*
pottery fâkh'khâr; ~ **workshop** fakhûra
pound (weight) raTl pl. arTâl; (currency) lîra
    ginêh
pour Sabb; ~ **me a glass of ...** Subb-li kubbâyit ...
    Subbi-li kubbâyet...; **it is ~ing down**
    (rain) id-dinyi kâbsi *id-dinya kulliha*
    naTar
poverty faqr
powder sufûf *bôdra*

power (physical strength) qudra; (authority) Hukm;
  that is not in my ~ haida mâ hû bi-yaddi
  di mâ yiTlaH'shê min îdi; **~ful** qadîr,
  'azîm

praise (n.) madH; (of God) Hamd; (v.) madaH;
  (~ God) Hamad; **to ~ oneself** madaH nafso;
  God be ~d il-Hamdillah *il-Hamdo lil-lâh*

pray Salla; (~ for someone) da'a la *da'a li*; **~er** Sala
  pl. Salawât; **to say one's ~er** Salla

preach (rel.) khaTab; **~er** khaTTâb

precaution iHtiyâT; **for ~** lil- iHtiyâT

precede (in rank) taqaddam; (in time) sabaq

preceding sâlif

precious tamîn, nafîs

prefer faDDal; **~ s.th. to** faDDal 'an, faDDal 'ala

pregnancy Habl

pregnant Hibli *Hibla*

prepare hayya'

prescription waSf, ritshetta

presence HaDar

present (adj.) HâDir; **to be ~** HiDir *HaDar*; **the ~
  time** il-waqt il-HâDir; **at the ~ time** hallaq
  il-HâDir, bil-waqt il-HâDir *dil-waqt*

present (n.) hadîyi *hadîya* pl. hadâya

preserve Hafaz (v.); (fruit, etc.) kabas, kabbas

preserved fruit murabba pl. murabbayât *murabbât*

preserved in vinegar makbûs *mukhallal*

president ra'îs *re'îs*, raiyis

press (n., for oil, wine, etc.) ma'Sara pl. ma'âSir;
　　　(printing ~) maTba'a; (v.) 'aSar, kabas,
　　　shadd
previous sâlif
pretty kwaiyis *kuwaiyis*, zarîf
prevent 'auwaq, mana'
price (n.) taman *temen*; **set ~** si'r; **what is the ~?** kam
　　　tamano? *kam temeno?*; **that is an excessive**
　　　~ haida taman fâHish *di temen fâHish*; **don't**
　　　you have s.th. at a cheaper ~? mâ 'indak
　　　minno bi-taman arkhaS? *mâ 'andak shi*
　　　minno bi-temen arkhaS?
pride (haughtiness) kibriya; (self-esteem) 'izza
priest kâhin pl. kahana; (catholic ~) qassîs pl. qusus
prince amîr *emîr* pl. umara
princess amîri *emîra*
principal (n.) raiyis *re'is*; (adj.) aSli, akbar; **~ly**
　　　bil-akhaSS
print (v.) Taba'; **~er** (profession) Tabbâ'
prior sâlif
prison Habs, sijn *sign*; **~er** maHbûs, asîr
private khâSS, khuSûSi; **~ lessons** durûs khuSûSiya
probable il-aRlab
proclamation manshûr
professor ustâz *ustâd* pl. asatza
program birnâmij *birnâmig* pl. barâmij *barâmig*
progress (n.) taqaddum; (v.) taqaddam; **~ive**
　　　mutaqaddim

project mashrû'
prolongation iTâla
promise (n.) wa'd; (v.) wa'ad
promotion taraqqi
pronunciation talaffuz, lafz
proof (evidence) burhân pl. barahîn
proper muwâwiq
property mâl, mulk
prophet nabi *nebi* pl. imbiyi *ambiya*; **by (the life of
    the)** ~ wan-nabi *wan-nebi*, wiHyât in-nabi
    waHyât in-nebi
proportion - **in ~ to** bi-qadr *qadde ma*; **~al** munâsib
protect s.b. Hâma 'an; ~ion Himâyi *Himâya*
protest (n.) iHtijâj; (against, v.) iHtajj 'ala
proud (conceited) mutkabbir *mutakabbir*
prove (v.) barhan
provided that iftaraDna in ... *nifriD in ...*
province wilâyi *wilâya*
provisions mûni *mûna*
proximity qurb
psychiatry it-Tibb in-nafsi
psychic nafsi, nafsâni
psychology 'ilm in-nafs
psychotherapy il-'ilâj in-nafsi
public (adj.) 'umûmi; **~ly** quddâm in-nâs
publish nashar; **~ing** house dâr in-nashr
pull (v.) shadd
pulpit mimbar *mambar*

pulse nabD; **to feel the ~** dass in-nabD
pumpkin(s) (coll.) qar'
punctual - to be ~ Hâfiz 'ala mawa'îd
punish jâza *gâza*; **~ment** jiza *giza, gazaa'*
pupil talmîz pl. talamza, talâmîz
purchase (n.) shiri, shrâyi *shirâya*, mushtara
pure nDîf *naDîf*, Sâfi
purity naDâfi *naDâfa*
purple (adj.) urjuwâni *urguwâni*
purpose qaSD; **on ~** makhSûS, qaSDan
purse kîs pl. ikyâs *akyâs*
push (v.) zaqqa; (vehicle, v.) dafa'; (door) zaqq
put (place, lay) HaTT; **~ away** (hide) khabba; **~ on
    one's clothes** libis**; ~ up with** iHtamal; **I
    cannot ~ up with that** mâ fîni iHmal haida
    mâ aRdarsh aHmil di
putrid 'ifin
pyramid haram pl. ahrâm

Q

qualification mu'ah'hil, mu'ah'hal pl. mu'ah'halât
qualified persons (persons with a diplomas, etc.)
    mu'ah'hilât
quality Sifa pl. Sifât; khaSla
quantity miqdâr, kammiya
quarantine Hajr SiH'Hi *Hagr SiH'Hi*
quarrel (n.) khiSâm; (v.) 'imil kalâm *'amal kalâm*

quarter (a fourth part) rub' pl. erbâ'; (of town) Hai
    Hâra

queen maliki *malika*

quench s.th. - that ~es thirst *Hâga tbarrad il-qalb*

question su'âl pl. is'ili *as'ila*; **that is the** ~ haida
    il-mas'ili *di il-mes'ela*; (v.) sa'al

quick sarî'; ~**ly** qawâm, bil-'ajel *bil-'agel*; ~! yalla

quiet hâdi, sâkit; **be** ~! irtâH! *uskut!*

quite (adv.) bil-khâliS, khâliS

R

rabbi khakhâm, khikhâm

rabbit arnab pl. arânib

racket miDrab

radiator (heating) tadfiya; (mot.) radyatêr

radio radyu

rage (annoyance) RaiZ *Rêz*

railway sikket il-Hadîd; ~ **station** maHatte *maHatta*

rain (n.) shiti *maTar*; (v.) shatta *maTTar, naTTar*; **it is**
    ~**ing** 'am bitshatti *id-dinya bitmaTTar*; **it**
    ~**ed** shattit id-dinyi *id-dinya maTTarit*; ~**bow**
    qaus qadaH *qôs qazaH*; ~**coat** mi'Taf Didd
    il-maTar

raisin(s) (coll.) zbîb *zebîb*

ram kabsh *kebsh*

rampart sûr pl. aswâr

rank rutbi *rutba*

rare nâdir, qalîl il-wujûd *qalîl il-wugûd*

rat fa'r pl. fîrân; jirdaun pl. jarâdin *girz* pl. *girzân*

raven Rurâb pl. aRribi *aRriba*

raw nai

razor mûs pl. mwâs *imwâs*

read qiri *qara* (v.); **can you ~?** bta'rif tiqra? *beta'ra
        tiqra?*; **~ing** qrâyi *qirâya*

ready HâDir, musta'idd; **to be ~** khalaS; **to get ~**
        khallaS, kammal *kammil*

real (genuine) SaHîH

reason (faculty) 'aql; (cause) sabab pl. isbâb *asbâb*;
        for what ~? li-ai sabab? *li-aiyi sabab?*;
        ~able 'aqîl

receipt waSl 'ala, waSl 'an; **notify me of the ~**
        'arrifni 'an il-wuSûl *'arrafni 'an il-wuSûl*;
        give me a ~ a'Tîni waSl, idîni waSl; **to give
        a ~** a'Ta waSl

receive (accept, take) akhad *khad*; (a visitor, guest)
        qibil, qabal *qabil*; (find, get) lâqa; **I ~d your
        letter** wiSil-li maktûbak *wiSil-li gawâbak*

receiver (telephone) sammâ'a

reception istiqbâl; **~ desk** istiqbâl

recipe waSfa

recite qiri *qara*; **~r of prayer** (before congretation of
        Muslims) muballir

recognize 'irif

recommend waSSa; **~ation** tûSyi *tauSiya*; **can you ~
        a good restaurant to me?** btiqdir twaSSîni

'ala maT'am mlîH? btiqdar tewaSSîli 'ala
maT'am yekûn Taiyib?; **do you have a**
recommendation? ma'ak tûSyi? *ma'ak*
tausiya?

reconcile - to be ~d tSalaH *iSTalaH*

reconciliation muSâlaHa, SulH

recover (after sickness) SaHH; (to rest) irtâH
isteraiyaH; (to get back) HaSSal; **~y** (after
sickness) shifa

record (v.) (register) sijill *sigill*; **~ing-tapes** sharâyit
tasjîl *sharâ'it tasgîl*

red aHmar f. Hamra pl. Humr

reddish aHmarâni

reduce (price) nazzal *nazzil*

reduction khaSm

refresh raTTab, barrad; **~ment** (drinks) shî mubarrid
Hâga muraTTaba

refrigerator tillâja *tallâga*

refugee lâji' *lâgi'*; **~ camp** mukhayyam

refuse (v.) rafaD, imtana' 'an

region mintaqa pl. manâtiq; **~al** iqlîmi

register (n.) daftar pl. dfâtir *defâtir*; (v.) sajjal *siggil*;
~ed letter maktûb msajjal *gawâb musaggal*

regret (v.) t'assaf 'ala *itassif 'ala*

regular qiyâsi, 'al qyâs *'al qiyâs*

regulation nizâm, qânûn

reign (v.) Hakam

rein ljâm *ligâm* pl. aljima *algima*

relative (family member) qarîb pl. qarâyib *qarâ'ib*
reliable amîn
relic Dakhîri *Dakhira*
religion dîn, dyâni *diyâna* pl. adyân
religious dîni
rely (on) ittakal 'ala *i'tamad 'ala*; **I ~ on you** bittakil
'alaik *ba'tamid 'alêk*
remain biqi, Dall, fiDil; **~der** baqiya *bâqi*
remark (n.) mulâHaza; (v.) lâHaz *lâHiz*
remedy (n.) 'ilâj *'ilâg*; (v.) 'âlaj *'âlig*
remember iftakar, tzakkar *itzakkar*; **I cannot ~ his
name** mâ bitzakkar ismo *mush mutazakkir
ismo*
remind fakkar; **~ me of ...** fakkirni fi ... *fakkarnini fi
...* (with acc.)
remote control iD-dabT il-ba'îd
remove (a tooth) qala'; (out of a house) naqal, 'azal
removal hair ~ (with depilatory paste made from
sugar, water and lemon juice) Halâwa
renegade murtadda
renew jaddad *gaddad*
rent (n.) ujra *ugra*; (v.) ajjar *aggar*, istâjar *istagar*
repair (n.) tiSlîH *taSlîH*; (v.) SallaH
repeat karrar
repent s.th. nidim 'ala, tnaddam 'ala *itnaddim 'ala*
reply (n.) radd pl. rudûd; (v.) radd
represent massil; **~ative** mumassil; **~ation** tamsîl
reproach (n.) 'itâb; (v.) 'atab *'itib*

reputation Sît

request (n.) Talab; (v.) Talab

require iHtâj *iHtâg*; **~ment** iHtijâj *iHtigâg*

resemblance mushâbaha

resemble shâbah *ashbah*

reserve (v.) Hajaz *Hagaz*; **~d** maHjûz *maHgûz*

resident - **~al area** mantiqa sakaniya

resign ista'fa

resist khâlaf *khâlif*; **~ance** mukhâlafi *mukhâlafa*

respiration tanaffus; **artificial ~** tanaffus Sinâ'i

respite mahl; **give ~ to s.b.** amhal

rest (remainder) bâqi, baqîyi *baqîya*

rest (break) râHa; **I need some ~** btilzamni râHa *ana 'â'iz râHa*; **we will ~ a little** baddna nistrîH shwaiyi *'âuzîn nisteraiyaH shuwaiye*

restaurant maT'am pl. maTâ'im

restore SallaH

resurrection qiyâma

retailer bîyâ' *baiyâ'*

retire Tala' il-ma'âsh *Tili' il-ma'âsh*; **~ment** ma'âsh

return (coming back, n.) rujû' *rugû*; (reply) radd; (v.) riji' *rigi'*; **~ ticket** tizkri rauHa wa-rujû' *tezkira râyih gâiy*

revenge (n.) intiqâm; **to take ~** intaqam

rheumatism dâ il-mafâSil

rhinoceros karkadann

rhyme qâfiyi *qâfiya* pl. qawâfi

rib Dil'n pl. Dulû'

ribbon shirîT *sherîT* pl. ashriTa

rice ruzz, rizz

rich Râni pl. *iRniya* aRnîya

riddle laRz *luRz* pl. ilRâz

ride (n.) mishwâr *mushwâr* pl. mshâwir *meshâwir*;
 (v.) rikib

ridiculous muDHiq

rifle bunduqiya

right (n.) Haqq pl. Huqûq; **you are ~** il-Haqq ma'ak;
 you have no ~ to act like this mâ ilak Haqq
 ta'mil haik *mâlakshi Haqq ti'mil kide*

right (adj.) **the ~ hand** yamîn; **on the ~** 'al yamîn;
 on your ~ hand 'ala îdak il-yamîn; (correct,
 true) SaHîH; **quite ~!** tamâm! (straight,
 sincere) mustaqîm; **~ on the top** fauq khâliS
 fôq khâliS; **to make ~** (adjust) sauwa

rigid shedîd

rim Hâffa

rind qishr

ring (finger ~) khâtim pl. khawâtim

ring (v.) daqq; **to ~ the bell** daqq il-jaras *daqq
 il-garas*

ripe mistwi *mustawi*

ripen (v., trans.) istawa

rise (stand, get up) qâm; (sun, moon) Tili'; **when
 does the sun ~?** aimta btiTla' ish-shams?
 emta tiTla' ish-shams?; **when does the
 moon ~?** aimta byiTla' il-qamar? *emta
 yiTla' il-qamar?*; **the Nile has ~n** in-nîl zâd

river nahr pl. nuhûr

road Tarîq pl. Turuq; **does this ~ lead to…?** biwaddi
haT-Tarîq la…? *biwaddi iT-Tarîq di li…?*;
the first ~ on the left auwal darb bitridd
'ash-shmâl *auwal darb 'ahs-shemâl*; **how
is the ~ to?** kîf id-darb la…? *ezai id-darb
li…?*; **is the ~ dry?** id-darb nâshfi? *id-darb
nâshif?*; **is the ~ very steep?** id-darb daraj
ktîr *id-darb darag ketîr?*

roast (adj.) mishwi *mashwi*; (meat, v.) shawa;
(coffee) HammaS; **~ me a chicken** ishwî-li
jâji *ishwî-li farkha*

robber Harâmi pl. Harâmiya

rock (n.) Sakhr pl. Sukhûr, Skhûr

rocket sarûkh pl. sawârîkh

roof saTH

room ûDa *ôDa* pl. uwaD *owaD*

rooster dîk pl. diyûk

root jidr *gidr* pl. judûr *gudûr*, aSl pl. uSûl

rope Habl pl. Hibâl

rosary (rel.) masbaHa

rose(s) (coll.) ward

rotten mut'affin

rough khishin

round mudauwar; (around) Hawalaih *Hauwalê*, dâyir
mindâr *dâ'ir mindâr*; **~ the town** dâyir min
dâr il-balad *dâ'ir min dâr il-beled*

row (line) Saff pl. Sufûf; (v.) qaddaf *qaddif*; **~ing
boat** qârib pl. qawârib

royal mulûki

rubber maTTât

rubbish (garbage) zibâla

rude faZZ

rug sajjada *saggada*

ruin (destruction) kharâb; (v.) kharrab; ~s (historical
      remains) asâr

rule (law) qânûn; (principle) qâ'idi *qâ'ida*;
      (command) Hukm; (~ over, v.) Hakam 'ala

ruler (governor) Hâkim pl. Hukkâm

ruler (stationary) musTra *masTara*

rush hour zahmit il-muwâSlât

S

sacrifice (n.) dabH

sad Hazîn

saddle (n.) sarj *sarg* pl. srûj *surûg*; (v.) saraj *sarrag*;
      ~ the horses! isruj il-khail! *sarrag il-khêl!*;
      ~bag khurj *khurg*

safe (trustworthy) amîn; (free from danger) sâlim

safety amnîyi *amniya*; ~ **belt** Hizâm amân

saffron za'farân, kurkum

sail (v.) abHar; (n.) qala' pl. qulû'; **small boat with**
      ~s filûka pl. falâyik; **~boat** markab qulû'i
      markib qilâ'i; **~or** baH'Hâr

saint (adj.) mâr; **St. Joseph, etc**. mâr yûsuf, etc.;
      Christian ~ qaddîs pl. qadâdîs; **Muslim** ~
      wali pl. ûliya

salad salaTa; **lettuce or other green** ~ khass

salamander samandar
salary râtib; **monthly ~** mâhiya
sale bai' *bê*; **is this for ~?** haida lish-shiri? *di lish-shira?*
sales tax Darîbat bai' *Darîbet bê'*
salt milH *malH*; (v.) mallaH; **~y** mâliH
salutation salâm
salute s.b. sallam 'ala
same (with def. noun) **the ~ ...** nafs il-...; **at the ~**
       time fi-nafs il-waqt; **that is not the ~** haida
       mush mitl ba'Do *di mush zai ba'Do*; **it is all**
       the ~ to me kullo 'indi sawa *kullo 'andi zai*
       ba'Do
sample 'aiyyina; **a cloth ~** 'ayyinit qumâsh
sand raml pl. rimâl; **~y** ramli; **~stone** Hjar raml
       Hagar raml
sandal Sandal pl. Sanâdil
sanitary SiH'Hi; **~ appliances** adawât SiH'Hiya
satan shîTân *shêTân* pl. shiyâTîn *sheyâTîn*
satiated (with food or drink) shab'ân
satin aTlas
satisfied with râDi bi, mabsûT min; (with food) shibi'
Saturday yaum is-sabt *yôm is-sabt*
sauce marqa
saucer SaHn il-finjân *SaHn il-fingân*
sausage(s) (coll.) sujuqq *suguqq*
savage mutwaH'Hish
save (rescue) najja *nagga*; (spare, economize) waffar;
       God ~ you! Allah ysallmak! *Allah yisallimak!*

savings wafr pl. wufurât

saw minshâr

say qâl; **what did you ~?** shû qult? qult ê?; **what does one ~ in Arabic for…?** kîf bîqûlu bil-'arabi 'an? ê biqûlu bil-'arabi 'an?; **that is to ~** ya'ni; **he/she is said to …** bîqûlu … biqûlu …

scale mîzân

scandal faDîHa, jursa gursa

scarf wishâH

scarab ju'rân gu'rân pl. ja'ârîn ga'ârîn

scarcely anjaq yâ dûb; (with difficulty) biz-zûr; **~ had we arrived** auwal mâ wiSilna

scholar 'âlim pl. 'ulamâ

school madrasa pl. madâris

science 'ilm pl. 'ulûm

scissors maqaSS

scold s.b. zajar zagar

scorpion 'aqrab pl. 'aqârib

scratch (n.) khadsh pl. khudûsh; (v.) khadash; **the cat ~ed me** il-qutt kharbishni; **~mark** kharbûsha

screen (n.) shâsha

screw mismâr musmâr pl. masâmîr; **~driver** mufakk

sculpture timsâl pl. tamasîl

sea baHr pl. bHûr biHâr; **the Dead ~** il-baHr il-mayyit; **the Mediterranean ~** il-baHr il-abyaD; **the Red ~** il-baHr il-aHmar; **~side** sâhil il-baHr

seal (n.) khâtim

seamstress khiyâTa *khaiyâTa*

search s.th. fattash 'ala *fattish 'ala*

season (of the year) faSl pl. fuSûl; (for s.th.) mausim
     mûsim; **~al** mausimi *mûsimi*

seat maq'ad pl. maqâ'id

second tâni f. tânyi *tânye*; **~hand** musta'mal

secret (n.) sirr pl. isrâr; (adj.) sirri, mukhfi; **~ly**
     bil-mukhfi

secretary kâtib *sekretêr*

secular 'âlami

security amân

see shâf; **do you ~ the ... there?** bitshûf haunik...?
     bitshûf henâk...?; **I do not ~ it** mâ bshûfo
     mâ bashûfush; **I ~ nothing** ana mâ bshûf
     ana manish shâ'if Hâga; **have you seen...?**
     shuft...?, shift...?; **when can I come to ~
     you?** aimta biqdir itsharraf la'andkon? *emta
     aRdar atsharraf 'andukum?*; **why don't you
     come to see us more often?** *laish mâ
     bitsharr'fu la'andna aktar? lê mâ
     tisharrifûsh 'andina aktar?*

seed bizâr, bizr, zarî'a; (what is sown) mazrû'a

seek dauwar 'ala

seem baiyan, tabaiyan *itbaiyin*; **it ~s so** mbaiyin haik
     il-baiyin kide, iz-zâhir haik *iz-zâhir kide*; **it
     ~s to me** (lit.: I think so) biftkir *baftikir*

seize misik

seizure qabd

self nafs, zât, Hâl (Syr. only); **I my~** ana nafsi, **you**
(m.) **yourself** inta nafsak, etc.

sell s.th. to s.b. bâ' (with acc. of thing and person);
~**er** bîyâ' *baiyâ'*

send arsal, wadda, ba'at; ~ **me ...** waddî-li ...,
ib'at-li; **I wish to ~ s.th. to ...** baddi waddi
shî la ... *'âyiz ab'at Hâga li...;* **to ~ for**
wadda wara, râH wara; ~ **for s.th.** rûH
wara, ib'at wara, khallîhon yjîbu *khallîhum
yegîbu*

sensation (feeling) shu'ûr

sense (intellect) 'aql; (meaning) ma'na; (feeling)
iHsâs; **the five ~s** il-Hawâss il-khamsi
il-khawâss il-khamsa

sensitive (person) Hassîs

sentence (phrase) jumla *gumla*; (verdict) Hukm

separate (adj.) la-waHdo, la-Hâlo *liwaHdo*;
(v., trans.) faSal; (intrans.) infaSal

September ailûl *sebtember*

sepulchre qabr pl. qubûr; **the Holy ~** (in Jerusalem)
il-qabr il-muqaddas

serene râyiq *râ'iq*, Sâhi

sermon wa'z

servant khâdim *khaddâm*

serve (meal) qaddam iT-Ta'âm; (intrans.) khadam

service khidmi *khidma*; khadâmi *khidâma*;
(**I am**) **at your ~** taHt il-amr, amrak,
HâDir

sesame simsim; ~ **oil** zait simsim *zêt simsim*

set (v., put, place) waDa'; (moon, sun) Rarab, Râb
setting (of the sun) Rurûb, Ryâb *Riyâb*
settle (sink to the bottom) rasab; **~ an account with**
  s.b. Hâsab *Hâsib* (with acc.); **~ accounts**
  with one another itHâsib; (people, land)
  sakkin; (take up residence) istautan; **~ment**
  iskân; **~r** mustautan
seven sab'a
seven hundred sab'mîyi *sub'emîya*
seventeen sabaTa'sh *saba'tâsher*
seventh sâbi' f. sâb'a *sab'a*
seventy sab'în
several ba'D
severe qâsi
sew khaiyat
sex jins *gins*; **the fair ~** il-jins il-laTîf *il-gins il-laTîf*;
  ~ual jinsi *ginsi*; **~ually transmitted**
  diseases amrâD siriya
shade (n.) fai *Dill*; (a shadow thrown by some object)
  khayal; **to sit in the ~** istaDal
shady matraH fîh fai *matraH fîh Dill*
shake (trans.) hazz; (intrans.) ihtazz
shaky mahzûz
shall - **~ I speak?** hal lâzim aHki? *lâzim akallim?*;
  ~ I do this? baddi a'mil haik? *a'mil
  kide?*
shame 'aib *êb*; **~less** qalîl il-Haya
shape (n.) hai'a

---

share (portion) naSîb pl. anSiba; (allotment) HiSSa
     pl. HiSaS; (v.) qassim, qâsim

shark qirsh

sharp Hâdd; **a ~ knife** sikkîna HâDDa; **~en** (v.) sann;
     could you ~en the knife? mumkin tisinn is-
     sikkîna?

shave (n.) Halqa; (v.) Halaq; **give me a ~ and a**
     haircut iHlaq-li daqn wa-sha'r; ~n Halîq;
     clean-~n Halîq id-daqn

shaving cream ma'jûn Hilâqa *ma'gûn Hilâqa*

shawl shâl

she hî, hiyi *hîya, hîye*

sheep(s) (coll.) Ranam

sheet - **~ of paper** waraqa; **bed~** milâya

shell(s) (coll.) Sadaf; (bomb) qunbila, qunbula

shepherd râ'i

shield turs, tirs

shine limi' *lama'*

shiny lam'i

ship (n.) markab *markib* pl. mrâkib *merâkib*; sefîni
     sefîna pl. sufun; (v.) arsal

shirt qamîS pl. qumSân

shoe (pair of ~s) Hidâ' *gazma*; **~maker** jazmâti
     gizamâti

shoot rama; **~ing** rimâya; **~ing star** nijm zârik *nigm*
     zârik

shop (n.) dikkân *dukkân* pl. dkâkîn *dekâkîn*; **to go**
     ~ping itsawwaq

shore shaTT, shâTi

short qaSîr *quSaiyar* pl. quSâr; ~en qaSSar

shorts (coll.) banTalôn shurt, banTalôn qaSîr
　　　　banTalôn quSaiyar

shortage naqS

shoulder kitf pl. iktâf

shout (n.) za'qa; (v.) za'q; **~ing** zi'îq; **~ of joy**
　　　　zalRûT *zarRûTa* pl. zalâRîT *zarâRît*

shovel (n.) mijrafi *magrafe*

show (v.) warra; **~ me** warrîni; **to ~ the way** dall; **is
　　　　there anyone who could ~ me the way?**
　　　　fî Hada bîdillni? *fîh Haddi yidillini?*

shrimp(s) (coll.) qraydis *rêdis*

shrink inkamash *kash'sh*

shut (trans.) Ralaq; **to be ~** inRallaq

shutter darfi *darfa*

shy yijfil *yigfil*

sick marîD, 'alîl; **~ness** marD

side jamb *gamb*, jânib *gânib*, Saub *naHya*; **on this ~**
　　　　fî haS-Saub *bin-naHya di*; **on that ~** fî
　　　　haidâk iS-Saub *bin-naHya dik-hâ*; **to this ~**
　　　　la haS-Saub *lin-naHya di*; **go on the other ~**
　　　　rûH la haidâk iS-Saub *rûH lin-naHya dik-
　　　　hâ*; **on the ~** 'al-jânib *'alal-gamb*; **on my ~**
　　　　'ala jambi *'ala gambi*

sieve Rirbâl *Rurbâl*

sift Rarbal

sigh (n.) tanhîda; (v.) tnah'had *itnah'hid*

sight (vision) baSar; (aspect) manzar
sign 'alâmi *'alâma* pl. alâmât; (v.) amDa
signature imDa
silence (n.) sukût; (v.) sakkit
silent - to be ~ sakat *sukut*; **be ~!** uskut!
silk Harîr; **of ~** min Harîr
silly (stupid) Rabi
silver fiDDa *faDDa*
similar mshâbih *mushbih*
simple basîT
simplicity basâTa
simply (solely) faqaT
sin (n.) khaTîyi *khaTîya* pl. khaTâya; (v.) khaTa,
          akhTa
Sinai sîna
since (prep.) ~ **that time** min Haidâk il-waqt *min*
          il-waqt dik-ha; ~ **the time when** min waqt
          illi *min waqt mâ*;; ~ **when?** min aimta? *min*
          emta?; **a year ~** min sini *min sana*; **some**
          time ~ min middi *min mudda*
since (adv.) min Hais *min Hês*
sincere mustaqîm; **~ly** bi-kull ikhlâS
sincerity Sadâqa, Sidq
sing Ranna; **~er** muRanni f. muRannîyi muRannîya
          pl. maRâni; **~ing** Rina
single (not double) mufrad, munfirid *munfarid*; (not
          married) 'âib pl. 'uzzâb
singly waHdo, laHâlo *bi-nafso*

sink (n.) HauD *HôD*; **kitchen** ~ HauD matbakh *HôD matbakh*; **bathroom** ~ HauD Hammâm *HôD Hammâm*

sink (v.) nizil; (ship) Ririq

Sir yâ sîdi

sister ukht pl. akhawât *ukhwât*; ~**-in-law** silfi *silfa*

sit qa'ad; ~ **down!** u'qud!

situation waD'

six sitti *sitta*

six hundred sittmîyi *suttemîya*

sixteen siTTa'sh *sittâsher*

sixth sâdis f. sadsi *sadsa*

sixty sittîn

skin jild *gild*

skirt junilla *gunilla*

skull jimjimi *gimgima*

sky sama pl. samawât; (atmosphere) falak *felek*

slave 'abd pl. 'abîd; ~**ry** 'ubudiya

sleep (n.) naum *nôm*; (v.) nâm; **I need to get some** ~ baddi nâm *'âyiz anâm*; **I have not slept the whole night** mâ nimt Tûl il-lail *mâ nimtish Tûl el-lêl*; **I have not yet slept enough** ba'd mâ shbi't mnin-naum *lissa mâ istaufêtshi in-nôm*; **I wish to** ~ **late** baddi nâm ktîr *'âyiz anâm ketîr*; **how did you** ~? kîf aSbaHt il-yaum? *kêf aSbaHt in-naharda?*; **to** ~ **with** nâm ma'a; ~**y** na'sân; ~**ing pill** munawwim pl. munawwimât

sleeve kumm pl. akmâm; **a short-~d shirt** qamîS
     bi-nuSS kumm

slender raqîq

slipper shibshib

slow 'almahl *bishwêsh*; **my watch is ~** sâ'ati
     bitakh'khir *sâ'ati mitakh'khara*; **~ly!** 'ala
     malak! shwai shwai! *shuwaiye shuwaiye!*

small zRîr *zuRaiyar* pl. zRâr *zuRaiyerîn, zuRâr*; **~er**
     than azRar min

smell (odor) rîHa pl. rawâyiH *rawâ'iH*; (scent)
     shamm; **bad ~** rîHa kerîha; **this flower has**
     a very pretty ~ haz-zahra ilha rîHa jamîli
     ktîr *iz-zahra di liha rîHa gemîla qawi*;
     (v., trans.) shamm; **it ~s bad here** haun fî
     rîHa mush Taiybi hene *fîh rîHa mush*
     Taiyiba hene

smile (n.) ibtisâma; (v.) tabassam *itbassam*

smoke (n.) dukhân; (v.) shirib dukhân; **~r** shirrîb
     dukhân; **~-free** mâ fîhi dukhân

smoky mudakh'khan

smooth (adj.) mâlis, laiyin

smuggle (v.) harrab; **~d tobacco** dukhân muharrab

snail Halazûn *Halazôn*

snake Haiyi *Haiya*, ta'bân; **~ charmer** (in Egypt)
     Hâwi

sneeze 'aTas *'aTTas*

snow talj *telg*; **it is ~ing** 'am btitlij id-dinyi, nâzil talj
     nâzil telg

so haik *kide*

soap (n.) Sâbûn; ~ **opera** musalsala

sock kalsa pl. kalsât *gaurab* pl. *gawârib*

social security Damân ijtimâ'i *Damân igtimâ'i*

sofa arîka *kanaba*

soft nâ'îm

soil (n.) trâb *turâb*, arD; (v.) wassakh; ~**ed** wusikh
                wisikh

soldier 'askari

sole (n.) na'l

sole waHîd; ~**ly** faqaT

solicitor wakîl da'âwi

solitude waHshi *waHsha*

some ba'D; ~ **days** kam yaum *kâm yôm*; ~ **people**
                ba'D in-nâs; ~**body** aHad, wâHid; ~**thing**
                shî *shê*, *Hâga*; ~**where else** makân tâni

son ibn pl. abnâ, walad pl. aulâd; ~**-in-law** Sahr *Sihr*

song uRnîyi pl. aRâni

soon qarîb, ba'd shwaiyi *ba'd shuwaiye*

sorcerer sâHir, saH'Hâr

sorcery siHr

sore (adj.) maqrûH; (n.) qarHa pl. quraH

sorrow Ramm *Huzn*; ~**ful** Hazîn

sorry âsif, muta'assif

soul nafs (f.) pl. infus, rûH

sound (n) Saut *Sôt*

sound (adj.) SaHîH

soup shorba

sour HâmiD

south janûb *ganûb*

sovereign Hâkim pl. Hukkâm

space wasa‘a

spare parts quTa‘ Riyâr *Hitat Riyâr*

spare tire Dûlâb ziyâda *‘agala ziyâda*

spark sharâri *sharâra*

sparrow ‘uSfûr pl. ‘asâfîr

speak Haka, tkallam *kallim, itkallim*; **you ~ too quickly** inta bitrauwij ktîr bil Haki *inta betista‘gil ketîr bil-Haki*; **~ slowly so that I can understand** iHki shwai shwai tâ ifhamak *iHki shuwaiye shuwaiye ‘ala shân afhamak*; **is there anyone here who ~s English?** fî Hada haun yiHki inglîzi? *fî Haddi hene yiHki ingelîzi?*; **I wish to ~ to Mr. ...** baddi kallim is-saiyid ... *‘âyiz akallim is-saiyid...;* **~er** khâTib

special (adj.) KhâS; **~ly** khâSSatan, khuSûSan

speech (language, words) kalâm; (discourse) khiTâb

speed (n.) sur‘a; **to ~ up** asra‘; **~ limit** Hadd lis-sur‘a

spend (money) Saraf

sphinx abul haul *abul hôl*

spice baHâr pl. baHârât

spicy Hârr

spider ‘ankabût; **~web** bait il-‘ankabût

spinach sbânikh *sabânikh*

spirit rûH (f.) pl. irwâH; **the Holy ~** ir-rûH il-qudus; **~ual** rûHâni

spit (v.) bazaq *taff*

spittle bizâq *tifâf, tifâfa*

split (trans.) shaqq

spoil (go bad) fassad *fisid*; **~ed** mafsûd *fasdân*;
        (pamper) dallil; **~ed** (pampered) midallil

sponge(s) (coll.) sfinj *safing, sifing*

spoon mal'aqa, ma'laqa pl. ma'âliq; **~ful** mal'aqa

spot (v.) (stain) buq'a pl. buqa'; **~ remover** muzîl
        lil-buq'a; (locality) buq'a, maHall

spouse (husband) jauz *gôz*; (wife) jauzi *gôza*

spread (v., trans.) madd, farash

spring (season) rabî'

sprinkle rash'sh

spy jâsûs *gâsûs*

square (n., adj.) murabba'; (public space) sâHa;
        ~ meter mitr murabba'

stable (n.) yâkhûr *iالسTabl*

stairs daraj *darag*, sullam *sellim*

stamp (n.) Tâbi' pl. Tawâbi'

stand (v.) waqaf; **to ~ up** qâm; (bear) iHtamal

star nijmi *nigma* pl. nujûm *nugûm*

start (n.) bidâya; (v.) bada; **~ with …** istabda bi …

state (condition) Hâl, Hâli *Hâla*; (nation) dauli *daula*

station maHatta

stationary adawât maktabiya

statue timsâl

stature qâmi *qâma*

stay (n.) iqâma; (v.) biqi; **~ here until I come back**
        khallîk haun Hatta tâ irja' *khallîk hene lamm*
        arga'; **we will ~ at this place two or three**

days baddna niksir fî hal-balad yaumain tlâti
        'auzîn nifDal fil-beled di yômên telâta

steal saraq; **stolen** masrûq

steam bukhâr; **~ship** bukhârîya

steel bulâd

step (n.) khaTwa; (v.) khaTTa; (gradation) daraji
        daraga

stepson rebîb; **~daughter** rebîba; **~father** râb;
        ~mother râba

steward muDîf; **~ess** muDîfa

stick (n.) qaDîb pl. quDbân; **walking ~** 'aSâyi *'aSâya*
        pl. 'iSi

stick (v., trans.) lazaq, liziq; **to be stuck** tlazzaq
        itlazzaq

still (yet) lissa, kamân, ba'd; (nevertheless) ma'a
        zâlik; **are you ~ ill** ba'dak marîd? *lissa*
        'aiyân?

still (silent) sâkit

sting (of insects) las'a; (v.) lasa'

stirrup rikâb pl. rikâbât

stock (of goods) makhzin *makhzan* pl. mkhâzin
        makhâzin

stock market bôrSa

stomach mi'di *mi'da*

stone Hajar *Hagar* pl. aHjâr *aHgâr*

stool skamli *targil*

stop (v., intrans.) waqaf *wiqif*; (trans.) waqqaf; **~!**
        qif!; **~ping place** mauqif pl. mawâqif; **my**
        watch has ~ped waqfit sâ'ati *wiqfet sâ'ati*

story (floor) tabaqa *dôr*

stork laqlaq

storm zauba'a *zôba'a*

story Hikâyi *Hikâya*; qiSSa pl. qiSaS; **~teller**
        Hakawâti *muHaddit*

straight mustaqîm; **~ ahead** dôgru, dugri

strand shâTi

strange Rarîb

stranger ajnabi *agnabi* ajânib *agânib*

strangle khanaq

strap (of leather) jildi *gilda*

straw qash'sh

strawberry(ies) (coll.) fraiz *faraula*

street shâri' pl. shawâri'

strength qûwi *qûwa*; (~ to endure s.th.) Tâqa

stretch (trans.) madd; (intrans.) imtadd
        itmadd

strike (n.) iDrâb; (v., go on ~) aDrab; (hit) Darab;
        the lightening has struck nizlit zâ'iqa
        nizilet SaHqa

striped muqallam *miqallim*

stroke Darbi *Darba*

stroll - go for a ~ shamm il-hawa

strong qawi, shedîd

student Tâlib pl. Tullâb

study (n.) dirâsa; (v.) daras

stuffed (food) miHshi *maHshi*

stumble ta'assar, itka'bil

stupid Rashîm

stutter ladaR
subject (matter, theme) mauDû' pl. mawâDi'
submission (handing over) taslîm
submit sallim
submissive mutwaDi'
subtract TaraH; **~ed** maTrûH
subway mitrô
suburb Dahya pl. DawâHi
succeed najaH *nagaH*
success najâH *nagâH*
successive mittâbi'
such haik *kide*
suck maSS; (child at the breast) riDi'
suckle raDDa'
Suez Canal qanât suwîs
suddenly 'al faur *fag'a*
suffer iHtamal, Tâq
sufficient kâfi
suffocate khanaq, faTas *fiTis*
sugar sukkar
suicide - to commit ~ qatil nafso
suit (man's suit, woman's pants-suit) badla pl. bidal
suit (v.) waafiq; **that does not ~ me** haida mâ
          bîwâfiqni *di mâ yifâwiqnîsh*
suitable munâsib
sultry mufaTTis
sum (total) jimli *gumla*; (amount) mablaR pl. mbâliR
          mebâliR
summer Saif *Sêf*

summit râs pl. ru'ûs

summon - **~ to court** jalab lil-maHkama *Talab lil-maHkama*

sun shams; **the ~ is very hot today** ish-shams il-yaum Hârra ktîr *ish-shams in-naharda Hârra ketîr*; **to walk, sit in the ~** mishi, qa'ad bish-shams; **what time does the ~ rise?** aimta bitiTla' ish-shams? *emta tiTla' ish-shams?*, aimta Tlû' ish-shams *emta Tulû' ish-shams*; **what time does the ~ set?** aimta bitRib ish-shams *emta teRîb ish-shams* aimta Rurûb ish-shams *emta Rurûb ish-shams*

sunbeam shi'â' pl. ashi''a

Sunday yaum il-aHad, yaum il-Hadd *yôm il-Hadd*, *il-Hadd*

sunrise Tlû' ish-shams *Tulû' ish-shams*

sunset Rurûb ish-shams

sunstroke - **I have a ~** khadni ish-shams

supper 'asha

supply (n.) mûni *mûna*; (v.) warrad; **to be supplied** itwarrad

supposing that faraDan … *faraDna in …*

surgeon jarrâH *garrâH*

surgery jirâHa *girâHa*

surprise (n.) mufâj'a *mufâg'a*; (v.) fâja' *fâ'gi'*

suspect (v.) Zann

suspicion Zann pl. Zunûn

swallow bala'

swear Hilif; **~ at s.b.** sabb

sweep (v.) kannas *kanas*
sweet Hulu, Hilu
sweets Halawiyât
swell waram *wirim*; **~ing** waram pl. aurâm
swim sabaH; **can you ~?** bta'rif tisbaH? *beta'raf*
        tisbaH?; **~ming** sibâHa; **~ming pool**
        Hammâm sibâHa
swing (n.) marjûHa *murgêHa*
swollen wârim
sword saif *sêf* pl. syûf *siyûf*
Syria sûrya, shâm
Syrian shâmi pl. shwâm
syringe miHqân
system niZâm pl. anZima; **~atically** bi-niZâm

T

table Tauli *Tarabêza*; **dining ~** sufra; **~cloth** mafrash
        sufra
tablet lauH
tail daneb, dambi *dêl*
tailor khiyâT *khaiyât, tarzi*
take akhad *khad*; **~!** khôd! *khod!*; **~ off** (v.) qâm
tale qiSSa pl. qiSaS
talent mauhiba pl. mawâhib; **~ed** mauhûb
talk (n.) kalâm; (v.) takallam, Haka; **to ~ big** fashar;
        this man ~s too much hal-insân byiHki ktîr
        il-insân di biHki ketîr; **~ative** mutakallim
tall Tawîl pl. Tuwâl

tamarind tamar hindi

tamarisk Tarfa

tar (pitch) qaTrân

tariff ta'rifa

taste (of s.th.) Ta'mi *Ta'ma*; (of s.b.) zauq *zôq*; **that
has a good ~** haida Ta'mtoTaiybi *di Ta'meto
Taiyiba*; **that is not my ~** haida mush 'ala
khâTri *di mush 'ala khâTri*; (v.) zâq,
istaT'am; **it ~s like** haida Ta'mto ... *di
Ta'meto...;* **that ~s bad** haida ilo Ta'mi
radîyi *di lo Ta'ma baTTâla*

tasty (food) zâqi *lazîz*

tattoo (v.) daqq

tax Darîbi *Darîba* pl. Darâ'ib

tea shây

teach 'allam *allim*; **~er** m'allim *me'allim*; **~ing** ti'lîm
ta'lîm

tear (n.) dam'a pl. dmû' *dumû'*

tear (v.) qaTa', khazzaq *sharmaT*

tedious bîza"il *biza"al*

telephone (n.) tilifôn; **~ call** mukâlami tilifôniyi
tilifôn; **~ booth** kishk tilifôn; **~ directory**
dalîl tilifôn *daftar tilifôn*; (v.) talfan *talfin*;
by ~ tilifôni

television tilifizyôn

tell qâl, Haka, aHka; **could you please ~ me ...** iza
kân bitrîd qulli...; **~ him to come** qullo tâ
yiji *qullo yigi*; **~ me the story from the
beginning to the end** iHkîli il-qiSSa

mnil-auwal lil-âkhir *iHkîli il-Hikâya min*
il-auwal lil-âkhir

temper (anger) za'l

temperature darajit il-Harâra *daragit il-Harâra*

temple (edifice) ma'bad pl. ma'âbid

temple (anat.) maSdaR pl. maSâDir

temporary muwaqqat

temporarily bi-Sifa muwaqqata, muwaqqatan

ten 'ashra *'ashara*

tenant musta'jir *musta'ger*

tender Tari

tent khaimi *khêma* pl. khiyam

tenth 'âshir f. 'ashra

terrace tirâs

test (n.) imtiHân; (v.) imtahan; **medical** ~ faHs Tibbi
pl. fuHûs Tibbiya

testament (last will) waSiya *wiSiya*; **the Old** ~
il-'ahd il-'aTîq; **the New** ~ il-'ahd il-jadîd
il-'ahd il-gadîd

testimony shihâdi *shihâda* pl. shihâdât

text matn

texture nasîj *nasîg*

than min; **better** ~ aHsan min; **bigger** ~ aktar
min

thank (v.) shakar, tshakkar *itshakkar*; **~ful** shakûr,
shâkir; **~s** shukr; **~ you** shukran

that (pron.) hadâk, haidâk *dik-hâ, duk-hâ, duk-hauwa*
f. hadîk, haidîk *dik-hâ, dik-haiya* pl. hadolîk,
haudîk *duk-hamma*

that (conj.) in (before vowels: inn); ~ **I** inni; ~ **you**
(m.) innak; ~ **you** (f.) innik; ~ **he** inno; ~ **she**
inha *innâha*; ~ **we** inna; ~ **you** inkon
innûkum; ~ **they** inhon *innûhum*; **in order** ~
tâ, Hatta, min shân *'ala shân*

the il

the … the … kullma … kullma

theater masraH

theft sirqa

then haidâk il-waqt *dok hal-waqt*

there haunîk *hunâk*, *henâk*; ~, **take!** khôd!; ~ **he is**
hai hû *âho*; ~ **she is** hai hî *âhi*; ~ **and back**
bir-râyiH u-bijjâyi *bir-râ'iH wa-biggâ'i*;
is ~ … **here?** fî haun…? *fîh hene…?*, byûjad
haun….? *yûgad hene…?*; **what is** ~ **to eat?**
shû fî lil-akl? *êsh fîh lil-akl?*

therefore fa izan

thereupon ba'do, ba'd minno, ba'dên

thermometer mîzân il-Harâra

they hinni *hum*, *huma*

thick takhîn, smîk, Dakhm; ~**ness** sumk, tukhn

thief Harâmi pl. Haramîyi *Harâmiya*

thigh fakhd pl. afkhâd

thimble kishtbân *kustebân*

thin rafî' *rufaiya*; (flowing, fluid) sâyil; (not
numerous) qalîl

thing shî *shê* pl. ishya *ashya*, Hâji *Hâga* pl. Hawâyij
Hâgât; **take my** ~**s upstairs** waddi Hawâyji
la-fauq *waddi Hâgâti li-fôq*; **these are my**

     ~s, three pieces hai Hawâyji tlât qiTa' *di*
        Hagâti telâta qiTa'; (matter) amr pl. umûr

think iftakar; **I ~** biftikir *baftikir*

third tâlit f. tâlti *talta*

thirst 'aTash; **~y** 'iTshân *'aTshân*

thirteen tlaTTa'sh *telatâsher*

thirty tlâtîn *telâtîn*

this hâda, haida *da* f. hâdi, haidi *di* pl. hadôl, haudi
        dôl; **~ day** il-yaum, han-nahâr *in-naharda*; **~
        evening** il-'ashîyi *il-misa*; **~ morning** il-
        yaum 'ala bukra *in-naharda iS-SubH*

thorn shauki *shôka*

though ma'a in

thought fikr pl. ifkâr; **~ful** mutafakkir

thousand alf

thread khaiT *khêT* pl. khîTân

threaten haddad, khauwaf

three tlâti *telâta*, talât

three hundred tlâtmîyi *tultemîya*

threshold 'atabi *'ataba*

throat Hulqûm

throne takht

through min, bi; (~ means of) biwâsTa

throughout Tûl; **~ the week** Tûl il-jum'a *tûl il-gum'a*

throw (v.) rama

thumb ibhâm pl. ibhâmât

thunder ra'd; **it is ~ing** in-dinyi 'am btir'ad *id-dinya
        betirad*; **~storm** zauba'a

Thursday yaum il-khamîs *yôm il-khamîs*

thus haik *kide*

ticket tizkri *tezkira* pl. tzâkir *tezâkir*

ticket window shubbâk tzâkir *shubbâk tezâkir*

tie (n.) krâfât

tie (v., shoes) rabaT

tiger nimr

tight (drawn) mash

till (conj.) Hatta, Hatta tâ

time waqt, zamân *zemân*; **what's the ~?** qaddaish
        is-sâ'a? *is-sâ'a kâm?*; **it is ~ to go** Sâr
        il-waqt tanrûH *âho il-waqt nerûH*; **do you**
        have ~? ilak waqt? *ma'âk waqt?*; **we still**
        have ~ ba'd ma'na waqt *lissa ma'âna waqt*,
        ba'd mâ Sâr il-waqt *lissa mâ gâsh il-waqt*;
        in due ~ ma'a il-waqt; **at the same ~** fi nafs
        il-waqt; **appointed ~** mîqât; **for a long ~**
        min zamân *min zemân*; **summer ~** tauqît
        Saifi *tauqît sêfi*; **local ~** tauqît maHalli;
        three ~s tlâti marrât *telâta marrât*

timetable jadwal *gedwal*

timid khajûl *mistHi*

tin qazdîr *qazzîr*, tanek *SafîH*

tip baqshîsh

tire (n.) iTâr pl. itârât

tire (v., trans.) ta'ab *at'ab*; (intrans.) ti'ib; **~d** ti'bân
        ta'bân; **~d of** (annoyed with) zi'lân min
        za'lân min

tiring - **that is very ~** haida shî yit'ib ktîr *di shê*
        yit'ib ketîr

tissue mandîl pl. manâdîl

to la *li*, ila, laHadd *liHadd*; (in order ~) tâ; **from …
to ~** min … la *li…*; **from two ~ three** tnain
tlâti *itnên telâta*; **go ~ the doctor** rûH la'and
it-tabîb; **up ~ ten pieces** la-Hadd il-'ashra
qiTa' *li-Hadd il-'ashara qiTa'*; **how far is
it ~ …?** qaddaish fî ba'd la…? *qaddi e lissa
li…?*

tobacco dukhân

today il-yaum, han-nahâr *in-naharda*

toe iSba' ir-rijl *iSba' ir-rigl* pl. Sâbî' ir-rijl *Sawâbi'
ir-rigl*

together sawa, ma'a ba'D

toilet (lavatory) marHâD pl. marâHîD (more
commonly used in the pl.), tuwalitt; **~ paper**
waraq tuwalitt

tolerate iHtamal, Tâq; **I cannot ~ that** mâ fîni Tîq
haida *mâ aRdarsh aTîq di*; **why do you ~
that?** laish tiHmal haida? *tiHmil di lê?*

tomato(es) (coll.) banadûra *Tamâtim*

tomb tirbi *turbe*

tomorrow bukra, Rada, Radi; **~ morning** bukra 'ala
iS-SubH *bukra iS-SubH*

tongs (coll.) malqâT *mâsha* pl. melâqiT *mâshâT*,
kimmâshi *kammâsha*

tongue lisân

tonight il-laili *il-lêla*, hal-laili *il-lêla di*

too (also) kamân *kemân*; **~ big, ~ small**: generally
rendered by the simple adjective, sometimes

'biz-ziyâdi *biz-ziyâda*' is added; **one ... ~
much** ziyâdi bi ... *ziyâda bi...*

tool âla pl. âlât, adâ pl. adawât

tooth sinn pl. snân *sinân*; **~brush** furshit snân *furshit
sinân*; **~paste** ma'jûn snân *ma'gûn sinân*

top râs pl. ru'ûs

torch mish'al *mash'ala* pl. mshâ'il *mashâ'il*

torn mukhazzaq

tortoise ZilHifi *ZilHifa*

total kullîye; (adj.) kull

tourism siyâHa

tourist sâyiH pl. suwwâH; **~ic** siyâHi

towel minshifi pl. mnâshif *fûTa* pl. *fuwaT*

tower burj *borg* pl. ibrâj *ibrâg*

town balad *beled*; mdîni *medîna* pl. mudun

trade (commerce) tijâra *tigâra*

traffic murûr; **~ jam** zaHmit il-muwâSalât, izdiHâm;
~ light Dau il-murûr; **~ officer** zâbit
il-murûr; **~ violation** mukhâlafit il-murûr;
~ signal 'alâmât murûr

train (n.) qaTr pl. quTurât

train (v.) rabba

traitor khâyin *khâ'in*

translate tarjam *targim*

translation tarjimi *targama*

transport (v.) naqal; **~ation** (n.) naql

trap fakh'kh pl. fkhâkh *fukhûkh*

travel (n.) safra; (v.) sâfar *sâfir*; **~er** musâfir; **~
agency** wikâlit siyâhiya; **~ companion** rafîq

treasure kinz pl. kunûz
treat (n.) mukâfa
treatment (med.) mu'âlaji *mu'âlaga*
treaty mu'âhadi *mu'âhada*
tree(s) (coll.) shajar *shagar*
tremble rijif *irta'ash*
trial muHâkma
tribe qabîli *qabîla* pl. qabâyil *qabâ'il*
tribunal maHkami *maHkama*
trouble (n.) kadar; (v., trans.) kaddar; **to ~ oneself**
    ijtahad, 'imil juhdo *'amal guhdo*
trousers (coll.) banTalôn
truck shâHina
true SaHîH
truly (really) Haqqan; (as an oath) wallâhi!
trumpet bûq
trunk qurmi, qurmîyi *qurma* pl. qarâmi
trust (n.) ittikâl, i'timâd; **to ~ in** twakkal 'ala
    itwakkal 'ala, i'timad 'ala *i'tamad 'ala*
trustworthy amîn
truth haqîqa
try jarrab *garrab* (v.)
Tuesday yaum it-tlâti *yôm il-talât*
tumor waram pl. aurâm
turban 'amâmi *'imma* pl. 'amâyim *'imâm*
Turkish turki pl. atrâk
turn (n.)daur *dôr*; **it's your ~** hallak ija daurak
    dil-waqti ga dôrak; (v., trans.) dauwar;
    (intrans.) dâr; **~ red** iHmarr; **~ round!**

        (trans.) dûr!; ~ round! (intrans.) dauwir!;
        ~ **aside** Haiyad, Hâyad *Hauwad*; ~ **back** riji'
        rigi'; ~ **over** (trans.) qalab; ~ over (intrans.)
        inqalab; ~ **on the radio** fataH ir-radyu

turnip(s) (coll.) lift
turtle sulaHfât
twelve Tnâsh *itnâsher*
twenty 'ishrîn
two tnain f. tintain *itnên*
two hundred mîtain *mîtên*
typhus tîfûs
tyranny zulm

U

ugly qabîH
ultimate akhîr
umbrella miZalla
unable Rair qâdir *Rêr qâdir*
unbeliever kâfir pl. kuffâr
uncle (father's brother) 'amm pl. 'umûmi *a'mâm*;
      (mother's brother) khâl pl. akhwâl
uncooked nai
under (prep.) taHt; (adj.) taHtâni; ~ **the table** taHt
      iT-Tauli *taHt iT-Tarabêza*
underneath min taHt
understand fihim; **did you ~ me?** fhimt 'alaiyi?
      fihimt?; **I ~ but little Arabic** mâ bifham

'arabi illa qalîl *mâ afhamshe 'arabi ill qalîl*;
I do not ~ you mâ fhimtak *mâ fhimtish*; **is**
there anyone here who ~s English? fî hada
haun yifham inglîzi? *fîh haddi hene yifham*
ingelîzi?

undress shalaH
unfortunate maskîn pl. msâkîn *mesâkîn*; **~ly** li-sû
il-Hazz
uniform badali rasmîyi *badla rasmiya*
uninhabited mâHada sâkin fîh *mâHaddish sâkin fîh*
unite jama' *gama'* (v.)
United Nations il-umam il-mutaH-Hida
United States of America il-wilayât il-muhtaHHida
university jâmi'a *gâmi'a*
unknown mush ma'rûf, majhûl *maghûl*
unlawful Harâm
unnecessary mush lâzim
unoccupied fâDi
unripe fijj *'agr*
unscrew fakk il-barRi *Hall il-barrîma*
untie fakk
until (prep.) la-Hadd *li-Hadd*; (conj.) Hatta, Hatta tâ
untrue Rair SaHîH *kidb*
up fauq *fôq*
uphill murtaqa
upper fûqâni *fôqâni*; **~ Egypt** is-si'îd
upset (v., trans.) qalab
upside down munqalib

urinate bâl
urine baul *bôl*
usage isti'mâl
use (n.) nafa', fâyidi *fâ'ida*; (habit) 'âdi *'âda* pl.
  'âdât; (v.) ista'mal
used to mut'auwid 'ala *mit'auwid 'ala*
useful nâfi', mufîd
useless mush nâfi'
usual musta'mal; **as ~** Hasab il-âdi *Hasab il-'âda*;
  ~ly 'âdatan, 'al-Râlib, il-aRlab
utmost Râyi *Râya*, âkhir

V

vacation 'uTla
vacant khâli
vaccination taT'îm
vacuum cleaner 'âlit tanDîf kahrabâ'iya
vain (adj.) mutkarrib *mutkebbir*; **in ~** bilâsh *balâsh*,
  ba-la fâyidi *ba-la fâ'ida*, bala nafa'; **all in ~**
  kullo bi-lâsh *kullo ba-lâsh*
valid mu'tabir
valley wâdi pl. widyân; **Nile ~** wâdi in-nîl; **~ of the**
  Kings wâdi il-mulûk
value qîmi *qîma*
vanguard Talî'a
varnish (v.) dahan
vault qubbi *qubba*

veal laHm 'ijil *laHm 'igl*
vegetable khuDra pl. khuDar
veil Hijâb *Higâb*
vein 'irq pl. 'urûq
velvet makhmal, mukhmal *qatîfa*
venerable muHtaram
very ktîr *ketîr*, jiddan *giddan*, qawi
vessel markab
vexed - to be ~ zi'il; **I am very ~ about that** ana ktîr
       zi'lân min haida *ana za'lân qawi min di*
vice 'aib *'êb* pl. 'iyûb
video recorder jihâz vidyô *gihâz vidyô*
village qarya pl. qura
vine leaves waraq 'ainab *waraq 'ênab*
vinegar khall
vineyard karm pl. kurûm
violent shedîd, qawi
violet (adj.) bnafsaji *binafsagi*
violin kamân
viper af'a pl. afâ'i
virgin bikr
virtue faDîli *faDîla* pl. faDâyil *faDâ'il*
virtuous faDîl
virus fîrûs
visible yinshâf
visit (n.) ziyâra; (v.) zâr, ija la'and *gi 'and, ga 'and*,
      râH la'and *râH 'and*; **I want to ~ Mr. ...**
      biddi zûr is-saiyid ... *biddi azûr is-saiyid ...*

vocabulary mufradât
voice Saut *Sôt*
volcano jabal nâr *gebel nâr*, burkân
volume (of a book, magazine etc.) mjallad *megallad*
voluntary ihtiyâri
vomit istafraR
vow (n.) nadr pl. nudûra; (v.) nadar
vulture nisr

W

wages (coll.) ijra *ugra*
wait instanZar, istanna; **~ a little** uSbur shwaiyi
     istanna shuwaiye; **how long shall I ~ for**
     you? qaddaish baddi inZurak qaddi ê
     astannak?; **I have been ~ing a quarter of**
     an hour Sarli rub' sâ'a nâZir *rub'a sâ'a*
     mustanni; **I cannot ~ any longer** mâ biqdir
     instanZir aktar *mâ aRdash astanna aktar*; **he**
     keeps us ~ing a long time hû bîTauwil ktîr
     hûwe biTauwil ketîr; **~ for me!** inZurni!
     Istannâni!
waiter sufraji *sufragi*
wake up istayqaZa
walk (n.) mishwâr *mushwâr* pl. mshâwir *meshâwir*;
     (v.) mishi; **~ing** mâshi; **you ~ too fast**
     bitrauwij ktîr *betista'gil ketîr*; **you ~ too**
     slowly btimshi 'ala mahlak ktîr *betimshi*

bishwêsh ketîr; **are you a good ~er?** btimshi
Taiyib? *betimshi Taiyib?*

wall (in a room) HaiT *HêT* pl. HîTân; (around a
town) sûr

walnut jauz *gôz*

want (v.) riRib, râd, 'âz, badd *bidd*; **what do you ~?**
shû bitrîd?, shû baddak? *'âyiz ê?*; **I still ~**
ba'd baddi, ba'dni 'âyiz *lissa biddi, lissa
ana 'âyiz*

war Harb pl. Hurûb; **Holy ~** jihâd *gihâd*

warm (adj.) Hâmi, dâfi; (v.) daffa; **to get ~** difi; **~ing**
mudaffi; **~th** shaub *shôb*

wash (v., trans.) Rasal, Rassal; **to ~ oneself** tRassal
itRassal; **~ing** (of clothes) Rasîl; **~ing
machine** Rassâla

wasp dabbûr pl. dbâbir *debâbîr*

watch (n.) sâ'a

watch over (v.) sahar 'ala, Haras

water mayy *mayya*

watermelon(s) (coll.) baTTîkh

waterfall shillâl *shalâl*

watering can marash'shi *mirash'sha*

waterproof mushamma' *mishamma'*

wax shama'

way Tarîq pl. Turuq, Turuqât; (manner) Tarîqa; **is
this the right ~ to…?** Haidi id-darb la…?
di id-darb li…?; **where does this ~ lead to?**
lawain bitwaddi had-darb *'ala fên yiwaddi*

id-darb di?; **which is the best ~ to…?** aina
hî aHsan darb la…? *anhû aHsan darb li…?*;
to lose one's ~ Dâ' *Tâh*; **a long ~ off** b'îd
be'îd; **~ out** khurûj *khurûg*

we niHna *iHna*

weak Di'îf pl. D'âf *Du'âf*; **to ~en** Da''af; **~ness**
Du'uf

wealth Rina

weapon silâH pl. isliHa *asliHa*

wear (clothes) libis

weary (adj.) ti'bân *ta'bân*

weather hawa, Taqs; **how is the ~?** kîf it-Taqs?
il-hawa ezai?; **the ~ is fine** it-Taqs Taiyib
il-hawa Taiyib; **the ~ is bad** it-Taqs Radi
il-hawa baTTâl; **~ forecast** tanabbu' iT-Taqs

weave Haiyak; **~r** Hîyâk *Haiyâk*

wedding 'irs *faraH*; **~ procession** zaffi *zeffa*

Wednesday yaum il-arba'a *yôm il-arba'a, l-arba'a*

week usbû'a pl. esâbî'; **~ly** usbû'i

weigh (v., trans.) zân *wazan*; (intrans.) wazno … (lit.:
its weight is …); **what does this ~?**
qaddaish wazno? *kâm wazno?*

weight (n.) wazn, tiql *tuql*

welcome ahlan wa-sahlan

welfare khair *khêr*

well (n.) bîr pl. biyâr

well (adv.) Taiyib; **I as ~** ana kamân *ana kemân, ana*
bardo; **as ~**; mitl; **~!** (come, go on) yalla!

well (adj.) sâlim; **to get ~** shifi

well-mannered Hayy, zarîf

west Rarb, maRrib; **~wind** hawa Rarbi

wet (n.) ruTûbi *ruTûba*; (adj.) mablûl; (v.) ball

what shû, aish *êsh*, *ê*; **~ is that?** shû haida? *di ê?*, *di
       êh di?*; **~ sort of ... is that?** min hal...?, shû
       hal...?, *êsh di...?;* **~ is going on?** shûfi?
       khabar ê?; **~ should we do now?** shû
       baddna na'mil hallaq? *ni'mil ê dil-waqt?*;
       ~ did you say? kîf qult? *qult ê?*; **~ for?**
       laish? *'ala shân ê?, lê?*

wheat HinTa *qamH*

wheel dûlâb *'agala* pl. dwâlîb *'agel*

when (in questions) aimta *emta*; (conj.) limma
       lamma; **~ can we see it?** aimta mniqdir
       nshûf haida? *emta neshûf di?*; **since ~?** min
       aimta? *min emta?*; **~ever it may be possible**
       lamma yimkin

where ain, wain, fain *fên*; **~ are you?** wainak?
       fênak?; **~ do I find...?** wain blâqi...? *fên
       altiqi...?;* **~ is there...?** wain fî...? *fên...?*
       ~ shall we meet? wain nitlaqa? *fên nitlaqa?*;
       ~ does ... live? wain sâkin...? *fên sâkin...?*;
       ~ do you want to go? la-wain biddak trûH?
       'ala fên 'âyiz trûH?; **~ is ... coming from?**
       mnain jâyi *min ên gâ'i?*

while mâ dâm

whisper (v.) washwash

whistle (n.) Saffâra; (v.) Safar, Saufar *Sôfar*

white abyaD f. baiDa *bêDa* pl. bîD

whitish abyadâni

who (in questions) mîn; (in relative sentences) Hada
 Haddi; **~ever it may be** mînma kân, mînma
 yekûn

whole kull; **the ~ house** kull il-bait *kull il-bêt*,
 il-bait kullo *il-bêt kullo*; **as a ~** (altogether)
 bil-kullîyi *bil-kullîya*, jamî'an *gamî'an*

why laish *lê*, *lêh*, li'ai sabab *li'aiyi sabab*, 'ala
 shân êh

wicked sharîr; **~ness** fasâd, shar

wide wâsi'

width 'arD, 'urD

widow armili *armila*; **~er** armil

wife jauzi *gôza*, mara; **my ~** il-madâm bita'ti; **how is
 your ~?** kîf Hâl martak? *ezai mirâtak?*, kîf
 Hâl madâmtak *ezai madâmtak?*

wild (animal) waHshi; (land) barr, barri

will (n.) irâdi *arâda*; (testament) waSîyi *waSîya*;
 (v.) arâd: **I ~** brîd *'âyiz*, baddi *biddi*; **I ~
 not** mâ brîd *mush 'âyiz*, mâ baddi *mâ biddîsh*

willingly (certainly) tikram!, 'ala râsi

willingness RiDa

willow SafSaf

win fâz; **~ner** fâyiz *fâ'iz*

wind hawa, rîH (f.) pl. aryâH

window shubbâk pl. shbâbîk; **open the ~** iftaH ish-
 shubbâk; **close the ~** sakkir ish shubbâk;
 leave the ~ open khalli ish-shubbâk maftûH

windshield izâz is-sayyâra *izâz il-'arabiya*; **~ wiper**
    mamsahat izâz is-sayyâra *mamsahat izâz*
    il-'arabiya

wine nbîd *nebîd*

wing jinâH *ganâH* pl. ijniHi *agniHa*

winter shiti *shita*

wire shirîT Hadîd *silk*; **~less** lâ silki

wisdom Hikmi *Hikma*

wise 'âlim, shâTir

wish (n.) Rarbi *Rarba*; (v.) Ririb, Râd, badd *bidd*, 'âz;
    as you ~ mitl mâ bitrîd *zai mâ terîd*

with ma', ma'a, 'ind *'and*; **~ me, ~ you, ~ him** ma'i
    ma'âya, ma'ak, ma'o, etc.; (instrumentally)
    bi; **~ the hand** bil-îd

without bala, min Rair *min Rêr*, min dûn

witness shâhid pl. sh'hûd *shuhûd*

wolf dîb pl. dyâb *diyâb*

woman mara *mar'a*, imra'a pl. nisa *niswân*

wonder 'ajîbi *'agiba*; **~ful** 'ajîb *'agîb*

wool Sûf; **~en** min Sûf

word kilmi *kilma* pl. kilmât

work (n.) shuRl pl. ishRâl, shRâl (Syr. only);
    (v.) ishtaRal *ishtiRil*; **~shop** warsha

world dinyi, dini *dunya*

worm(s) (coll.) dûd

worse than arda min

worth (n.) qîmi *qîma*; **to be ~** sawa; **~less** baTTâl,
    mâ-lo qîmi *mâ-lôsh qima*

wound(s) (coll.) jurH *gurH*
wrap up in laff bi
write katab; (books) allaf; **~r** kâtib pl. kuttâb
writing (calligraphy, document) ktîbi *kitâba*;
       in ~ bil-ktîbi *bil-kitâba*; **hand~** khaTT
wrong Ralat, mush SaHîH

X

x-ray ash'iya iks

Y

yawn tâwab *titâwib*
year sini *sana* pl. sinîn, sanawât; **this ~** is-sini,
      has-sini *is-sana di*; **last ~** 'âm il -uwal;
      next ~ sint ij-jâyi *is-sana ig-gâi'a*; **~ly**
      sanawi; **every ~** kull sini *kull sana*
yellow aSfar f. Safra pl. Sufr
yes aiwa, bala; (certainly) na'am
yesterday ams, mbâriH *imbâriH*
yet kamân *kemân*, lissa; (nevertheless) ma'a zâlik
yogurt laban *zabâdi*
you (m.) inta, (f.) inti, (pl.) intu
young zRîr *zuRaiyar* pl. zRâr *zuRaiyerîn*, zuRâr;
      a ~ man shabb *shabâb* pl. shubbân, shibâb;
      a ~ girl Sabîyi pl. Sabâya, Sbaiyât *Sibâyât*
younger azRar

Z

zero Sifr
zip sûsta
zone mintaqa pl. manâtiq
zoo bustân il-Haiwânât *bustân il-Hêwânât*
zucchini (coll.) kôsa

ARABIC-ENGLISH
DICTIONARY

The Arabic-English vocabulary is arranged according
to the following order:

**a b d/D e f g h/H i j k/kh l m n o q
r/R s/S t/T u w y z/Z '**

to make the finding of words easier for users unfa-
miliar with the Arabic alphabet and Arabic word
forms.

Both the Syrian (Syr.) and Egyptian (Egypt.)
dialects are given, the latter in italics. Where there is
no Arabic in italics or the entry is not identified, the
Syrian and Egyptian are alike. Words which are very
similar in the Syrian and Egyptian dialect are listed
under one single entry.

a

a'lan announce
a'ma pl. 'imyân blind
a'rag *a'raj* lame (adj.)
a'Sâb (coll.) nerve(s)
a'Ta waSl give a receipt
a'waj *'awag* f. 'auja *'ôga* pl. 'ûj *'ôg* crooked
a'zab *'âzib* bachelor

âb (Syr.) August
ab pl. âbâ' father
ab'ad farthest
abadan never, not at all
abadi eternal (without end)
abawi paternal
abHar sail (v.)
abjadiya *abgadiya* alphabet
abrîl (Egypt.) April
abTal abolish
abu farwe (Egypt.) chestnut
abul haul *abul hôl* sphinx
abyaD f. baiDa *bêDa* pl. bîD white
abyadâni whitish
abzîm pl. abâzîm (Egypt.) buckle (n.)
adâ pl. adawât tool
aDâf ila enclose, join
adâr (Syr.) March
âdatan usually
adawât maktabiya stationary
adawât SiH'Hiya sanitary appliances
addib (Egypt.) educate
âdemi kind (adj.)
aDrab strike, go on strike
af'a pl. afâ'i viper
afriqya Africa
agâza (coll.) (Egypt.) holiday(s)

aggar (Egypt.) rent (v.)

agîba (Egypt.) miracle

agnabi (Egypt.) pl. agânib stranger, foreigner

agnabi (Egypt.) foreign

aHad any

ahâli inhabitants

ahâna (Egypt.) offence

aHât enclose, surround

aHka tell

ahl family; **ahl il-bait** *ahl il-bêt* family

**ahl la … *ahl li …* able

ahlan wa-sahlan welcome

ahli national

ahlîyi *ahlîya* ability

aHmar f. Hamra pl. Humr red

aHmar shafâyif *aHmar shafâ'if* lipstick

aHmarâni reddish

aHsan better

aHsin (Syr.) better

ailûl (Syr.) September

aimta (Syr.) when (in questions)

ain (Syr.) where

aina 'am yes, indeed

aish (Syr.) what

aiwa yes

aiyan *'aiyin* nominate

ajbar force (v.)

ajjar (Syr.) rent (v.)

ajnabi (Syr.) pl. ajânib stranger, foreigner

ajnabi (Syr.) foreign

akal (Syr.) eat

akbar principal (adj.)

akh pl. ikhwi *ikhwe*, ikhwân brother

akh'khar delay (v.)

akhad (Syr.) receive, accept, take

akhad bard (Syr.) catch a cold

âkhar f. ukhra pl. ukhar other, another

akhatt izn? Have you received permission?

akhbar inform

akhDar f. khaDra green

âkhir extreme, final, last, ultimate, utmost

akhîran lately

akhras dumb

akhTa sin (v.)

akîd sure, certainly

akkad confirm

akl (Egypt.) food

akli *akla* meal

akmal complete (v.)

aktar biktîr *aktar biketîr* much more

aktar min longer than (time), more than

aktar most; aktar in-nâs *aktar in-nâs* most people

alf thousand

âli *âla* pl. âlât tool, machine, engine

alîm painful

alkuhûl alcohol
allaf write (books)
allâh God
allah ybârik fîk! *allah yebârik fîk!* God bless you!
allah yil'anak! God curse you!
allâh ysallmak! *allah yisallimak!* God save you!
allim (Egypt.) teach
almâs diamond
âlô hello
alRa cancel
amal hope (n.)
amal hope (v.)
âman bi believe in God
amân safe conduct, security
amâni fidelity
amar command, order (v.)
ambar (Syr.) barn
amDa sign (v.)
amhal give respite to s.b.
amîn honest, faithful, reliable, safe, trustworthy
amîr (Syr.) pl. umara prince
amîri (Syr.) princess
amma but
ammal hope (v.)
amnîyi *amnîya* safety
amr pl. 'umûr affair, thing, matter
amr pl. awâmir order, command (n.)
amrâD siriya sexually transmitted diseases

amrak (I am) at your service
amrâr ktîri (Syr.) often
amrîkâni American
ams yesterday
amti'a baggage, luggage
ana I
ana nafsi I myself, myself
anf (Egypt.) pl. unûf nose
anîs kind (adj.)
anjaq (Syr.) scarcely
antibiyôtîk antibiotics
antîkât antiquities
aqaddimlak ê? (Egypt.) What can I offer you?
aqall mâ yekûn at least
aqall min less than
aqrab min nearer than
arb'a *arba'* four
arb'amîyi (Syr.) four hundred
arb'în *arba'în* forty
arbaTa'sh *arba'tâsher* fourteen
arD pl. arâDi ground, soil, land, floor (of a room),
        surface, real estate, planet earth
arda min worse than
arDeshôke (Syr.) artichoke
arîka (Syr.) sofa
armil widower
armili *armila* widow
arnab pl. arânib rabbit, hare

aRosstos (Egypt.)
arsal send, ship
arzi *erza* pl. arz *erz* cedar
asad lion
asaf grief
asansêr (Egypt.) elevator
asâr ruins, historical remains
asâs bottom, foundation, basis, ground
aSfar f. Safra pl. Sufr yellow
ash'iya iks x-ray
ashbah (Egypt.) resemble
ashma kân (Syr.) anything
ashqar f. shaqra pl. shuqr fair, blond
âsif sorry
âSimi *'âSima* capital (town)
asîr prisoner
âsiya Asia
aSl pl. uSûl root, origin
aSli original, principal
asmar f. samra pl. sumr brown (of the human
         complexion)
asra' accelerate, speed up
assas (Syr.) found (v.)
assis (Egypt.) found (v.)
aswad *iswid* f. sauda *sôda* black
aswân Aswan
at'ab (Egypt.) tire (v., trans.)
aTash thirst

aTlas satin
aTrash deaf
aTwal min longer than (measure)
auwal anterior
auwal darb bitridd 'ash-shmâl *auwal darb*
'ahs-shemâl the first road on the left
auwal, aulâni *auwalâni* f. aulânîyi *auwalâniya* first
auwil imbâriH *auwal* imbâriH, **auwal** *ams* the day
before yesterday
auwil'ma as soon as
ayy Hâga (Egypt.) anything
azali eternal (without beginning)
azraq f. zarqa pl. zurq blue
azRar min smaller than, younger than

b

b'îd (Syr.) far; **qaddaish b'îd min haun la…?**
How far is it from here to…?; **ba'do b'îd?**
Is it far?
b'îd *be'îd* distant
ḅâ' (with acc. of thing and person) sell s.th. to s.b.
ba'at send
ba'd after, past
ba'd bakkîr (ktîr) (Syr.) it is yet (much) too early
ba'd bukra *ba'de bukra* day after tomorrow
ba'd iD-Duhr *ba'd iD-Duhr* afternoon, p.m.
ba'd minno thereupon

ba'D several, a few, some

ba'd shwaiyi *ba'd shuwaiye* soon

ba'd still, yet

ba'dên afterwards, later, thereupon

ba'do ili ma'ak shî, ba'do ili 'indak shî (Syr.) You
      still owe me s.th.

ba'do thereupon

ba'îd (Egypt.) far; **qaddi ê il-mesâfe min hene li…?**
      How ~ is it from here to…?; **lissa ba'îd?** Is
      it yet far?

ba'îd far off

bâb pl. ibwâb, bwâb door

bâbâ pope

babâRa, babRâl *babaRân* parrot

bada start (v.)

baDâ'a (Syr.) merchandise

baDâ'a goods

badali rasmîyi *badla rasmiya* uniform

badawi *bedawi* pl. badu Bedouin

badd (Syr.) want, wish (v.)

baddal *baddil* change, alter, exchange (v.)

badfa'lak … fîh (Egypt.) I offer you … for it.

badla pl. bidal suit (man's suit, woman's pants-suit)

badlit RaTs diving suit

badr full moon

baftikir (Egypt.) it seems to me

baH'Hâr sailor

baHâr pl. baHârât spice

bâhas (Syr.) discuss
baHr il-muhîT ocean
baHr pl. bHûr *biHâr* sea
baHSa (Syr.) pebble
bai' (Syr.) sale
baiD *bêD* (coll.) egg(s); **baiD brisht** *bêD birisht* soft
      boiled eggs; **baiD maslûq Taiyib** *bêD*
      maslûq Taiyib hard boiled eggs; **baiD**
      mishwi *bêD mashwi* fried eggs
bain (Syr.) among, between
bait (Syr.) pl. biyût, buyût home, house; **fil-bait** at
      home
bait il-'ankabût spiderweb
baiyâ' (Egypt.) retailer, seller
baiyan seem
baka (Egypt.) cry (v.)
bakhash dig
bakht happiness
bakkîr (Syr.) early; **bakkîr iS-SubH** early in the
      morning
bâl mind (n.)
bâl urinate
bala without
bala yes
bala fâyidi *ba-la fâ'ida* in vain
bala nafa' in vain
bala RaraD impartially
bala shakk certainly, no doubt

ba-lâ taman (Syr.) gratis
bala zamb innocent, not guilty
bala' swallow
balad (Syr.) town
baladîyi (Syr.) municipality
balaH *beleH* date (fruit)
bâlaR exaggerate
balâsh (Egypt.) gratis, in vain
balîyi *belîye* calamity
balkûn *balakôn* balcony
bana (Egypt.) build
banadûra (coll.) (Syr.) tomato(es)
bangar (coll.) (Egypt.) beet(s)
bank pl. bunûk bank
banTalôn pants
banTalôn qaSîr *banTalôn quSaiyar* shorts
banTalôn shurt shorts
banzîn petrol
bâqa bunch of flowers
baqara cow
baqbûqa *buqbêqa* blister
baqdûnis parsley
bâqi, baqîyi *baqîya* rest, remainder
baqq (coll.) bug(s)
baqshîsh tip
bâr bar
bâr hawk
baRaD hate (v.)

bârak *bârik* bless
bard (Egypt.) also
bard cold, flu (n.); **id-dinyi bard** *id-dinya bard* it
     is cold
barhan prove (v.)
bârid cold, cool (adj.)
barîd jauwi *barîd gauwi* airmail
barîd mail
barîd messenger
barmîl pl. barâmîl barrel
barq flash, lightning
barr land, continent, shore
barr, barri wild (land)
barra out; **min barra** from outside
barrad refresh
barrâni outer, external
BarRût pl. brâRît *berâRît* flea
barTal bribe (v.)
bartTîl bribe (n.)
bârûdi (Syr.) pl. bwârîd gun
barzûla (Syr.) cutlet
bâs (Egypt.) kiss (v.)
basal (coll.) onion(s)
baSar sight, vision
basâTa simplicity
bashar mankind
bashari human (not divine)
basîT modest, simple
bass (Syr,.) enough

bass *bess* but, only

bâT *ibâT* armpit

bât spend the night, pass the night

baTâni *baTâna* lining (of clothes)

baTâTis (coll.) Egypt.) potato(es)

baTîHa (Egypt.) bog

bâTin inside (n.)

baTn abdomen, belly

baTrak pl. baTârki *baTârika* patriarch (rel.)

baTT (coll.) duck(s)

baTTa (Syr.) calf (of the leg)

baTTâl worthless

baTTîkh (coll.) watermelon(s)

baTTîkh aSfar (coll.) (Syr.) melon(s)

baul (Syr.) urine

bausi *bôsa* kiss (n.)

bauwâb doorman, janitor

bauwâbi *bauwâba* gate

bauwas kiss (v.)

bâyin (Egypt.) evident

bâyit *bâ'it* old, not fresh

bazaq spit (v.)

bâzella (coll.) (Syr.) pea(s)

bdâl (Syr.) for, in place of, instead

bê' (Egypt.) sale

beden body

bedri (Egypt.) early; **bedri iS-SubH** early in the
morning

beled (Egypt.) town

beledîya (Egypt.) municipality

belki perhaps

bên (Egypt.) among, between

berqûq (coll.) (Egypt.) plum(s)

bess (Egypt.) enough

bêt (Egypt.) pl. biyût, buyût home, house;
      fil-bêt at home

betrôl (Egypt.) oil, petrol

b-Hais *bi-Hês* as, since, because

bi by, through, with (instrumentally)

bi-âkhir il-... at the end of

bidâl (Egypt.) for, in place, instead

bidâya start (n.)

bidd (Egypt.) want, wish (v.)

bidfa'lak ... fîh (Syr.) I offer you ... for it.

biftkir (Syr.) it seems to me

bi-Hasb after, according to

bi-iznak with your permission

bîkallif *bîkellif* expensive

bi-kâm *bi-qaddaish* What does it cost?

bi-khuSûS about, concerning, as far as ... is
      concerned

biki (Syr.) cry

bikr virgin

bi-kull ikhlâS sincerely

bi-kull il-iHwâl by all means

bil- âli loudly

bil-'agel (Egypt.) quickly

bil-'ajel (Syr.) quickly
bi-lâ temen (Egypt.) gratis
bilâd (Egypt.) native country
bil-akhaSS principally
bil-âkhir at the end
bil-aqall at least
bi-lâsh *ba-lâsh* for nothing
bil-Haqîqa indeed
bil-îd with the hand
bil-ishtirâk in common
bil-izn with your permission
bil-khâliS quite (adv.)
bil-ktîbi *bil-kitâba* in writing
bil-kullîyi *bil-kullîya* as a whole, altogether, entirely
bil-lail *bil-lêl* in the night, at nighttime
billôr crystal
bil-marra all at once
bil-mîyi *bil-mîye* percent
bil-qalîli at least
bil-qur'a by lot
bil-Ralat by mistake
bil-Rasb by force
bi-luRatên bilingual
bil-wâTi noiseless
bi-mazîd is-surûr *be-mezîd is-surûr* with the
        greatest pleasure
bi-mûjib (Egypt.) after, according to
bina *bine*, *bunya* pl. ibnyi *abniye* building

binafsagi (Egypt.) violet (adj.)

bi-niZâm systematically

binj *bing* anesthetic

binn (Syr.) coffee beans, unground coffee

bin-nâzil downhill

bin-nihâyi (Syr.) at last

bint pl. bnât *banât* daughter, girl

bint il-'amm cousin (daughter of father's brother)

bint il'-ammi *bint il-'amma* cousin (daughter of
    father's sister)

bint il-akh niece (daughter of the brother)

bint il-khâl cousin (daughter of mother's brother)

bint il-khâli *bint il-khâla* cousin (daughter of
    mother's sister)

bint il-ukht niece (daughter of the sister)

bi-qadr (Syr.) in proportion to

biqi remain, to be over, stay

bîr pl. biyâr well (n.)

bîra beer

birdân *bardân* to be cold

birdâyi (Syr.) curtain

birka pond, pool

birnâmij *birnâmig* pl.barâmij *barâmig* program

birwâz pl. barâwîz frame

bishwêsh (Egypt.) slow

bi-Sifa muwaqqata temporarily

bisilla (coll.) (Egypt.) pea(s)

bismillâh in the name of God

biS-Sudfi *biS-Sudfa* by chance
bi-Su'ûbe hardly
bi-suhûli *bi-suhûla* easily
bi-tadrîg (Egypt.) bit by bit
bitâqat hawiyat (Syr.) identification card
bitrûl (Syr.) oil, petrol
bit-tâbi' (Syr.) bit by bit
bit-tamâm as much as
bit-tidrîj *bit-tedrîg* gradually
bi-wafra galore
bîwajji' *biwaggi'* painful
bi-wâsiTat (Egypt.) by means of
bi-wâsTa by, through, by means of
bîyâ' (Syr.) retailer, seller
bîyâ' *baiyâ'* dealer
bîza"il *biza"al* tedious
bizâq (Syr.) spittle
bizâr seed
bizr seed
biz-ziyâdi *biz-ziyâda* too ... (followed by adjective)
biz-zûr with difficulty
bkhâTrak as you please
blâd *bilâd* pl. bildân *buldân* country, native country
blâstîk plastic; **min blâstîk** made of plastic
blâT *balâT* pavement
b-maujib *bi-mûgib* according
bnafsaji (Syr.) violet (adj.)
bôdra (Egypt.) powder

bôl (Egypt.) urine

bolîs (Egypt.) police; **markaz il-bolîs** police station

borg (Egypt.) pl. ibrâg tower

bornêTa (Egypt.) hat

bôrSa stock exchange, stock market

bortuqân (coll.) (Egypt.) orange(s)

brîq (Syr.) jug

bta'rif inglîzi? *beta'raf ingelîzi?* Do you know
        English?

bu'd distance

buDâ'a (Egypt.) merchandise

buHaira *buHêra* lake

bukhâr steam

bukhârîya steamship

bukli pl. bukal (Syr.) buckle (n.)

bukra 'ala SubH *bukra is-SubH* tomorrow
        morning

bukra tomorrow

bulâd steel

bulbul nightingale

bûlîs khafîya *bolîs sirri* detective

bûm (coll.) owl(s)

bunduqiya (Egypt.) pl. banâdiqa gun, rifle

bunn (Eygpt.) coffee beans, unground coffee

bûq trumpet

buq'a pl. buqa' spot, stain

buq'a locality

bûr sa'îd Port Said

buRD hate (n.)

burdqân (coll.) (Syr.) orange(s)

burguma (Egypt.) pl. barâgim knuckle (hand)

burhân pl. barahîn proof, evidence

burj (Syr.) pl. ibrâj tower

burjuma (Syr.) pl. barâjim knuckle (hand)

burkân volcano

bursa exchange, stock exchange

buS (Syr.) bus

bûsi *bûsa* kiss (n.)

bûSla compass

busTa post office

bustân il-Haiwânât *bustân il-Hêwânât* zoo

bustân pl. bsâtîn *besâtîn* garden, orchard

buTâTa (coll.) (Syr.) potato(es)

bûz mouth (of animals)

bûZa (Syr.) ice cream

b-wâsTit (Syr.) by means of

byi'di *bi'di* contagious

d/D

D'îf ill, weak

da f. di pl. dôl (Egypt.) this

dâ il-mafâSil rheumatism

dâ rabwi asthma

Dâ' (Syr.) lose one's way

da' invite
Da"af weaken
da'a la *da'a li* pray for s.b.
Da'îf ill, weak
da'wa invitation
da'wa pl. da'âwi lawsuit, claim
dâb melt
Dab' pl. Dibâ' hyena
Dabâb fog
dabaH kill, slaughter
Dabb (Syr.) pack (v.)
dabbar manage, negotiate
dabbûr pl. dbâbir *debâbîr* wasp
dabbûs pl. dababîs pin
dabdab crawl
dabH sacrifice(n.)
dâdâ pl. dadawât nurse, nanny
Dâdad (Syr.) contradict
dafa' 'an defend
dafa' fî offer, bid for
dafa' offer (n.)
dafa' pay (n.); **qaddaish lâzim idfa'?** (Syr.) How
much do I have to pay?; **baddi idfa' *'âyiz
adfa'*** I want to pay; **dafa't ana** I have paid;
bidfa' waqt it-tislîm *adfa' waqt it-teslîm*
I shall pay on receipt; **la-mîn baddi idfa'
haida?** *limîn adfa'di?* To whom do I have
to pay that?

dafa' payment

dafa' push (v., vehicle, etc.)

dafan bury

daffa warm (v.)

dâfi warm (adj.)

dafn funeral

daftar pl. dfâtir *defâtir* register (n.)

daftar tilifôn (Egypt.) telephone directory

dahab (Syr.) gold

dahan varnish(v.)

Dahr back (part of the body)

Dahrak! Look out!, Watch out!

dahsshar (Syr.) let alone, let go

Dahya pl. DawâHi suburb

Daif *Dêf* pl. Diyûf guest

dain *dên* pl. dyûn *diyûn* debt

daini (Syr.) ear pl. dainât

dair *dêr* pl. idyuri, dyûra *diyûr* monastery

Daiya' lose

daiyân (Syr.) durable

Daiyik narrow (adj)

dakar pl. dukûra male

dakh'khal (Egypt.) bring in

dakhal enter

Dakhîri *Dakhira* relic

dakhl income

Dakhm thick

dalîl pl. dulala (Egypt.) guide

dalîl tilifôn (Syr.) telephone directory

dall direct, guide; **dillni 'ala Tabîb** *dillini 'ala Tabîb* direct me to a doctor

Dall remain

dall show the way, direct

dallil spoil, pamper

dâlûl (Syr.) pl. dwâlîl guide

dâm last (v.)

dam'a pl. dmû' *dumû'* tear (n.)

Damân (Egypt.) guarantee (n.)

Damân ijtimâ'i *Damân igtimâ'i* social security

Daman li guarantee (v.)

dambi (Syr.) tail

Dâmin (Egypt.) one who stands bail

damm blood

daneb (Syr.) tail

daqîq (Egypt.) flour (n.)

daqîqa daqâyik *daqâ'iq* minute, moment

daqn beard

daqn chin

Daqq il-bâb knock at the door

daqq il-jaras *daqq il-garas* ring the bell

daqq mismâr bil-HaiT *daqq musmâr bil-HêT* drive a nail in the wall

daqq ring (v.)

daqq tattoo (v.)

daqqâra bolt (door)

dâr bâlo 'ala (Syr.) pay attention to

dâr house
dâr il-bâl 'ala (Syr.) look after s.b., take care of
dâr in-nashr publishing house
dâr manage
dâr turn (v., intrans.)
Darab beat, strike, hit
Darab multiply
darabukka (Egypt.) drum
darag (Egypt.) stairs
daraga (Egypt.) step, gradation
daragit il-Harâra (Egypt.) temperature
daraj (Syr.) stairs
daraji (Syr.) step, gradation
daraji *darage* pl. darajât *daragât* degree
darajit il-Harâra (Syr.) temperature
Darar damage, harm (n.)
daras study (v.)
Darb, Darbi *Darba* blow, stroke
darfi *darfa* shutter
Darîbat bai' *Darîbet bê'* sales tax
Darîbi *Darîba* pl. Darâ'ib tax
Darr damage, harm (v.); **mâ yiDurrish** (Egypt.)
        there is no harm
darrâja bukhârîya motorcycle
darrâje (Syr.) bicycle
dars pl. durûs lesson
Darûri necessary
darwîsh *derwîsh* pl. darâwîsh dervish

dash'shar (Syr.) chase, drive away
dash'shar (Syr.) leave (v., trans.)
dashîshi (Syr.) measles
dass in-nabD feel the pulse
Dau (Syr.) daylight, light
Dau il-murûr traffic signal
daukha *dôkha* giddiness
daukhan *dôkhan* giddy
dauli *daula* state, nation
daur (Syr.) turn (n.)
dauriya patrol
dausha (Egypt.) noise
dauwar 'ala look for, seek
dauwar turn (v., trans.)
dauwir! Turn round! (intrans.)
dawa pl. idwyi *adwiya* medicine, drug
DawâHi neighborhood, outskirts
Dâyan hold, last, to be strong
dâyi *dâya* midwife
Dâyi' lost
dâyim *dâ'im* eternal, immortal
dâyir mindâr *dâ'ir mindâr* round, around; **dâyir min dâr il-balad** *dâ'ir min dâr il-beled* round the town
dâyman *dâ'iman* always
dâyri *dâ'ira* pl. dawâyir *dawâ'ir* circle
dêl (Egypt) appendix (of a book), tail
deshîsha (Egypt.) measles

dessember (Egypt.) December

di maSlaHti (Egypt.) That is my business.

di mush Hâga (Egypt.) It does not matter.

Di'îf pl. D'âf *Du'âf* weak

dîb pl. dyâb *diyâb* wolf

dibbân (Syr.) (coll.) fly(ies)

Didd against, contrary (n.)

Difda' (Syr.) pl. Dafâdi' frog

difi get warm

difl oleander

Difr (Syr.) pl. aDâfir fingernail

diheb (Egypt.) gold

DiHik laugh (v.); **DiHik 'ala** laugh at

dihn fat (n.)

dîk pl. diyûk cock, rooster

dik-hâ, duk-hâ, duk-hauwa (Egypt.) f. dik-hâ, dik-haiya pl. duk-hamma that (pron.)

dikkân (Syr.) pl. dkâkîn shop (n.)

Dil' pl. Dulû' rib

dilfîn *dolfîn* dolphin

Dilim (Egypt.) dark, obscure

Dill (Egypt.) shade (n.)

dil-waqt (Egypt.) just, at this moment, at the time, now

dil-waqti ga dôrak (Egypt.) It's your turn.

Dimâdi *Dimâda* bandage

dimâr (Syr.) brain

dimashq Damascus

dimmi *dimma* conscience
dîmûqrâTiya democracy
dîn religion pl. adyân religion
dîni religious
dinis immoral, obscene
dinyi, dini *dunya* world
dîr bâlak! (Syr.) Take care!
dirâsa study (n.)
dirbekki (Syr.) drum
Diyâfa hospitality
diyi *diya* blood money
dôgru straight ahead
dôr (Egypt.) story, floor
dôr (Egypt.) turn (n.)
Du'uf weakness
dubb bear
dubbân (Egypt.) fly
dûd (coll.) worm(s), caterpillar
Dufda' (Egypt.) pl. Dafâdi frog
Dufr, Difr (Egypt.) pl. Dawaafir fingernail
dugri straight ahead
duhn (Syr.) grease
Duhr midday, noon
duhûn ointment
dukhân muharrab smuggle tobacco
dukhân smoke (n.)
dukhân tobacco
dukhûl entrance

dukhûlîyi (Syr.) admission fee

dukkân (Egypt.) pl. dekâkîn shop, store (n.)

dukkân ma'kûlât grocery store

dûlâb (Egypt.) pl. dewâlîb cupboard

dûlâb (Syr.) pl. dwâlîb wheel

Dûlâb ziyâda (Syr.) spare tire

dumyât Damietta

duqq il-jaras! *duqq il-garas!* ring the bell!

dûr! Turn round! (trans.)

durra corn

durrâq (coll.) (Syr.) peach(es)

durûs khuSûSiya private lessons

durzi pl. drûz *durûz* Druse

dûta dowry

dyâni *diyâna* pl. adyân religion

e

ê 'umrak? (Egypt.) How old are you?

ê fîh gedîd? (Egypt.) What is the news?

êb (Egypt.) pl. 'iyûb shame, vice

ebrîq (Egypt.) jug

edeb good manners

elli mâlôsh nihâya (Egypt.) endless, finite

embâreH fil-lêl (Egypt.) last night

ekîd (Egypt.) sure, certainly

emîn (Egypt.) honest

emîr (Egypt.) pl. umara prince

emîra (Egypt.) princess
emta (Egypt.) when (in questions)
êsh (Egpyt.) bread
êsh (Syr.) what
ezai (Egypt.) how
ezai il-ishRâl? (Egypt.) How is business?
ezaiyak? (Egypt.) How do you do?

f

fa izan therefore
fa"âl efficient
fâ'gi' (Egypt.) surprise (v.)
fa'inn for (conj.)
fâ'iq awake (adj.)
fa'r pl. fîrân rat, mouse
fabrîka (Egypt.) factory
faDDa (Egypt.) silver
faDDal prefer; **faDDal 'an, faDDal 'ala** prefer s.th.
       to s.th. else
fâdi empty, unoccupied, hollow
faDîHa scandal
faDîl virtuous
faDîli *faDîla* pl. faDâyil *faDâ'il* virtue
faDl excellence, goodness
faDl pl.afDâl kindness, favor
faDlan 'an notwithstanding
fag'a (Egypt.) suddenly

fagr (Egypt.) dawn

faHas examine, inquire

faHaS investigate

fâHish immoral, indecent, obscene

faHm coal

faHs examination, investigation

faHs Tibbi pl. fuHûs Tibbiya medical exam

fai (Syr.) shade (n.)

fâida advantage

failasûf (Syr.) pl. fêlasûf philosopher

fain (Syr.) where

fâja' (Syr.) surprise (v.)

fajr (Syr.) dawn

fakh'kh pl. fkhâkh *fukhûkh* trap

fâkh'khâr pottery

fakhd pl. afkhâd thigh

fakhr glory

fakhûra pottery workshop

fâkiha pl. fuâki *fewâkih* fruit

fakk il-barRi (Syr.) unscrew

fakk untie

fakka change, small money

fakkar remind; ~ **fakkirni fi …** *fakkarnini fi …*
      remind me of … (with acc.)

falaH plough (v.)

falak (Syr.) sky, atmosphere

falayki boatman

fall flee

fallâH (Syr.) pl. fallaHîn peasant

falsafa philosophy

falsu false, counterfeit

fann pl. fnûn *funûn* art

fannân pl. fannânîn artist

faqa' (intrans.) burst

faqad il-wa'i lose consciousness

faqad miss. lose, lack

faqaT only, but, simply, solely

faqîr pl. fuqara poor (without money)

faqr poverty

fâr pl. *firân* mouse, rat

far' (Egypt.) big branch

fara'ôni pharaonic; **asâr fara'ôniya** relics of the pharaonic period

faraD interest, premium

faraDan (Syr.) supposing that

faraDna in (Egypt.) supposing that

faraH (Egypt.) wedding

faraH joy

faras il-nahr hippopotamus

faras pl. afrâs horse

farâsh (coll.) butterfly(ies)

farash spread (v., trans.)

faraula (coll.) (Egypt.) strawberry(ies)

fard odd (number)

fardan fardan one by one

farHân (Egypt.) glad, merry

fâriR empty, hollow
farkha (Egypt.) hen
farmala brake
farmalat Tawâri emergency brake
farmalit yad handbrake
farq difference (between two things)
farraR empty (v.)
farrûj *farrûg* pl. frârîj *farârîg* chicken
farshi (Syr.) bed
farshi, firâsh pl. furûsh (Syr.) mattress
farwi (Syr.) fur
fasâd wickedness
faSal separate (v., trans.)
fasdân (Egypt.) spoiled, bad
faSl pl. fuSûl season (of the year)
fasqiya (Egypt.) fountain
fassad (Syr.) spoil, go bad, go off
fassar explain
faSûlya (coll.) haricot bean(s)
fât (Syr.) come in
fât il-waqt It is already late.
fataH ir-radyu turn on the radio
fataH open (v.)
fataHat 'ulab *fataHat 'ilab* can opener
faTas (Syr.) suffocate
fâtiH light, bright, of color
fâTir lukewarm
fattash *fattish 'ala* search s.th.

fauq (Syr.) above, beyond, over, up, on

fauq haida (Syr.) in addition to this

fauq il-'âdi *fôq il-'âde* extraordinary

fauq khâliS (Syr.) right on the top

fauq min (Syr.) above, beyond, over

fauwaT (Syr.) bring in

fâyidi *fâ'ida* use

fâyiz *fâ'iz* interest, premium

fâyiz *fâ'iz* winner

fâz win

fazz jump (v.)

faZZ rude

fazzi (Syr.) jump (n.)

febrâ'ir (Egypt.) February

feddân acre

felek (Egypt.) sky, atmosphere

fellâH (Egypt.) pl. fellaHîn peasant

fên (Egypt.) where

fên buddi yekûn? (Egypt.) Where may that be?

fezze (Egypt.) jump (n.)

fî at, in

fî blâd ajnabîyi *fî bilâd barra* abroad

fî in (at a place)

fî nafs il-waqt in the mean time

fî wasT *fî wusT* in the middle

fiDDa (Syr.) silver

fiDil remain, to be over

fihim understand; **fhimt 'alaiyi?** *fihimt?* Did you
        understand me?

fihrist catalogue

fijj (Syr.) unripe

fikr belief, opinion; **shû fikrak?** *fikrak ê?* What is
      your opinion?

fikr pl. afkâr idea, thought

fîl pl. ifyâl elephant

filasTîn Palestine

filasTîni Palestinian

fil-bait *fil-bêt* at home

filfil pepper (n.)

fill (Syr.) jasmine

fillîn *filli* cork

film pl. aflâm movie

fil-mâDi once, in the past

fil-qadîm once, in the past

filûka pl. falâyik small boat with sails

finjân *fingân* pl. finâjîn *finâgîn* cup

fir'aun *far'ôn* Pharaoh

firHân (Syr.) glad

firiH to be pleased

firshâyi (Syr.) brush

fîrûs virus

fisid (Egypt.) spoil, go bad, go off

fiTis (Egypt.) suffocate

flâsfi (Egypt.) pl. felâsifa philosopher

flâsh flashlight

flûs (Egypt.) money

fonduq (Egypt.) hotel

fôq (Egypt.) above, beyond, over, up, on

fôq khâliS (Egypt.) right on the top
fôq min (Egypt.) above, beyond, over
fôqâni (Egypt.) upper
fraiz (coll.) (Syr.) strawberry(ies)
frinsâwi *feransâwi* French
fûl dry broad beans
full (Egypt.) jasmine
fulûs (Syr.) money
fumm (Egypt.) mouth
fûqâni (Syr.) upper
furn oven
furSa pl. furaS occasion
furshe (Egypt.) brush
furshit snân *furshit sinân* toothbrush
furtai'ki (Syr.) fork
fusaH (Syr.) (coll.) holiday(s)
fuStân pl. faSâTîn (ladies') dress
fustuq (coll.) pistachio(s)
fûTa (Egypt.) pl. fuwaT towel
fûTa apron
fuTr mushroom
fuTûr breakfast
fuTûr lunch

g

gâ (Egypt.) come
ga 'and (Egypt.) visit (v.)

gâ'iz (Egypt.) allowed

gâb (Egypt.) bring, fetch

gâb sîret (Egypt.) mention (v.)

gabân (Egypt.) coward

gadd (Egypt.) earnest

gaddad (Egypt.) renew

gahannam (Egypt.) hell

gahil (Egypt.) ignorant

gala (Egypt.) polish (v.)

gama' (Egypt.) add, collect, gather

gamâ'at mûsîqa (Egypt.) orchestra

gamâl (Egypt.) beauty

gamal (Egypt.) pl. gimâl camel

gamb (Egypt.) beside, side; **'ala gambi** on my side;
        'alal-gamb on the side

gamb (Egypt.) by, near

gamb min (Egypt.) near to, close to

gambûn (Egypt.) ham

gamî' (Egypt.) all

gâmi' (Egypt.) pl. gawâmi' mosque

gâmi'a (Egypt.) college, university

gamî'an (Syr.) as a whole, altogether

gâmid (Egypt.) durable

gâmid (Egypt.) lifeless

gamîl (Egypt.) beautiful

gammâl (Egypt.) camel driver

gâmûs pl. gawâmîs (Egypt.) buffalo

ganâ'ini (Egypt.) flower garden

ganâH (Egypt.) pl. agniHa wing

gânib (Egypt.) side

ganna (Egypt.) paradise

ganûb (Egypt.) south

ganzabîl (Syr.) ginger

gâr (Egypt.) pl. gîrân neighbor

gara (Egypt.) occur

garab (Egypt.) itch (n.)

garad (Egypt.) locust

garaH (Egypt.) injure

garas (Egypt.) bell

garâsh garage

gargîr (Egypt.) cress

garH (Egypt.) pl. girâH injury

garr (Egypt.) drag

garrab (Egypt.) try (v.)

garrâH (Egypt.) surgeon

gasîm (Egypt.) corpulent

gasûr (Egypt.) bold

gâsûs (Egypt.) spy

gau (Egypt.) atmosphere

gaurab pl. gawârib (Egypt.) sock

gawâb (Egypt.) pl. gawâbât letter, note

gawâb pl. agwiba (Egypt.) answer (n.)

gawâb musaggal (Egypt.) registered letter

gawâz (Egypt.) marriage

gâwib (Egypt.) answer (v.)

gâz (Egypt.) gas

gâza (Egypt.) punish

gazaa' (Egypt.) punishment

gazar (coll.) (Egypt.) carrot(s)

gazma (Egypt.) shoes, a pair of shoes

gêb (Egypt.) pocket; **HaTT bi-jaib** *HaTT bi-gêb* put
     in the pocket

gebel (Egypt.) pl. gibâl mountain

gebel nâr (Egypt.) volcano

gedîd (Egypt.) pl. gudâd, gudud new

gedwal (Egypt.) timetable

gelâti (Egypt.) ice cream

gemâ'a (Egypt.) party, company

genâze (Egypt.) funeral

genêne (Egypt.) flower garden

gêsh giyûsh (Egypt.) army

geza naqdi (Egypt.) fine (n.)

gezîra (Egypt.) pl. gezâ'ir island

gi (Egypt.) come

gi 'and (Egypt.) visit (v.)

gi'ân, gî'ân (Egypt.) hungry

gibîn, gibîna (Egypt.) forehead

gibn (Egypt.) cheese

gibs (Egypt.) gypsum

gidd (Egypt.) grandfather

giddan (Egypt.) very

gidr (Egypt.) pl. gudûr root

gifn (Egypt.) pl. gifûn eyelid

gihâd (Egypt.) Holy War

gihâz vidyô (Egypt.) video recorder

gîl pl. **igyâl** (Egypt.) age, generation

gila (Egypt.) polish (n.)

gild (Egypt.) leather; **min gild** of leather (adj.)

gild (Egypt.) skin

gilda (Egypt.) strap (of leather)

gimgima (Egypt.) skull

ginâya (Egypt.) crime

ginêh (Egypt.) pound (currency)

ginn (coll.) (Egypt.) ghost(s)

gins (Egypt.) sex, gender; **il-gins il-laTîf** the fair sex

ginsi (Egypt.) sexual

ginsiya (Egypt.) nationality

gîr (Egypt.) lime

girâHa (Egypt.) surgery

girz (Egypt.) pl. **girzân** rat

gism (Egypt.) body

gîtâra guitar

gîz (Egypt.) beetle

giza (Egypt.) punishment

gizamâti (Egypt.) shoemaker

gîzeh Giza

gogrâfiya (Egypt.) geography

gôhar (Egypt.) pl. **gawâhir** jewel

gôhargi (Egypt.) jeweller

gôz (Egypt.) couple

gôz (Egypt.) husband

gôz (Egypt.) nut, walnut

gôz hindi (Egypt.) coconut
gôz it-Tîb (Egypt.) nutmeg
gôza (Egypt.) spouse, wife
gû' (Egypt.) hunger
gu'rân (Eygpt.) pl. ga'ârîn scarab
gubha (Egypt.) forehead
gumla (Egypt.) sentence, phrase
gumla (Egypt.) sum, total
gumruk (Egypt.) customs
gûn (Egypt.) gulf
gunilla (Egypt.) skirt
gurH (coll.) (Egypt.) wound(s)
gurnâl (Egypt.) journal
gursa (Egypt.) scandal
gurtûma garâtim (Egypt.) bacteria
gûwa (Egypt.) inside, in, within
gûwâni (Egypt.) inner
guz' (Egypt.) pl. agzâ' part
guz'i (Egypt.) partial

h/H

Ha'iT fence
Habas (Egypt.) imprison
Habb like, love (v.)
Habba sôdâ (Egypt.) fennel
Habbi *Habba* grain

Habbi *Habba* pill
Habîbi my dear
Habl pl. Hibâl cord, rope
Habl pregnancy
Habs arrest (n.)
Habs prison
Hada (Syr.) any
Hada (Syr.) who (in relative sentences)
hâda, haida (Syr.) hâdi, haidi pl. hadôl, haudi this
hadâk, haidâk (Syr.) f. hadîk, haidîk pl. hadolîk, haudîk that (pron.)
HaDar (Egypt.) to be present
HaDar presence
Hadas (Syr.) happen
Hadd (Egypt.) any
Hadd lis-sur'a speed limit
HaDD luck (n.)
Hadd pl. Hudûd border, frontier
Hâdd sharp; **sikkîna HâDDa** a sharp knife
Haddâd l(Egypt.) locksmith
haddad menace, threaten
Haddi (Egypt.) who (in relative sentences)
hâdi quiet
Hadîd anchor
Hadîd iron (metal)
HâDir (I am) at your service
HâDir present, ready; **il-waqt il-HâDir** the present time; **hallaq il-HâDir, bil-waqt il-HâDir** (Syr.) at the time

Hâdis (Syr.) conversation
Hâdis accident
Hâdisi *Hadsa* pl. Hawâdis event
hadîyi *hadîya* pl. hadâya present, gift
haDm digestion
HafaD (Egypt.) keep, retain
Hafar dig
Hafaz (Syr.) keep, retain
Hafaz preserve (v.)
Haffi *Haffa* edge, rim
Hâfi barefoot
Hafîd grandson
Hafîda granddaughter
Hâfiz 'ala mawa'îd to be punctual
Hafla performance (theater)
Hafla pl. Hafalât party, social gathering
Haflit 'îd mîlâd birthday party
Haflit mûsîqa (Egypt.) concert
Hâga (Egypt.) pl. Hâgât thing
Hâga muraTTaba (Eygpt.) refreshment, drinks
Hâga tbarrad il-qalb (Egypt.) s.th. that quenches
            thirst
Hagal (Egypt.) partridge
Hagar (Egypt.) pl. aHgâr stone
Hagar raml (Egypt.) sandstone
Hagaz (Egypt.) reserve (v.)
Hagg (Egypt.) pilgrimage
Hâgg (Egypt.) pl. Huggâg pilgrim
Hâgib (Egypt.) pl. Hwâgib eyebrow

Hagr SiH'Hi (Egypt.) quarantine

Hai (Syr.) quarter of a town

Hai alive

hai'a (Syr.) look, appearance, aspect

hai'a figure, aspect, form

hai'a shape (n.)

haida kâri (Syr.) That is my business.

Haida mâ hu shî (Syr.) It does not matter

haidâk il-yaum (Syr.) the other day

haik (Syr.) so, such, thus

Hais *Hês* as, since

Hais kân by all means

HaiT (Syr.) pl. HîTân wall (in a room)

Haiwân *Hêwân* pl. Haiwânât *Hewânât* animal

Haiyad (Syr.) turn aside

Haiyâk (Egypt.) weaver

Haiyak weave

Haiyi *Haiya* (Syr.) snake

Hajal (Syr.) partridge

hajam 'ala *hagam 'ala* attack s.b.

Hajar (Syr.) pl. aHjâr stone

Hâjar *Hâgar* emigrate

Hajaz (Syr.) reserve (v.)

Hâji (Syr.) enough

Hâji (Syr.) pl. Hawâyij thing

Hâjib (Syr.) pl. Hwâjib eyebrow

Hajj (Syr.) pilgrimage

Hâjj (Syr.) pl. Hujjâj pilgrim

Hajr SiH'Hi (Syr.) quarantine

Haka (Syr.) speak, talk, tell
Hakam 'ala condemn, rule over command
Hakam decide
Hakam reign
Hakawâti (Syr.) storyteller
Hâkim pl. Hukkâm ruler, governor, sovereign
Hâl (Syr.) self
Hâl, Hâli *Hâla* pl. aHwâl case, state, condition,
          circumstance, state
Hâla iDTirâriya emergency
Halab Aleppo
Halaf yamîn *Hilif yemîn* to take the oath
Halam *Hilim* (v.) dream
Hâlan as soon as, at once, directly
Halaq earrings; **jauz Halaq** *gôz Halaq* a pair of
          earrings
Halaq shave (v.)
Halâwa hair removal with depilatory paste made
          from sugar, water and lemon juice
Halawiyât sweets
Halazûn *Halazôn* snail
halbatt certainly
Halîb (Syr.) milk
Halîq shaven; **Halîq id-daqn** clean shaven
Hall il-barrîma (Egypt.) unscrew
hallaq (Syr.) just, at this moment
Hallûf boar
Halqa shave (n.)
hals nonsense

hal-waqt (Syr.) now

Hâma 'an defend, plead a cause

Hâma 'an protect s.b.

Hamad praise God (v.)

Hamal carry

Hamal lamb

Hamâm (coll.) dove(s), pigeon(s)

Hamât mother-in-law

Hamd praise of God

Hâmi warm (adj.)

HâmiD acid (n. + adj.), sour

Hamli *Hamla* load (n.)

Hammal *Hammil* load (v.)

Hammâl pl. Hammâlât braces

Hammâm bath

Hammâm sibâHa swimming pool

HammaS roast coffee (v.)

Hamu father-in-law

hanna congratulate

han-nahâr (Syr.) today

Haqan inject

Haqîqa (Egypt.) fact

haqîqa truth

Haqîr contemptuous

Haqli pl. Huqûl field, arable land

Haqq pl. Huqûq right (n.); **il-Haqq ma'ak** You are right. **mâ ilak Haqq ta'mil haik** *mâlakshi Haqq ti'mil kide* You have no right to act like this.

Haqqan truly, really

Hâra (Egypt.) quarter or a town

Harab escape (v.)

harab flee

Haraki (Syr.) about, near to; **Harakit 'ashra qiTa'**
     about ten pieces

haram pl. ahrâm pyramid

Harâm unlawful

Harâm! (Syr.) What a pity!

Harâmi pl. Haramîyi *Harâmiya* thief, robber

Haraq burn (trans.)

Haras watch over (v.)

Harat plough (v.)

Harb ahliye *Harb ahliya* civil war

Harb pl. Hurûb war

Harbân (Egypt.) fugitive

Hardûn (Egypt.) lizard

Harf pl. Hurûf letter, character

Harfi literal

Harfîyan literally

Harîm harem

Harîq *Harîqa* fire

Harîr silk; **min Harîr** of silk

Harr heat (n.)

Hârr spicy

harrab smuggle (v.)

Harrak move (v., trans.)

Hâsab (with acc.) (Syr.) settle an account with s.b.

Hasab according

Hasab enumerate
Hasab il-âdi *Hasab il-'âda* as usual
Hasab, Hâsab *Hâsib* calculate
Hasad envy
Hasal (Egypt.) happen
HaSal 'ala obtain
Hasharât insects
Hashîsh grass, hay
Hâsib (with acc.) (Egypt.) settle an account with s.b.
HaSîdi *HaSîda* harvest, harvesting (n.)
HaSîri *HaSîra* pl. HuSr mat
Hâsis mâ-li (Syr.) I do not feel well
Hass feel
HaSSal obtain, recover, get back
Hassâsi allergic
Hassâsiye *Hassâsiya* allergy
Hassîs sensitive (person)
Hasûd envious
HaSwa (Egypt.) pebble
HaTT put, place, lay
Hatta even, also
Hatta in order, that, until (conj.)
Hatta tâ until (conj.)
Hatta, Hatta tâ till (conj.)
HauD (Syr.) sink (n.); **HauD matbakh** kitchen sink;
       HauD Hammâm bathroom sink
Haud *HôD* bathtub
haun (Syr.) here

haunîk (Syr.) there
Haur (Syr.) poplar
Haush *Hôsh* courtyard
Hauwad (Egypt.) turn aside
Hauwalê (Egypt.) around, round
hawa (Egypt.) climate
hawa air
hawa amorousness
hawa il-aSfar cholera
hawa passion, affection, love
hawa Rarbi west wind
hawa shmâli north wind
hawa weather
hawa wind
Hawalai *Hauwalê* around
Hawalai' *Hawâli* about, around
Hawalaih (Syr.) around, round
Hâwi snake charmer (in Egypt)
Hâyad (Syr.) turn aside
hayât life
Hayy well-mannered
hayya' prepare
Hayyak knit
Hazam pack (v.)
Hazar guess (v.)
Hazîn sad, sorrowful
Hâziq clever
Hazîrân (Syr.) June

Hazz fortune, luck, happiness, pleasure
hazz shake (trans.)
hazzar (Egypt.) joke (v.)
Hd'ash *Hdâsher* eleven
hene (Egypt.) here
HêT (Egypt.) pl. HîTân wall (in a room)
hî she
Hibli *Hibla* pregnant
Hidâ' (Syr.) shoes, a pair of shoes
Hidâye conduct, guidance
Hiddâd (Syr.) locksmith
HiDir (Syr.) to be present
Hifyân (Syr.) barefoot
Higâb (Egypt.) veil
Hijâb (Syr.) veil
Hijji (Syr.) plea
Hikâyi *Hikâya* story
Hikmi *Hikma* wisdom
hilâl crescent
hilâl new moon
Hîli *Hîla* pl. Hiyal cunning (n.)
Hilif swear
Hillâq *Hallâq* barber
Hilm (Egypt.) pl. aHlâm dream
hilu sweet
Hilw dessert
Himâr, Hmâr *Humâr* pl. Hamîr donkey
Himâyi *Himâya* protection

Himl burden
Himmâm (Syr.) bath
Hinklîz (Syr.) eel
hinni (Syr.) they
HinTa (Syr.) wheat
Hirâm, Hrâm pl. aHrima blanket
Hirbân (Syr.) fugitive
Hirdaun (Syr.) lizard
Hirfa pl. Hiraf craft, skill
Hirz (Syr.) amulet
Hisâb (Egypt.) invoice
Hisâb account
Hisâb estimate (n.)
HiSSa pl. HiSaS share, allotment
Hitat Riyâr (Egypt.) spare parts
hiTTet laHm (Egypt.) a piece of meat
Hîyâk (Syr.) weaver
hiyi *hîya, hîye* she
Hizâ' 'âlî sâq pl. aHzîya 'âlî sâq boot
Hizâm amân safety belt
Hizb pl. aHzâb political party
Hjar raml (Syr.) sandstone
Hkâyi *Hikâya* fairy tale
HôD (Egypt.) sink (n.); **HôD matbakh** kitchen sink;
        HôD Hammâm bathroom sink
Hôr (Egypt.) poplar
hôtello (Syr.) hotel
Hsâb (Syr.) invoice

Hsâb *Hisâb* bill, calculation
Hsân il-baHr (Syr.) hippopotamus
hû (Syr.) he
Hubb love (n.)
hubûT Tawâri emergency landing
HuDn lap (n.)
hudû calm (n.)
Hufra pl. Hufar hole
Hugga (Egypt.) plea
Hukm authority, power, jurisdiction, rule, command
Hukm pl. aHkâm decision, sentence, verdict
Hukûmi *Hukûma* government
hukûmi, hkûmi *hukûma* authorities
Hulm (Syr.) pl. aHlâm dream (n.)
Hulqûm palate
Hulqûm throat
Hulu sweet
hum, huma (Egypt.) they
Humma fever
HummuS (coll.) chickpea(s)
hunâk, henâk (Egypt.) there
Huqna pl. Huqan injection
Hurr free
Hurrîyi *Hurrîya* freedom
Husân il-baHr (Egypt.) hippopotamus
hûwa, hûwe (Egypt.) he
Huzn (Egypt.) sorrow

i

i'lân advertisement

i'tabar esteem (v.)

i'tamad 'ala (Egypt.) rely on, trust in; **ba'tamid 'alêk** I rely on you.

i'tana mind (v.)

i'taraf acknowledge, confess

i'tâz need (v.)

i'tazar excuse oneself

i'tibâr esteem (n.)

i'timad 'ala (Syr.) trust in

i'timâd trust (n.)

i'tirâf acknowledgement

i'tiyâdi ordinary

ib'at wara send for s.th.

ibhâm pl. ibhâmât thumb

iblîs devil

ibn il-'amm cousin (son of father's brother)

ibn il-'ammi *ibn il'-amma* cousin (son of father's sister)

ibn il-akh nephew (son of the brother)

ibn il-khâl cousin (son of mother's brother)

ibn il-khâli *ibn il-khâla* cousin (son of mother's sister)

ibn il-ukht nephew (son of the sister)

ibn pl. abnâ son

ibri *ibra* pl. ibar needle

ibta'ad 'an (Syr.) keep far from

ibta'ad 'an (Syr.) absent oneself from

ibtada begin (intrans.)

ibtisâma smile (n.)

îd pl. iyâdi *eyâdi, ayâdi* arm, hand

idâre *idâra* administration

idda' claim (v.)

iD-dabT il-ba'îd remote control

id-delta delta

iddi'â claim (n.)

id-dinya kulliha naTar (Egypt.) it is pouring down,
      it is raining heavily

id-dinyi kâbsi (Syr.) it is pouring down, it is raining
      heavily

id-dunya Dilmet (Egypt.) It has grown dark.

iDrâb strike (n.)

ifriqya Africa

iftaH an-nûr (Egypt.) Switch on the light!

iftakar remember, think, suppose

iftakar think; **biftikir** *baftikir* I think

iftaraDna in (Syr.) provided that

iftikhâr glory

igtimâ' (Egypt.) meeting

ihâni (Syr.) offense

iHmarr blush, turn red

iHna (Egypt.) we

iHsân alms

iHsân charity

iHsâs feeling, sense

iHtafal celebrate, party (v.)

iHtâg (Egypt.) need, require

iHtâj (Syr.) need, require

iHtajj 'ala protest against (v.)

iHtajj *iHtagg* argue; **mâ aqder ahâjjak** *mâ aqder ahâggek* I cannot argue with you

iHtamal bear, suffer, stand, put up with, tolerate

iHtaram esteem, honor (v.)

iHtaraq (Syr.) become consumed by fire

ihtazz shake (intrans.)

iHtifâl celebration

iHtigâg (Egypt.) requirement

iHtijâj (Syr.) requirement

iHtijâj protest (n.)

iHtirâm esteem (n.)

ihtiyâri voluntary

iHtiyâT precaution; **lil- iHtiyâT** for precaution

ija come (Syr.)

ija daurak (Syr.) It's your turn.

ija la'and (Syr.) visit (v.)

ijr (Syr.) pl. irjul foot

ijra (Syr.) lease, wages, pay (n.)

ijraiyi wârmîn (Syr.) My feet are swollen.

ijrit busTa (Syr.) postage

ijtahad (Syr.) trouble oneself

ijtihâd *ightihâd* diligence

ijtimâ' (Syr.) meeting

ikhta'ra' invent

ikhtafa (Egypt.) disappear

ikhtalaf (Egypt.) disagree

ikhtâr choose

ikhtirâ' invention

ikhtirâ' patent, invention

ikhtiyâr choice

iktashaf discover

iktishâf discovery

il the

il-'ahd il- jadîd (Syr.) the New Testament

il-'ahd il-'aTîq the Old Testament

il-'ahd il-gadîd (Egypt.) the New Testament

il-'ilâj in-nafsi psychotherapy

ila to

ilâhi divine

il-aHsan best, the best

il-aqall least

il-aRlab probable, usually

il-baHr il-abyaD the Mediterranean Sea

il-baHr il-aHmar the Red Sea

il-baHr il-mayyit the Dead Sea

il-baiyin kide (Egypt.) it seems so, it appears

il-etnên (Egypt.) both

il-Hamdillah *il-Hamdo lil-lâh* God be praised

ili (Syr.) I have

ili khâTir ktîr (Syr.) inclined to do s.th.

il-jum'al Hazîni *ig-gum'al Hazîna* Good Friday

il-khabar ê? (Egypt.) What is going on?

illa but, except (prep.)

illa qalîl (Syr.) almost

illa shuwwaiye (Egypt.) almost

il-lail *il-lêla* tonight

illi mâlo nihâyi (Syr.) endless, infinite

il-lubnân Lebanon

il-madâm bita'ti (Egypt.) my wife

il-qabr il-muqaddas the Holy Sepulchre (in
          Jerusalem)

il-qâhira Cairo

il-quds Jerusalem

il-qur'ân Koran

iltaqa (Syr.) meet

iltihâb inflammation

il-umam il-mutaH-Hida United Nations

il-urdun Jordan

il-wâldain *il-wâlidên* parents

il-wilayât il-muhtaHHida United States of America

il-yaum (Syr.) today

il-yaum 'ala bukra (Syr.) this morning

îmân belief

îmân faith

imbâriH (Egypt.) yesterday

imDa signature

imrâr ketîra (Egypt.) often

imsâk constipation

imtadd (Syr.) stretch (v., intrans.)

imtahan examine

imtana' 'an refuse (v.)

imtiHân examination, test

in that (conj.) (before vowels: inn)

in'ada (Syr.) catch a disease

inbasaT to be pleased

indâr alarm

infa'kashit ijri *itfa'raket rigli* I have sprained
         my ankle

infajar *infagar* explode

infakashit ijri *itfaraket rigli* I sprained my ankle

infaSal separate (v., intrans.)

infataH (Syr.) to be open

infazar burst (intrans.)

inglîzi pl. inglîz English

inha (Syr.) that she

inhon (Syr.) that they

inkamash (Syr.) shrink

inkâr denial

inkon (Syr.) that you (pl.)

inna that we

innâha (Egypt.) that she

in-nahâr dok-hâ (Egypt.) the other day

in-naharda (Egypt.) today

in-naharda is-SubH (Egypt.) this morning

innak that you (m. sg.)

inni that I

innik that you (f. sg.)

in-nîl Nile

in-nîl zâd The Nile has risen.
inno that he
innûhum (Egypt.) that they
innûkum (Egypt.) that you
inqalab turn over (intrans.)
inqata' cease (v.)
inRallaq to be shut
inSâf justice
insân pl. nâs mankind
insâni human (not animal)
insânîyi *insânîya* humanity
insaraf leave (v., intrans.)
insarr to be pleased
insh allah let us hope
instanZar wait
inta you (m.)
intakhab extract, draw out, pick, select
intaqam take revenge
intaZar (Egypt.) expect
inti you (f.)
intibâH attention
intifâkh (Syr.) inflation
intikhâbât elections
intiqâm revenge (n.)
intu you (pl.)
inwajad (Syr.) exist
inZurni! (Syr.) Wait for me!
iqâma stay (n.)

iqlîmi regional
iqtiSâd economy
irâd income
irâdi (Syr.) will (n.)
ir-raHmân (God) the merciful
ir-rûH il-qudus the Holy Spirit
irs heritage
irta'ash (Egypt.) tremble
irtâH (Syr.) recover, rest
irtâH! (Syr.) be quiet!
irtifa' altitude
irtiyâh comfort, ease (n.)
iSba' ir-rijl *iSba' ir-rigl* pl. Sâbî' ir-rijl *Sawâbi'*
　　ir-rigl toe
iSba' (Syr.) pl. aSâbî' finger
ish'al iD-Dau (Syr.) Switch on the light!
isHâl diarrhea
ishtâq la *ishtâq li* long for (v.)
ishtara buy (v.)
ishtaRal (Syr.) work (v.)
ishtiRil (Egypt.) work (v.)
iskân settlement
iskindiriya Alexandria
iskut! (Syr.) Hush!
ism pl. asmâ, asâmi name (n.)
isma'ni! Listen to me!
is-saiyid Mr.
is-saiyida Mrs.

is-sana elli fâtet (Egypt.) last year
is-si'îd Upper Egypt
ista'âr min borrow from
ista'fa resign
ista'mal use (v.)
ista'ma' (Egypt.) listen
ista'zan (Syr.) ask for permission
ista'zan *ista'zin* take leave
istabda bi start with
iSTabl (Egypt.) stable (n.)
iSTâd hunt (v.)
istaDal sit in the shade
istafraR vomit
istagar (Egypt.) hire, rent (v.)
istaHa to be ashamed
istaHamma (Egypt.) bathe, take a bath
istaHaqq deserve
istaHass feel
istaHsan (Syr.) approve
istaHsin (Egypt.) approve
istâjar (Syr.) hire, rent (v.)
istakhbar 'an inquire
istakhbar learn, hear
istakra hire (v.)
iSTalaH (Egypt.) to be reconciled
istanna expect, wait
istanna shuwaiye! (Egypt.) Wait a little!
istannâni! (Egypt.) Wait for me!

203

istanZar (Syr.) expect
istaqraf min disgusted with
istarHam to ask for mercy
istaSwab approve
istaT'am taste (v.)
istaula 'ala conquer
istautan settle, take up residence
istawa ripen (v., trans.)
istayqaZa wake up
istazin (Egypt.) ask for permission
isteraiyaH (Egypt.) recover, rest
isti'mâl usage
istiha (Egypt.) embarrassment
istiHsân (Syr.) approval
istiqbâl reception, reception desk
istiqlâl independence
istisnâ exception
istiSwâb (Egypt.) approval
istîzân leave (n.)
it'aiyin (Egypt.) to be nominated
it'allim (Egypt.) learn
it'aggib (Egypt.) to be astonished
it'akh'khar (Egypt.) to be late
it'ammal (Egypt.) hope (v.)
iTâla prolongation
iTâr pl. itârât tire (n.)
itassif 'ala (Egypt.) regret (v.)
itbâ'ad 'an (Egypt.) keep far from, absent oneself from

itbâhis (Egypt.) discuss
itbaiyin (Egypt.) seem
itbassam (Egypt.) smile (v.)
itfaDDal (Egypt.) please (to a male, speaker offering s.th.); *itfaddal khush'sh* please enter
itfaDDal (Egypt.) to have the kindness
itfataH (Egypt.) to be open
iTfi iD-Dau *iTfi in-nûr* Turn off the light!
itgaraH (Egypt.) to be injured
itgâsar (Egypt.) dare
itgauwiz (Egypt.) marry (intrans.)
itHâdit (Egypt.) chat (v.)
itHaraq (Egypt.) become consumed by fire
itHarrak (Egypt.) move (v., intrans.)
itHaSal 'ala (Egypt.) obtain
itHâsib settle accounts with one another
itHassan (Egypt.) improve (intrans.)
itjaraH (Syr.) to be injured
itka'bil stumble
itkaffal 'an (Egypt.) guarantee (v.)
itkallim (Egypt.) speak
itkhabba hide (intrans.)
itlazzaq (Egypt.) to be stuck
itmadd (Egypt.) stretch (v., intrans.)
itmakh'khaT (Egypt.) blow one's nose
itmatta' bi enjoy s.th.
itnaddim 'ala (Egypt.) repent s.th.
itnah'hid (Egypt.) sigh (v.)

itnashal (Egypt.) to have one's pocket picked
itnâsher (Egypt.) twelve
itnên (Egypt.) two
itqâbil (Egypt.) meet each other
itqâtil (Egypt.) fight
itRarraq (Egypt.) to be drowned
itRassal (Egypt. wash oneself, bathe, take a bath
itsamma (Egypt.) to be nominated
itsawwaq go shopping
itshaka min complain of
itshakkar (Egypt.) thank
ittafaq 'ala agree on s.th.
ittakal 'ala (Syr.) rely on; **bittakil 'alaik** I rely on
          you.
ittaSSal call (v.)
it-Tibb in-nafsi psychiatry
ittifâqan eventually
ittijâh *ittigâh* direction
ittikâl trust (n.)
iTTilâ' 'ala insight into
ittnain (Syr.) both
itwagad (Egypt.) exist
itwakkal 'ala (Egypt.) trust in
itwaqqa! (Egypt.) Take care!
itwarrad to be supplied
itzakkar (Egypt.) remember; **mush mutazakkir
          ismo** I cannot remember his name.
îyâk! Take care!

îyâr (Syr.) May
iza if (with indic.)
izâ'a broadcast
izâz il-'arabiya (Egypt.) windshield
izâz is-sayyâra (Syr.) windshield
izdiHâm traffic jam
izdiyâd increase (n.)
izn permission
iz-zâher (Syr.) evidently
iz-zâhir haik (Syr.) It seems so.
iz-zâhir kide (Egypt.) It seems so.

j

jâb (Syr.) bring, fetch
jâb sîrit (Syr.) mention (v.)
jabal (Syr.) pl. jibâl mountain
jabal nâr (Syr.) volcano
jabân (Syr.) coward
jadd (Syr.) earnest
jaddad (Syr.) renew
jadwal (Syr.) timetable
jahannam (Syr.) hell
jahil (Syr.) ignorant
jaib (Syr.) pocket
jaish pl. juyûsh (Syr.) army
jâji (Syr.) hen
jâkêt jacket

jala (Syr.) polish (v.)

jalab lil-maHkama (Syr.) summon to court

jama' (Egypt.) unite (v.)

jama' (Syr.) add, collect

jama' (Syr.) unite (v.)

jama' gather (v.)

jamâ'a (Syr.) party, company

jamâ'at mûsîqa (Syr.) orchestra

jamal (Syr.) pl. jimâl camel

jamâl (Syr.) beauty

jamb (Syr.) beside, side; **'ala jambi** on my side

jamb by, near

jamb min (Syr.) near to, close to

jambûn (Syr.) ham

jamî' (Syr.) all

jâmi'a (Syr.) university

jamî'an (Syr.) as a whole, altogether

jâmid (Syr.) lifeless

jamîl (Syr.) beautiful

jammâl (Syr.) camel driver

jamûs pl. jawâmîs (Syr.) buffalo

janainâti (Syr.) flower garden

jânib (Syr.) side; **'al-jânib** on the side

janni (Syr.) paradise

janûb (Syr.) south

jâr (Syr.) pl. jîrân neighbor

jarab (Syr.) itch (n.)

jarad (Syr.) locust

jaraH (Syr.) injure
jaras (Syr.) bell
jarH (Syr.) pl. jirâ injury
jarr (Syr.) drag (trans.)
jarrab (Syr.) try (v.)
jarrâH (Syr.) surgeon
jasîim (Syr.) corpulent
jasûr (Syr.) bold
jâsûs (Syr.) spy
jauhar (Syr.) pl. jawâhir jewel
jauharji (Syr.) jeweller
jauz (Syr.) couple
jauz (Syr.) nut, walnut
jauz (Syr.) spouse, husband
jauz hindi (Syr.) coconut
jauzi (Syr.) spouse, wife
jauzit iT-Tîb (Syr.) nutmeg
jawâb (Syr.) answer (v.)
jawâb pl. ijwibi (Syr.) answer (n.)
jâyiz (Syr.) allowed
jâza (Syr.) punish
jaza naqdi (Syr.) fine (n.)
jazar (coll.) (Syr.) carrot(s)
jazîri (Syr.) pl. jazâyir island
jazmâti (Syr.) shoemaker
jdîd (Syr.) pl. jdâd, judud new
jefsîn (Syr.) gypsum
jêzi (Syr.) marriage

jibîn, jibîni (Syr.) forehead
jibn (Syr.) cheese
jidd (Syr.) grandfather
jiddan (Syr) very
jidr (Syr.) pl. judûr root
jîfi (Syr.) corpse
jifn (Syr.) pl. jifûn eyelid
jigrâfiya (Syr.) geography
jihâd (Syr.) Holy War
jihâz vidyô (Syr.) video recorder
jîl pl. ijyâl (Syr.) age, generation
jila (Syr.) polish (n.)
jild (Syr.) leather; **min jild** of leather (adj.)
jild (Syr.) skin
jildi (Syr.) strap (of leather)
jimjimi (Syr.) skull
jimli (Syr.) sum, total
jinâH (Syr.) pl. ijniHi wing
jinâyi (Syr.) crime
jinâzi (Syr.) funeral
jinn (coll.) (Syr.) ghost(s)
jins (Syr.) gender
jins (Syr.) sex, gender; **il-jins il-laTîf** the fair sex
jinsi (Syr.) sexual
jinsiya (Syr.) nationality
jirâHa (Syr.) surgery
jirdaun (Syr.) pl. jarâdin rat
jirjîr (Syr.) cress

jism (Syr.) body

jisr pl. jusur (Syr.) bridge

jîz (Syr.) beetle

jiza (Syr.) punishment

jnaini (Syr.) flower garden

jû' (Syr.) hunger

jû'ân (Syr.) hungry

ju'rân (Syr.) pl. ja'ârîn scarab

jumla (Syr.) sentence, phrase

jumruk (Syr.) customs

jûn (Syr.) gulf, bay

junilla (Syr.) skirt

jurH (coll.) (Syr.) wound(s)

jurnâl (Syr.) journal

jursa (Syr.) scandal

jurtûma pl. jarâtim (Syr.) bacteria

jûwa (Syr.) in, within, inside (adv.)

jûwâni (Syr.) inner

juz' (Syr.) pl. ajzâ' part

juz'i (Syr.) partial

k/kh

ka'b cube, die

ka'b heel

ka'b pl. k'âb ankle, knuckle

ka'ka (Egypt.) cake

kabas press (v.)

kabas, kabbas preserve (fruit, etc.)

kabîr *kibîr* adult

kabsh (Syr.) ram

kadar trouble (n.)

kaddâb (Eygpt.) false (person)

kaddar annoy, trouble (v., trans.)

kafal backside

kaffâra atonement

kâfi sufficient

kafîl *kefîl* one who stands bail

kâfir pl. kuffâr unbeliever

kâfûr eucalyptus

kâhin pl. kahana priest

kahraba electricity

kahrabi electric

kahramân (Egypt.) amber

kahrubâ (Syr.) amber

ka-in (Syr.) as if

kal (Egypt.) eat

kalâm fâreR nonsense

kalâm speech (language, words), talk

kalb *kelb* pl. klâb *kilâb* dog

kallaf *kallif* cost (v.)

kallim (Egypt.) speak

kalsa pl. kalsât (Syr.) sock

kâlûn (Egypt.) lock (n.)

kâm (Egypt.); **kâm yôm** some days

kam (Syr.) some; **kâm yaum** some days

kâm 'alêye? (Egypt.) How much do I have to pay?

kâm how many, how much

kam *kâm* a few

kâm lâk 'alêye? kam lâk 'andi? (Egypt.) How much do I owe you?

kamân (Syr.) also, yet, more, too, still

kamân violin

kâmil entire, complete, perfect

kamîra camera

kammal kammil get ready

kammal *kammil* continue, conclude, finish, execute, accomplish, complete

kammâsha (Egypt.) pincers

kammâsha (Egypt.) tongs

kammiya quantity

kân be (past tense)

kanaba (Egypt.) sofa

kanas (Egypt.) sweep (v.)

kannas (Syr.) sweep (v.)

karam liberality

karîm (Syr.) liberal

karîm generous

karkadann rhinoceros

karkand lobster

karm pl. kurûm vineyard

karra *karro* cart

karram honor (v.)

karrar repeat

kart 'uDwiya membership card
kart taHqîq ish-shakhSiya (Egypt.) identification
       card
karwân (Syr.) caravan
kasal laziness
kasar break (v.)
kasb gain (n.)
kâsh cash
kash'sh (Egypt.) shrink
kaslân (Egypt.) lazy
kasr pl. ksûr *kusûr* fraction
kassar break (v.)
kastalêta (Egypt.) cutlet
kastani (Syr.) chestnut
kasûl (Egypt.) lazy
katab write
kâtib (Syr.) clerk, secretary
kâtib pl. kuttâb writer
kattar increase (v., trans.)
kâtûlîki pl. kwâtli *katâlka* Catholic
kaukab (Syr.) planet
kawa iron (v.)
kâz (Syr.) gas
kazâlik *kazâlik* also, likewise
kbîr (Syr.) great, old (for persons), big, large
keber increase (v., intrans.)
kebîr (Egypt.) great, old (for persons), big, large
kebsh (Egypt.) ram

keddâb (Egypt.) liar

kêf (Egypt.) how

kêf comfort, ease (n.)

kelâm (Egypt.) language, speech, words

kemân (Egypt.) also, yet, too

ketîr (Egypt.) a lot, often, plenty, very much, too
        much; **ketîr min in-nâs** a lot of people;
        ketîr khâliS, ketîr giddan very much

kfâli (Syr.) guarantee (n.)

kfâyi *kfâya* enough

khabar ê? (Egypt.) What is going on?

khabar pl. akhbâr news

khabaT knock, beat

khabba conceal, put away, hide

khabbar *khabbir* inform

khabîr pl. khubarâ expert

khabîs (Syr.) cunning, low, mean

khad (Egypt.) receive, accept, take

khad bâlu (Syr.) to be mindful

khad bard (Egypt.) catch a cold

khadam serve (intrans.)

khadâmi (Syr.) service

khadash (v.) scratch

khadd pl. khudûd cheek

khaddâm (Egypt.) servant

khâdim (Syr.) servant

khadni ish-shams I have a sunstroke

khadsh pl. khudûsh scratch (n.)

khâf min be afraid of, fear s.b. or s.th.

khafîf light, not heavy

khail *khêl* (coll.) horse(s)

khaimi (Syr.) pl. khiyam tent

khair (Syr.) welfare

khair *khêr* good (n.)

khaiT (Syr.) pl. khîTân thread

khaiyât (Egypt.) tailor

khaiyat sew

khaiyâTa (Egypt.) seamstress

khaiyir benevolent, generous

khajûl (Syr.) timid

khakhâm, khikhâm rabbi

khâl pl. akhwâl uncle (mother's brother)

khâlaf (Syr.) resist, oppose

khalaq create

khalaS (Syr.) end (v., intrans.)

khalaS to be ready

khalaT mix (v.)

khalf after, behind

khalf min after, behind

khâli *khâla* aunt (on the mother's side)

khâli vacant

khalif (Egypt.) contradict

khâlif (Egypt.) resist

khâliS genuine

khâliS quite (adv.)

khall vinegar

khalla bâlo 'ala (Eypt.) pay attention to

khalla bâlu (Egypt.) to be mindful

khalla il-bâl 'ala (Egypt.) look after s.b., take care of

khalla let, permit (v.)

khallaS end, bring to an end, finish, get ready

khalli bâlak! (Egypt.) Take care!

khallîhon yjîbu (Syr.) send for s.th., ask s.b.
       to bring s.th.

khallîhum yegîbu (Egypt.) send for s.th., ask s.b. to
        bring s.th.

khallîni leave me alone

khalq creation

khâmis f. khâmsi *khamsa* fifth

khamsi *khamsa* five

khamsîn fifty

khamsmîyi *khumsemîya* five hundred

khamsTa'sh *khamstâsher* fifteen

khanaq strangle, suffocate

khandaq pl. khanâdiq ditch

khanSar little finger

khansîr pig

khanzîr berri boar

kharâb ruin, destruction

kharbûsha scratchmark

khardal (Syr.) mustard

kharîf autumn

khârig (Egypt.) outside

khârij (Syr.) outside

kharr id-damm (Egypt.) it is bleeding
kharrab ruin, destroy
kharshûf (Egypt.) artichoke
kharTa map
khâS special (adj.)
khasâra (Syr.) loss
khash (Egypt.) come in
khash'sh enter
khaSla quality
khaSm pl. ikhSâm opponent
khaSm reduction, discount
khaSS belong, concern (v.)
khass lettuce
khâSS personal, private
khâSSatan specially
khaTa sin (v.)
khaTa, khaTtîyi *khatîya khaTâya* fault
khaTab preach (rel.)
khaTaf hijack, kidnap
khatam close, finish
khatan circumcise
khaTar danger, hazard, peril
khâtim pl. khawâtim ring, finger ring
khâtim seal (n.)
khaTîyi *khaTîya* pl. khaTâya sin (n.)
khaTT (Egypt.) handwriting
khaTT line, stroke, stripe
khaTTâb preacher

khaTTâf hijacker, kidnapper

khaTwa step (n.)

khauf *khôf* fright, fear

khaukh (coll.) (Syr.) plum(s)

khauwaf threaten

khawâga (Egypt.) pl. khawâgât foreigner

khayal shade, a shadow thrown by some object

khâyif *khâ'if* afraid; **bkhâf nit'akh'khar** *bakhâf*
          nit'akh'khar I am afraid we will be late

khâyin *khâ'in* false person, traitor

khazzaq (Syr.) tear (v.)

khêma (Egypt.) pl. khiyam tent

khêr (Egypt.) welfare

khêT (Egypt.) pl. khîTân thread

khibbâz *khabbâz* baker

khidâma (Egypt.) service

khidma (Egypt.) service

khidmi (Syr.) service

khilâf (Syr.) difference, opposition

khiliS (Egypt.) end (v., trans.)

khiSâm quarrel (n.)

khishin gross, unrefined, impolite, rough

khisir lose (at a game)

khiTâb speech, discourse

khiTân circumcision

khiTTa plan

khiyâr (coll.) cucumber(s)

khiyâT (Syr.) tailor

khiyâTa (Syr.) seamstress
khizâni (Syr.) cupboard pl. khazâyin
khôd *khod* Take!
khôf (Egypt.) fear (n.)
khôkh (coll.) (Egypt.) peach(es)
khubz (Syr.) bread
khuDra pl. khuDar vegetables
khunfusa pl. khanâfis beetle
khurdâji *khurdâgi* haberdasher
khurg *khurj* saddlebag
khurq breach, opening
khurûg (Egypt.) exit, way out
khurûj (Syr.) exit, way out
khurûj *khurûg* exit (n.); **mnain il-khurûj?** *fên
         il-khurûg?* Where is the exit?
khusâra (Egypt.) loss
khuSS (Syr.) hut
khusûf il-qamar eclipse of the moon
khuSûSan specially
khuSûSi private
kibdi *kibda* liver
kibir grow (intrans.)
kibrît (Egypt.) lightning match
kibriya pride, haughtiness
kidb (Egypt.) untrue
kidba (Egypt.) lie (n.)
kide (Egypt.) so, such, thus
kidib (Egypt.) lie (v.)
kîf (Syr.) how

kîf Hâlak? (Syr.) How do you do?

kîf il-ishRâl? (Syr.) How is business?

kilâks horn (mot.)

kilfi (Syr.) expect

kilmi *kilma* pl. kilmât word

kils (Syr.) lime

kilwi *kilwa* pl. kalâwi kidney (food)

kilya kidney (anat.)

kimmâshi (Syr.) pincers

kimmâshi (Syr.) tongs

kinz pl. kunûz treasure

kirha aversion

kirmîd brick

kîs pl. ikyâs *akyâs* purse

kishk tilifôn telephone booth

kishtbân (Syr.) thimble

kisib earn, gain

kislân (Syr.) lazy

kiswi *kiswa* clothes

kitâba (Egypt.) inscription, writing (calligraphy, document)

kitf pl. iktâf shoulder

kittân linen (n.); **min kittân** linen (adj.)

kizbi (Syr.) lie (n.)

kizib (Syr.) lie (v.)

kizzâb (Syr.) false person, liar

knîsi *kenîsa* pl. knâyis *kenâyis* church

kofta meatballs

kôkab (Egypt.) planet

konsêr (Syr.) concert

korumb (Egypt.) cabbage

kôsa (coll.) zucchini

krâfât tie (n.)

krafs *karafs* celery

krêdito credit

ktâb il-mqaddas *kitâb il-muqaddas* bible

ktâb *kitâb* pl. kutb *kutub* book

ktâbe (Syr.) desk

ktâbet yad (Syr.) handwriting

ktîbi (Syr.) inscription, writing (calligraphy, document)

ktîr (Syr.) a lot, plenty, very much, too much, many, often; **ktîr min in-nâṣ** a lot of people; **nâs ktîr** many people; **ktîr khâliS, ktîr jiddan** very much

kû' *kô'* pl. kî'ân elbow

kubbâyi *kubbâya* glass (drinking glass)

kubri (Egypt.) bridge

kufr blasphemy

kufta meatballs

kulfa (Egypt.) expense

kull all; **il-kull** everything

kull each, either, entire, every, total, whole

kull iyâm 'umri (Syr.) in my whole life

kull sini *kull sana* every year

kull sini winta sâlim *kull sana winta Taiyib* Happy New Year!

kull wâhid *kulli wâHid* everybody
kulliyi *kulliya* academy
kullma … kullma the more … the more …
kullmîn everybody
kullo everything
kumbûter computer
kumm pl. akmâm sleeve
kummitra (coll.) (Egypt.) pear(s)
kuntrâtu contract
kura *kora* ball
kurat il-qadam football
kurk (Egypt.) fur
kurkum saffron
kursi pl. krâsi *karâsi* chair
kustebân (Egypt.) thimble
kutubi, kutbi bookseller
kuwafêr hairdresser
kwaiyis *kuwaiyis* beautiful, nice, pretty

l

la (Syr.) for, to
lâ … ulâ (Syr.) neither … nor; **lâ haida ulâ haida**
    neither one nor the other; **lâ haik ulâ haik**
    neither so nor so
lâ … walâ (Egypt.) neither …nor; **lâ di walâ di**
    neither one nor the other; **lâ kide walâ kide**
    neither so nor so

lâ ba's (Syr.) never mind
lâ no
lâ silki wireless
lâ tuSaddaq incredible
lâ twâkhidna (Syr.) excuse me
lâ yu'add innumerable
lâ yuHSa innumerable
la'b (Syr.) game, play (n.)
la'b iS-Sûlajân *la'b iS-Sôlagân* golf
la'ni *la'na* curse (n.)
la'in *li'in* because
laban (Egypt.) milk
laban (Syr.) yogurt
la-barra (Syr.) out
labbâd (Syr.) felt
labbas *labbis* dress
ladaR stutter
lafaz express oneself (v.)
laff bi wrap up in
lafz pronunciation
lafZi *lafZa* accent
lâgi' (Egypt.) refugee
lagl (Egypt.) in order to
la-Hadd (Syr.) as far as, until, to
la-Hâlo (Syr.) separate
lâHaz (Syr.) remark (v.)
lâHaz *lâHiz* observe
lahîb flame, blaze

lâHiz (Egypt.) remark (v.)
lahja *lahga* dialect
laHm (coll.) meat, flesh
laHm 'igl (Egypt.) veal
laHm 'ijil (Syr.) veal
laHm baqar beef
laHm Dâni mutton
laHm khanzîr pork
laHm kharûf lamb meat
laHm maslûq boiled meat
laHm midhin fat meat
laHm miqli roast meat
laHm Ranam mutton
laHm Sabb lean, boneless meat
laHm Tari fresh meat
laHmi *laHma* lump of meat
laHn pl. alHân melody
laHza moment
lail, laili pl. iyâli (Syr.) night
laimûn (coll.) (Syr.) lemon(s)
laimûnâDa *lêmûnâta* lemonade
laish (Syr.) why
laiyin smooth (adj.)
lâji' (Syr.) refugee
la-khalf *li-khalf* backwards
lâkin but, only
lâm (v.) blame
lam'i shiny

lama' (Egypt.) shine
lamba lightbulb
lamî' (Syr.) bright, shining
lamma (Egypt.) when (conj.)
lâmûn (coll.) (Egypt.) lemon(s)
lâqa meet, receive, find, get
laqlaq stork
la-quddâm (Syr.) forward
laRz (Syr.) pl. ilRâz riddle
las'a sting (of insects)
lasa' sting (v.)
laSaq paste (v.)
la-taHt (Syr.) down
laTîf amiable
laTîf kind, mild, pleasant, polite
lau *lô* (with subj.) if
lau mâ *lô'lâ in* if not
lauH i'lânât *lôh i'lânât* bulletin board
lauH tablet
lauHa (Syr.) painting
laum *lôm* blame (n.)
laun (Syr.) pl. alwân color, paint
lauz *lôz* almond
lawa bend (trans.)
la-waHdo (Syr.) separate (adj.)
la-wara *li-wara* backwards
lazaq stick (v., trans.)
lâzim must; **lâzim sâfir hallaq** *lâzim asâfir dil waqt*
    I must start now.

lâzim necessary

lazîz (Egypt.) tasty

lazqa plaster, cataplasm

lê, lêh (Egypt.) why

lêl, lêla pl. leyâli (Egypt.) night

li (Egypt.) for, to

li (Egypt.) I have

li'b (Egypt.) play, game

li'ib play (v.)

li'ai sabab *li'aiyi sabab* why, for what reason

li-ajl (Syr.) in order to

libd (Egypt.) felt

libis put on one's clothes, get dressed, wear
        (clothes)

libs pl. libâs clothes

lift (coll.) turnip(s)

ligâm (Eygpt.) pl. algima rein

liH'Hâm *laH'Hâm* butcher

liHaâf pl. luHûf bed cover

li-Hadd (Egypt.) as far as, until, to

liHiq follow

liHyi *liHya* beard

lil-Râyi extreme

limi' (Syr.) shine

limma (Syr.) when (conj.)

li-quddâm (Egypt.) forward

lîra (Syr.) pound (currency)

lisân pl. ilsini *alsina* language, idiom, tongue

lissa bedri (ketîr) (Egypt.) it is still too early

lissa lîye ma'ak shê, lissa lîye 'andak shê (Egypt.)
   You still owe me s.th.

lissa still, yet

li-sû il-Hazz unfortunately

liwaHdo (Egypt.) separate

lîye khâTir ketîr (Egypt.) inclined to do s.th.

liziq stick (v., trans.)

ljâm pl. aljima (Syr.) rein

lôHa (Egypt.) painting

lôn (Egypt.) pl. alwân color, paint

lûbyi *lûbyia* (coll.) French bean(s)

lukanda *lokanda* inn

lûliye (Egypt.) July

lûlu (coll.) pearl(s)

luRa pl. luRât language, idiom

luRz (Egypt.) pl. ilRâz riddle

luzûm necessity

m

m'allim *me'allim* master, teacher

mâ 'alêsh (Egypt.) It does not matter.

mâ 'indi khabar 'anno *mâ 'andîsh khabar 'anno* I
   know nothing about it.

mâ bîsâyil it does not matter, there is no harm, never
   mind

mâ byimkinni *mâ yimkinîsh* I cannot

mâ dâm as long as, while

mâ fîhi dukhân smoke-free

228

mâ fîsh khâTir ebeden (Egypt.) I do not feel
      inclined to

mâ fîsh mâni' There is no objection.

mâ Hada (Syr.) nobody, none

mâ Haddish (Egypt.) nobody, none

mâ ilak shuRl haun *mâlak shuRl hene* You have no
      business here.

mâ ili khâTir abadan (Syr.) I do not feel inclined to.

mâ not

mâ shi, mâshi (Syr.) nothing

mâ ti'âkhiznîsh (Egypt.) excuse me

mâ yidûrrish (Egypt.) never mind

ma', ma'a at, with

ma'a ba'D together

ma'a in though

ma'a zâlik however, still, nevertheless, yet

ma'âsh pension, retirement

ma'bad pl. ma'âbid temple (edifice)

ma'din pl. ma'âdin metal

ma'diye ferry

ma'jûn Hilâqa *ma'gûn Hilâqa* shaving cream

ma'jûn snân *ma'gûn sinân* toothpaste

ma'lûf familiar

ma'lûmât information

ma'lûmkon in *ma'lûmkum in* Is it known to you
      that…?

ma'mal laboratory

ma'mal factory

ma'na pl. ma'âni meaning

ma'nâh ê? (Egypt.) What does that mean?

ma'raD exhibition

ma'rifi *ma'rifa* pl. ma'ârif knowledge

ma'rûf familiar

ma'rûf favor, kindness

ma'Sara pl. ma'âSir press (n., for oil, wine, etc.)

ma'zi (Syr.) pl. ma'z goat

ma'zira excuse, apology

mabHûH hoarse

mablaR pl. mbâliR *mebâliR* sum, amount

mablûl wet (adj.)

mabrûk congratulations

mabsûT min content with, to be satisfied with

madad! Help!

madaH praise (v.); **madaH nafso** praise oneself

madâm Madam

madaR (Egypt.) chew

maDbûT *mazbûT* correct, exact

madd spread (v., trans.)

madd stretch (v., trans.)

madfa' *medfa'* pl. mdâfi' *medâfi'* cannon

madH praise (n.)

mâDi past (n.)

mâdni *mâdna* pl. meâdin minaret

madrasa pl. madâris school

maDrûr hurt, injured

mâfi Darar *mâfîsh Darar* there is no harm

mafrash sufra tablecloth

mafrûsh furnished

mafsûd (Syr.) spoiled, bad

maftûH open (adj.)

magalla (Egypt.) magazine

magbûr (Egypt.) obliged

maghûl (Egypt.) unknown

magnûn (Egypt.) pl. megânîn foolish, mad

magrafe (Egypt.) shovel (n.)

maHa erase

maHabbi *maHabba* love (n.)

mâHada sâkin fîh *mâHaddish sâkin fîh* uninhabited

maHall pl. maHallât place, spot, locality

maHatte *maHatta* station

maHaTTet buSât *maHaTTat ôtôbîs* bus station

maHattit banzîn gas station

maHbûb dear

mahbûl (Syr.) idiot

maHbûs prisoner

mahd cradle

maHgûz (Egypt.) reserved

mâhir clever

mâhiya monthly salary

maHjûz (Syr.) reserved

maHkami *maHkama* tribunal, court

mahl respite

maHlûq clipped, cut off

maHmûl loaded

mahr dowry

mahrajân *mahragân* festival
maHrami (Syr.) pl. mHârim handkerchief, tissue
maHshi (Egypt.) stuffed (food)
maHzana mourning
mahzûz shaky
mai'ûs desperate
maiyit corpse, dead
majalla (Syr.) magazine
majbûr (Syr.) obliged
majhûl (Syr.) unknown
majjânan *maggânan* gratis
majlis *meglis* council
majnûn (Syr.) pl. mjânîn foolish, mad
makân il-ijtimâ' *makân il- igtimâ'* meeting place
makbûs (Syr.) preserved in vinegar
makhdûm employer
makhlûT mixed
makhmal (Syr.) velvet
makhSûS on purpose
makhtûb engaged
makhzin *makhzan* pl. mkhâzin *makhâzin* stock
        (of goods)
mâkin durable, firm, solid
mâkina machine
makinisti mechanic
mâkiyâj (Syr.) make-up
makkar (Egypt.) cunning (adj.)
makseb gain (n.)

maksûr broken
maktab (Egypt.) desk
maktab busTa post office
maktab office
maktabi *maktaba* bookstore, library
maktûb (Syr.) pl. mkâtib letter, note
maktûb destiny
maktûb msajjal (Syr.) registered letter
makwa, mikwa (household) iron
mâl pl. amwâl goods, means, income, property
mal'aqa, ma'laqa pl. ma'âliq spoon, spoonful
mal'ûn cursed
mala (Egypt.) fill (v.)
malak have, possess
malak *melek* pl. mlâyiki *melâ'ika* angel
mâlak? (Egypt.) What's the matter with you?
malarya malaria
malfûf (Syr.) cabbage
malH (Egypt.) salt
mâliH salty
mâlik owner
malik pl. mulûk king
maliki *malika* queen
mâlis smooth (adj.)
mâ-lish kêf (Egypt.) I do not feel well.
malja' *malga'* asylum
malla (Syr.) fill (v.)
mallaH salt (v.)

mallaq flatter (v.)

mâ-lo qîmi *mâ-lôsh qima* worthless

mâlo RaraD *mâlosh RaraD* impartial

malqâT (Syr.) pl. melâqiT tongs

malyân (Egypt.) full; **malyân bi** filled with

mamarr passage, passageway

mambar (Egypt.) pulpit

mamlaki (Syr.) kingdom

mamnû' forbidden

mamsahat izâz il-'arabiya (Egypt.) windshield
            wiper

mamsahat izâz is-sayyâra (Syr.) windshield wiper

mamsha (Syr.) balcony

mana' prevent

manâkh (Syr.) climate

manâra lighthouse

mandîl pl. manâdîl tissue

manfaDa (Syr.) ashtray

manga (coll.) mango(s)

mâni' pl. mawâni' obstacle

manshûr proclamation

mantiqa sakaniya residential area

manzar pl. menâzir aspect, sight

manZar Tabî'i landscape

manzil (Syr.) pl. mnâzil inn

maq'ad pl. maqâ'id seat

maqaSS scissors

maqbaD pl. maqâbiD handle (of a basket, knife)

maqbara pl. maqâbir (Egypt.) cemetery

maqbûl pleasant

maqfûl locked

maqha coffeehouse

maqli fried

maqrûH sore (adj.)

maqSûd intention

maqSûS clipped, cut off

mâr saint (adj.)

mara *mar'a, imra'a* pl. nisa *niswân* woman, wife

maraD pl. imrâD illness

maRâra pl. maRâyir cave, cavern

maRas (Egypt.) colic

marash'shi (Syr.) watering can

marD sickness, ailment

marHâD pl. marâHîD toilet, lavatory (more commonly used in the pl.)

marham pl. marâhim ointment

marîD ill, sick

marîD pl. marDa patient (n.)

marj (Syr.) pl. mrûj meadow

marjûHa (Syr.) swing (n.)

markab (Syr.) pl. mrâkib ship, vessel

markab qulû'i (Syr.) sailboat

markaz *merkaz* pl. marâkiz *merâkiz* center

markib (Egypt.) pl. merâkib ship, vessel

markib qilâ'i (Egypt.) sailboat

---

maRlûT faulty

marqa sauce

marqit laHm *maraqat laHm* gravy, broth

marr go by, pass

marra once, in the past

marra waHdi *marra waHda* once, one single time

maRrib occident, west

maRribi occidental

mârs (Egypt.) March

marsa cord

martaba (Egypt.) pl. marâtib mattress

mârûni pl. mwârni *muwârna* Maronite

marwaHa (Egypt..) pl. marâwiH fan (mot.)

masa (Syr.) evening; **masal khair** good evening;
      il-masa in the evening

masalan (Syr.) for instance

masâni *mesâna* bladder

maSâri money

maSârîn (coll.) intestine(s)

masbaHa rosary (rel.)

maSbûR dyed

maSdaR pl. maSâDir temple (of the head)

masgid (Egypt.) pl. msâgid small mosque

mash tight (drawn)

mash'ala (Egypt.) pl. mashâ'il torch

mash'had funeral

mash'hûr popular

mâsha (Eygpt.) pl. mâshâT tongs

mâshi o.k.

mâshi pedestrian, walking

mashi, mashyi pace

mashkûk doubtful

mashlûl paralyzed

mashmûl included

mashrû' project

mashRûl busy, occupied (seat, bathroom, phone)

mashwara *mushâwara* consultation

mashwi (Egypt.) roast (adj.)

masîkh monster

masjid (Syr.) pl. msâjid small mosque

maskîn *meskîn* pl. msâkîn *mesâkîn* poor, miserable, unfortunate

maslûq boiled

maSna' (Syr.) cistern

masnid pl. msânid *mesânid* sofa cushion

maSnû' artificial

masnûn (Egypt.) pointed

masqi (Egypt.) irrigated

maSr Cairo

maSr Egypt

maSr gedîda Heliopolis

masraH theater

maSri Egyptian

maSrûf pl. maSârif expense

masrûq stolen

masrûr glad, eased

maSS suck
massil represent
masTara (Egypt.) ruler (stationary)
mâsurat il-'adim (Syr.) exhaust (n.)
mât die (v.)
maT'am pl. maTâ'im restaurant
matal (Syr.) pl. imtâl example; **matalan** for example
maTar (Egypt.) rain (n.)
maTâr airport
maTba'a printing press
maTbakh kitchen
maTbûkh cooked
matHaf pl. matâHif museum
matn text
matraH fîh fai *matraH fîh Dill* shady
maTrah tâni (Egypt.) elsewhere
maTrûH subtracted
maTTar (Egypt.) rain (v.); **id-dinya bitmaTTar** It
        is raining.
maTTât rubber
mauDi' position
mauDû' pl. mawâDi'subject, matter, theme, content
mauhiba pl. mawâhib talent
mauhûb talented
maukib pl. mwâkib *mewâkib* gathering, meeting
maulûd born
mauqef buSât *mauqef otobîs* bus stop
mauqid (Egypt.) fireplace

mauqif pl. mawâqif stopping place

mausim (Syr.) season (for s.th.)

mausim *môsem* pl. mwâsim *mewâsim* harvest, crop

mausimi (Syr.) seasonal

maut *môt* death

mauz *môz* (coll.) banana(s)

mawSûl joined

mâyi' liquid

mâyo (Egypt.) May

mayy *mayya* water

mazâd auction

mazaH (Syr.) joke (v.)

mazbûT exact (adj.)

mazra'a pl. mazâri' farm

mazrû'a what is sown

mazRûl false, counterfeit

mbaiyin haik (Syr.) it appears, it seems so

mbârHa fil-lail (Syr.) last night

mbâriH (Syr.) yesterday

mdîni (Syr.) pl. mudun town

mêdân (Egypt.) large, open space

medîna (Egypt.) pl. mudun town, city

megallad (Egypt.) volume (of a book)

memlaka (Egypt.) kingdom

mendîl (Egypt.) pl. menâdîl handkerchief, tissue

menzil (Egypt.) pl. menâzil inn

merg (Egypt.) pl. murûg meadow

mesel (Egypt.) pl. emsâl; **meselen** for example

meselen (Egypt.) for instance
mesîHi Christian
mî'âd appointment (time and place)
mi'di *mi'da* stomach
mi'Taf coat
mi'Taf Didd il-maTar raincoat
mi'za (Egypt.) pl. ma'z goat
midallil spoiled, pampered
mîdân (Syr.) large, open space
midhin fat (adj.)
miDrab racket
miflis (Syr.) bankrupt
miftâH (Syr.) pl. mfâtîH key
miHqân syringe
miHrât (Egypt.) plough (n.)
miHshi (Syr.) stuffed (food)
mijrafi (Syr.) shovel (n.)
mijwiz *migwiz* double (adj.)
miknsi *maknasa* broom
mikrofôn microphone
mîl pl. amyâl mile
mîlâd birth
milâya bedsheet
milH (Syr.) salt
milyân (Syr.) full; **milyân bi** filled with
milyûn pl. mlâyîn *melâyîn* million
mimbar (Syr.) pulpit
mimkin (Syr.) possible

min by, through, of

min since (prep.)

min dûn shakk no doubt

min dûn tiklîf no ceremony

min dûn without

min ên (Egypt.) where from

min faDlak please (to a male, speaker requesting s.th.)

min fauk *min fôk* from above

min fauq la-taHt *min fôq li-taHt* downwards

min gadd (Egypt.) in earnest

min Hadîd iron (adj.)

min Hais *min Hês* since (adv.)

min il-aSl originally

min jadd (Syr.) in earnest

min jihit *min gihet* as far as … is concerned

min jihit *min gihet* as for

min khalf behind (adv.)

min khârij *min khârig* external

min qabl before (conj.)

min qabl before (of time)

min quddâm in front of

min quddâm in front of

min Rair *min Rêr* without

min shân (Syr.) for, in favor of

min shân in order, that

min shân ta *min shân* in order to

min taHt underneath

min wara behind (adv.)

mîn who (in questions)

min yamm as far as … is concerned

min yamm as for

min zamân *min zemân* for a long time

min'ada except (conj.)

mîna enamel

mîna pl. mawâni harbor, port

minkhar (Syr.) pl. manâkhîr nose

minqar beak

minshâr saw

minshifi pl. mnâshif (Syr.) towel

minSif just (adj.)

mintaqa *mantiqa* pl. manâtiq region

miqallim (Egypt.) striped

miqdâf pl. maqâdîf oar

miqdâr quantity

mirabba jam, preserve

mîrâs heritage

mirash'sha (Egypt.) watering can

mirjân *morjân* coral

mirwaHa (Syr.) pl. marâwiH fan (mot.)

miS'ad (Syr.) elevator

mis'ad happy

misa (Egypt.) evening; **misal khêr** good evening;
       il-'ishe in the evening

miSbâH lamp

mish not

mish'al (Syr.) pl. mshâ'il torch

mishamma' (Egypt.) waterproof
mishi walk (v.)
mishmish (coll.) apricot(s)
mishwâr *mushwâr* **pl. mshâwîr** *meshâwîr* errand,
       walk
mishwi (Syr.) roast (adj.)
misik catch, hold, grasp, keep, seize
misik maraD (Egypt.) catch a disease
misk musk
mismâr pl. msâmir *mesâmir* nail, screw
misqi (Syr.) irrigated
miSrân pl. maSârîn gut, intestine
mistakhdim (Egypt.) clerk
mistwi (Syr.) ripe
mit'aSSeb fanatic
mit'auwid 'ala (Egypt.) used to
mîtain *mîtên* two hundred
mitgauwiz (Egypt.) married
mitl (Syr.) as, like, similar, as well
mitl mâ bitrîd (Syr.) as you like
mitlais polluted
mitlauwis contaminated
mitnabbih attentive
mitr murabba' square meter
miTraqa (Egypt.) hammer
mitrô subway
mittâbi' successive
mittâkil *mitâkil* edible

miTTallaq divorced
mitwâDi humble
miwaffaq matching
mîyi *mîya* hundred
miZalla umbrella
miZallat hubûT parachute
mîzân balance, scale
mîzân il-Harâra thermometer
miznib guilty
mizrâb gutter (n.)
mjallad (Syr.) volume (of a book)
mkhayyam *mukhayyam* camp
mlîH *melîH* good (adj.)
mnain (Syr.) where from
mnâsib (Syr.) fit, to be suitable
moi (Syr.) brook
moiye (Egypt.) brook
montaza park (n.)
môtôsîkl motorcycle
mrabba (Syr.) educated
msalli *mesalla* obelisk
mshâbih (Syr.) similar
mu'âhadi *mu'âhada* treaty
mu'âlaji *mu'âlaga* treatment (med.)
mu'ânid obstinate
mu'auwaq (Syr.) disabled
mu'di infectious
mu'tabir valid

mu'tadil moderate (adj.)

mu'ah'hil, mu'ah'hal pl. mu'ah'halât
      qualification

mu'ah'hilât qualified persons, persons with a
      diplomas

mu'aiyan certain, designated, fixed

mu'akkad certain, certainly

mu'allif author

mu'annas female (adj.)

mu'eddin *mu'ezzin* muezzin

mubâlaRa exaggeration

muballir reciter of prayer (before congregation of
      Muslims)

mubârak, mabrûk blessed

mubâsharatan directly

mubaTTan with lining (of clothes)

mûda fashion

muDâ'af (Syr.) double (adj.)

mudaffi warming

mudah'hab gilt

mudakh'khan smoky

mudauwar round

muDHiq ridiculous

muDîf host, steward

muDîfa stewardess

mudîr director, manager

mufaDDal favorite (adj.)

mufâg'a (Egypt.) surprise (n.)

mufâj'a (Syr.) surprise (n.)
mufakk screwdriver
mufattesh inspector
mufaTTis sultry
mufellis (Egypt.) bankrupt
mufîd useful
mufrad single (not double)
mufradât vocabulary
muftâH (Egypt.) pl. mefâtîH key
muHaddit (Egypt.) storyteller
muHâfaZa 'ala l-bî'a ecology
muHâkma trial
muHâl impossible
muHâmi lawyer
muhandis *muhandes* engineer, architect
muHarrik motor
muHarrir editor
muHibb lover
muhimm important, interesting
muHtall occupied (territory)
muHtaram venerable
mujarrib *mugarrib* experienced
mujtahid *mugtahid* diligent
mukabbir pl. mukabbirât loudspeaker
mukâfa treat (n.)
mukâlama (Egypt.) conversation
mukâlama khârîjiya *mukâlama khârîgiya* long-
      distance call

mukâlama maHalliya local call
mukâlama tilîfûniye phone call
mukarram honorable
mukarsaH *mukassaH* crippled
mukatâbi *mukâtaba* correspondence
mukayif hawâ' air-conditioning
mukh'kh (Egypt.) brain
mukh'kh marrow
mukhâlafi *mukhâlafa* resistance
mukhâlafit il-murûr traffic violation
mukhallal (Egypt.) preserved in vinegar
mukhâTara danger
mukhauwif perilous
mukhayyam refugee camp
mukhazzaq torn
mukhfi secret (adj.); **bil-mukhfi** secretly
mukhmal (Syr.) velvet
mukhûf hazardous
mulâHaza remark (n.)
mulk pl. imlâk, emlâk estate, possession
mulûki royal
mumarriDa nurse (in hospital)
mumassil representative
mumkin (Egypt.) possible
munâfaqa hypocrisy
munâfiq hypocrite
munâqsha discussion
munash'shaf dried

munâsib (Egypt.) fit, to be suitable, proportional
munawwim pl. munawwimât sleeping pill
munbasiT flat (level)
mûnet 'askar (Egypt.) ammunition
munfarid (Egypt.) single (not double)
munfirid (Syr.) single (not double)
mûni *mûna* provisions, supply
munqalib upside down
muntabih attentive
muntajât Halîb *muntagât laban* dairy products
muntij *muntig* efficient
muq'ad handicapped
muqabbil (Syr.) appetizer
muqaddam (Egypt.) front
muqaddam anterior
muqaddama introduction (book)
muqaddar certain, designated, fixed, fatal, destined
muqaddas holy
muqallam (Syr.) striped
muqâTa'a boycott
muqâtali *muqâtala* combat (n.)
murabba pl. murabbayât *murabbât* preserved fruit
murabba' square (n., adj.)
murabbi (Eygpt.) educated
muRaiyim foggy
mûrâni pl. mwârni *muwârna* Maronite
muRanni f. muRannîyi muRannîya pl. maRâni
        singer

murâqaba censorship
muraqqa' patched
murauwas (Syr.) pointed
murgêHa (Egypt.) swing (n.)
murr bitter
muRram fî in love with
murtadda renegade
murtaqa uphill
murûr traffic
mûs pl. mwâs *imwâs* razor
musâ'adi *musâ'ada* help, aid (n.)
musâfir traveler
musakkar locked
musakkin painkiller
muSâlaHa reconciliation
musalsala soap opera
musauwir photographer
musâwama bargain (n.)
mûsâwi equal
mushâbaha resemblance
mush Hâga (Egypt.) nothing
mush lâzim unnecessary
mush ma'rûf unknown
mush mumkin impossible
mush nâfi' useless
mush not
mush SaHîH wrong
mushahi (Egypt.) appetizer

mushamma' (Syr.) waterproof

mushâraka partnership

mushbih (Egypt.) similar

mushT *mishT* comb (n.)

mushtara purchase (n.)

mushwâr (Egypt.) pl. meshâwir ride, walk (n.)

muSîbi *muSîba* disaster, evil, misfortune

mûsim (Egypt.) season (for s.th.)

mûsimi (Egypt.) seasonal

musimm poisonous

mûsîqa music

muslim pl. muslimîn Muslim

musmâr (Egypt.) pl. masâmîr screw

musta'ger (Egypt.) tenant

musta'idd ready

musta'jir (Syr.) tenant

musta'mal secondhand

musta'mal usual

mustaHîl impossible

mustaqbal *mustaqbil* future; **bil-mustaqbal** in
       the future

mustaqill independent

mustaqîm honest, right, straight, sincere

mustarda (Egypt) mustard

mustashfa hospital

mustautan settler

mustawâ level

mustawi ripe

musTra (Syr.) ruler (stationary)

mustwi *mustewi* done, cooked
mut'affin rotten
mut'auwid 'ala (Syr.) used to
muta'assif sorry
mutafakkir thoughtful
mutakabbir (Egypt.) proud, conceited
mutakallim talkative
mutallim (Egypt.) blunt
mutaqaddim progressive
mutarjim *mutargim* interpreter
mutashâbih *mutshâbeh* alike
mutdaiyin pious
mutekabbir *mutkabber* arrogant
muthim distrustful
mutjauwiz (Syr.) married
mutkabbir (Syr.) haughty, proud, conceited
mutkarrib (Syr.) vain (adj.)
mutkebbir (Egypt.) vain (adj.)
mutnabbih careful, cautious
mutRaffil *muRaffal* negligent
mutRaiyir changeable
mutwaDi' submissive
mutwaH'Hish savage
muwaqqat temporary
muwaqqatan temporarily
muwâTin citizen
muwâwiq proper
muzîl lil-buq'a stain remover

n

na'am yes, certainly
na'am? I beg your pardon.
na'âmi *na'âma* ostrich
nâ'îm soft
na'l horseshoe
na'l sole (n.)
na'S (Syr.) bog
na'sân drowsy
na'sân sleepy
nabât plant (n.)
nabD pulse (n.)
nabi (Syr.) pl. imbiyi prophet
naDâfi *naDâfa* purity
nadar vow (v.)
naDâra (sg.) glasses
naDDaf clean (v.)
naDîf pl. nDîf clean (adj.)
nâdir rare
nadr pl. nudûra vow (n.)
naf' interest, concern, benefit, profit
nafa' use (n.)
nafas *nefes* breath
nâfi' useful
nafîs precious
nafkh (Egypt.) inflation
nafs (f.) pl. infus soul
nafs il- ... (with def. noun) same; **fi-nafs il-waqt** at
          the same time

nafs self

nafs shahîya (Egypt.) appetite; **mâ-lish nafs** I have
      no appetite

nafsâni psychic

nafsi psychic

naft oil, petrol, petroleum

nagaH (Egypt.) succeed

nagâH (Egypt.) success

nagga (Egypt.) save, rescue

nâH lament

nahab plunder (v.)

naHâs aSfar (Egypt.) bronze

nahîb plunder (n.)

naHîf lean (adj.)

naHl (coll.) bee(s)

nahr pl. nuhûr river

naHya (Egypt.) side; **bin-naHya di** on this side;
      bin-naHya dik-hâ on that side; **lin-naHya**
      di to this side; **rûH lin-naHya dik-ha** go to
      the other side

naHye *naHya* direction

nai (Egypt.) flute

nai raw, uncooked

naiyam *naiyim* lie down, go to sleep

naiyir (Egypt.) bright, shining

najaH (Syr.) succeed

najâH (Syr.) success

najja (Syr.) save, rescue

nakhâli *nakhale* bran

nakhl (coll.) palm tree(s)

nâl obtain, obtain

nâm sleep, lie, rest, go to bed; **nâm ma'a** sleep with

naml ant

nâmûs (coll.) mosquito(s)

nâmûsîyi *nâmûsîyia* mosquito net

naqal (Syr.) move (house)

naqal transport (v.)

nâqish (Eygpt.) discuss

naql damm blood transfusion

naql transportation (n.)

naqS shortage

naqsh ornamentation, pattern

nâr fire, incendiary

nâs (coll.) people, persons

nash'shaf (Syr.) dry (v., trans.)

nash'shâl pickpocket (n.)

nash'shif (Egypt.) dry (v., trans.)

nashar publish

nashîd anthem; **nashîd waTani** national anthem

nâshif dried, dry

naSîb destiny, fate

naSîb lot, luck, chance

naSîb pl. anSiba share, portion

nasîg (Egypt.) texture

nasîj (Syr.) texture

nasîj *nasîg* cloth, fabric

naSli *naSla* pl. niSâl blade (of a knife)

naSrâni pl. naSâra Christian
natîga (Egypt.) calendar
naTT jump (v.)
naTTar (Egypt.) rain (v.)
nau' *nô'* pl. inwâ' kind, sort, class
nauba qalbiya heart attack
naubi *nôbe* band of musicians
naufara *nôfara* fountain
naum (Syr.) sleep (n.)
nawar (coll.) gypsy(ies)
nayim *na'im* asleep
naZar expect
naZar pl. anZâr look, glance (n.)
nâzik neat
nâzil downward
nâzil talj *nâzil telg* it is snowing
nazz (Egypt.) leak (v.)
nazzal *nazzil* reduce the price of s.th.
nbîd (Syr.) wine
nDîf pure
nebi (Egypt.) pl. ambiya prophet
nebîd (Egypt.) wine
nehaito (Egypt.) at last
nhâr *nehâr* day (in opposition to night)
niddâbi *naddâba* mourning woman, hired female
                mourner
nidi *nida* dew
nidim 'ala repent s.th.

nifâq hypocrisy

nifriD in (Egypt.) provided that

nigis (Eygpt.) impure

nigm zârik (Egypt.) shooting star

nigma (Egypt.) pl. nugûm star

nihâ'i final

nihâyi *nihâya* end; **fin-nihâyi** *fin-nihâya* at the end

niHna (Syr.) we

nijis (Syr.) impure

nijjâr *naggâr* carpenter

nijm zârik (Syr.) shooting star

nijmi (Syr.) pl. nujûm star

nîl indigo

nimr tiger

niqâbat 'ummâl labor union

nisân (Syr.) April

nishif (Egypt.) dry (v., intrans.)

nishiT lively

nisi forget

nisr (Syr.) pl. nsûra eagle

nisr vulture

nîyi *nîya* intention

nîyti *nîyeti in* I have the intention of

niZâm pl. anZima system

nizil descend, sink (v.)

nizil spend the night, pass the night

nizûl descent

njâS (coll.) (Syr.) pear(s)

nôm (Egypt.) sleep (n.)

nôvember (Egypt.) November
nuHâs aSfar (Syr.) bronze
nuHâs aSfar brass
nuHâs *naHâs* copper
nukta pl. nukat gag, joke
numrit ôtombîl *nimrit ôtombîl* license plate
numro number (n.)
nuqra (Egypt.) neck
nuqrus gout
nuqta pl. nuqat point, dot (n.)
nûr (Egypt.) daylight, light
nuskha copy
nuSS half
nuSS lail *nuSS il-lêl* midnight
nûwâr (Syr.) May

o

ôDa pl. owaD (Egypt.) room
ôdit sufra (Egypt.) dining table
oksîjên oxygen
oktôber (Egypt.) October
ôtîl (Egypt.) hotel
ôtôbîs (Egypt.) bus

q

qâ'a hall
qa'ad live, dwell, sit

qâ'ide jauwiye *qâ'ida gauwiya* air base
qâ'idi *qâ'ida* rule, principle
qâ'ime catalogue
qabal (Syr.) receive (a visitor, guest)
qabbal (Syr.) kiss (v.)
qabbi (Syr.) collar
qabd seizure
qabîH infamous, ugly
qâbil (Egypt.) meet, receive (a visitor, guest)
qabîli *qabîla* pl. qabâyil *qabâ'il* tribe
qabl ago, before, earlier
qabl iD-Duhr a.m.
qabl il-kull above all
qabl mâ *qable mâ* before (conj.)
qabl min zamân *qabla min zemân* long ago, long
        before
qabla (Egypt.) midwife
qâblî'yi (Syr.) appetite; **mâ-li qâblî'yi** I have no
        appetite.
qabr pl. qubûr grave, sepulchre
qabu *qabwa* cellar
qâd lead (v.)
qadd as, as much as
qaddaf (Syr.) row (v.)
qaddaish (Syr.) how many, how much
qaddaish 'alaiyi? (Syr.) How much do I have to
        pay?
qaddaish 'umrak? (Syr.) How old are you?

qaddaish baddo yTauwil? (Syr.) How long will it last?

qaddaish ilak 'alaiyi? qaddaish ilak 'indi? (Syr.) How much do I owe you?

qaddam introduce a person

qaddam iT-Ta'âm serve a meal

qaddam *qaddim* offer (v.)

qaddâs pl. qadâdîs mass

qadde 'aiz minni? (Egypt.) How much do I have to pay?

qadde ma (Eygpt.) in proportion to

qadde yerîb (Egypt.) How long will it last?

qaddê yeTauwil? (Egypt.) How long will it last?

qaddi ê (Egypt.) how many, how much

qaddi mâ (Egypt.) as long as

qaddif (Egypt.) row (v.)

qaddîs pl. qadâdîs Christian saint

qaddmâ (Syr.) as long as

qaddma ... qaddma the more ... the more ...

qâDi judge

qaDîb pl. quDbân stick (n.)

 qadîm pl. qudm ancient, old (for things)

qâdir la ... *qâdir li ...* able

qadîr powerful

qadiya lawsuit

qafal lock with a padlock

qafas cage

qâfila (Egypt.) caravan

qâfiyi *qâfiya* pl. qawâfi rhyme

qahwi *qahwa* coffee

qahwi *qahwa* pl. qahâwi café

qâl tell

qal'a castle, fortress, citadel

qala fry

qala' extract, draw out, remove a tooth

qala' pl. qulû' sail (n.)

qalab turn over, upset

qalam pl. aqlâm pen

qalb pl. qulûb heart

qâlib pl. qwâlib *qawâlib* form

qalîl few

qalîl il-Haya shameless

qalîl il-wujûd *qalîl il-wugûd* rare

qalîl is-Sabr impatient

qalîl ktîr *qalîl ketîr* far too little

qallad invest

qallad *qallid* imitate

qâm pick up, lift, rise, stand, get up, take off

qamar moon

qamH (Egypt.) wheat

qâmi *qâma* figure, aspect, form, stature

qamîS bi-nuSS kumm a short-sleeved shirt

qamîS pl. qumSân shirt

qaml (coll.) lice

qâmûS dictionary

qanâ' canal

qanât suwîs Suez Canal

qannîni pl. qanâni (Syr.) bottle

qanTara pl. qanâTir (Egypt.) bridge

qanTara pl. qanâTir arch

qânûn il-auwal (Syr.) December

qânûn it-tâni (Syr.) January

qanûn pl. qawânîn law, rule, regulation

qâq pl. qîqân crow

qar' (coll.) pumpkin(s)

qara (Egypt.) read, recite (v.)

qarab b-khaimi *qârib b-khêma* houseboat

qarD loan

qarHa pl. quraH sore (n.)

qârib bi-muharrik motor boat

qârib pl. qawârib boat, rowing boat

qarîb min close, near to, soon

qarîb pl. qarâyib *qarâ'ib* relative, family member

qarn pl. qurûn century

qarn pl. qurûn horn (animal)

qarnabîT cauliflower

qarr confess

qarra continent

qarrab approach, draw near; **qarriib!** *qarrab!*
      approach!

qarya pl. qur village

qâs measure (v.)

qaSab cane

qasabi *qasaba* pipe (tobacco)

qaSad intend
qasam divide
qaSD intention, purpose
qaSDan on purpose
qash'sh straw
qash'shar peel (v.)
qâsi cruel, hard, severe
qâsim share (v.)
qaSîr (Syr.) pl. quSâr short
qaSS cut (v.)
qassam divide
qaSSar shorten
qassim share (v.)
qassîs pl. qusus Catholic priest
qaT'a pl. qiTa' piece
qat'an not at all
qaTa' cut, tear
qaTaf pick, gather
qatal execute, kill, fight
qâTî' herd (n.)
qatîfa (Egypt.) velvet
qatîl fatal, deadly, murdered
qâtil murderer
qatil nafso commit suicide
qatl murder (n.)
qaTr pl. quTurât train (n.)
qaTr sari' (Syr.) express train
qaTrân tar (pitch)

qaus qadaH *qôs qazaH* rainbow

qawâm quickly

qawi (Egypt.) very (adv.), strong (adj.)

qazdîr (Syr.) tin

qazzîr (Egypt.) tin

qibâl opposite

qibil (Syr.) receive (a visitor, guest)

qibil accept, consent to s.th. (v.)

qibTi pl. iqbâT Copt, Coptic

qidir can, may

qif! Stop!

qifl (Egypt.) padlock

qîmi *qîma* value, worth (n.)

qirâya (Egypt.) reading

qird pl. qurûd monkey

qiri (Syr.) read, recite (v.)

qirif min disgusted

qirsh pl. qurûsh piastre

qirsh shark

qishr peel (n.)

qishr pod, rind

qishTa cream

qism pl. aqsâm division, department, lot, share, portion

qiSSa pl. qiSaS tale, story

qitâl fight (n.)

qiyâma resurrection

qiyâsi regular

qizâz glass (material)
qizâza pl. qizâzât (Egypt.) bottle
qraydis (coll.) (Syr.) shrimp(s)
qrâyi (Syr.) reading
qubba'a (Syr.) hat
qubbâr caper
qubbi *qubba* cupola, dome
qubbi *qubba* vault
qubTân captain
quddâm before (of place)
quddâm in-nâs publicly
qudra power, physical strength
quffâz gloves
qufl (Syr.) padlock
qûlanj (Syr.) colic
qumâr gambling
qumâsh cloth
qunbila, qunbula pl. qanâbîl shell, bomb
qunbulat zarriyat *qunbula zarriya* atomic bomb
qunfud hedgehog
qunSul consul
qunsulâto *qonsolâto* consulate
quraiyib nearly
qurb proximity
qurfi *qirfa* cinnamon
qurmi, qurmîyi *qurma* pl. qarâmi trunk
qurS pl. iqrâS disk
qurunful clove

quSaiyar (Egypt.) pl. quSâr short
quTa' Riyâr (Syr.) spare parts
quTâr il-eksebriss (Egypt.) express train
quTb pole (geogr.)
quTn cotton
quTT cat
qûwi *qûwa* force, strength
qyâs *qiyâs* measure (n.)

r/R

ra'd thunder
râ'i shepherd
ra'îs (Syr.) president
ra'îs *re'îs* head, chief
Râb (Syr.) disappear
Râb last long
râb stepfather
râba stepmother
rabaT bind, tie, tie (shoes)
rabba (Syr.) educate
rabba grow (trans.)
rabba train (v.)
Rabi silly, stupid
râbi' f. râb'a *rab'a* fourth; **rub'** pl. erbâ', one fourth,
        fourth part
rabî' spring (season)
râd want, wish (v.)

Rada lunch
Rada tomorrow
RaDab anger
RaDbân furious
radd give back, reply, return
radd jawâb *raddê gawâb* answer
radd pl. rudûd reply (n.)
raDDa bruise (n.)
raDDa' suckle
râDi bi content with, to be satisfied with
radi pl. irdyi *ardiye* bad, evil
Radi tomorrow
raDî' pl. raDâ'i baby
radyatêr radiator (mot.)
radyu radio
rafaD refuse (v.)
râfaq *rafaq* accompany
rafî' (Syr.) fine, slender, lean, thin
rafîq travel companion
rafraf mudguard
râgil (Egypt.) pl. rigâla man
râH 'and (Egypt.) visit (v.)
râh go, leave
râH la'and (Syr.) visit (v.)
râH wara send for
râha comfort, ease, rest, break (n.); **btilzamni râHa**
    ana 'â'iz râHa I need some rest.
râhan bet (v.)

rahbâni *rahbâna* religious order
râhib pl. ruHbân monk
râhibi *râhiba* pl. râhbât nun
raHîl departure
rahîna pl. rahâyin hostage
raHmi *raHma* mercy, pity
rahn bet, deposit, pledge, mortgage
Raibi *Rêba* absence; **b-Raibti** *bi-Rêbeti*, *fî Riyâbi*
     during my absence
Raim *Rêm* pl. Ryûm *Riyûm* cloud
Rair (Syr.) different, else
Rair Harîf *Rêr Harîf* mild (taste)
Rair in (Syr.) except
Rair maTrah (Syr.) elsewhere
Rair mudakh'khin *Rêr mudakh'khin* non-smoking
Rair qâdir (Syr.) unable
Rair *Rêr* another, but, except
Rair SaHîH (Syr.) untrue
Rair zâlik *Rêr zâlik* in addition to this
RaiT *RêT* field
Raiyar alter, change, exchange (v.)
raiyis (Syr.) principal, head, chief
raiyis il-baladîyi *re'îs il-beledîya* mayor
Raiyûr jealous
RaiZ (Syr.) rage, annoyance
raka' kneel
rakan il- sayyâra *rakan il-'arabiya* park the car
rakhîS *rikhîS* cheap

râkib pl. rukkâb passenger
rakkab *rakkib* compose, put together
Râl pl. Râlât lock (n.)
Ralab overcome
Ralaq close, shut (v.)
RalaT error, wrong
RalaT, RalTa mistake
Râli expensive
Râliban commonly, in general
Ralîz (Egypt.) awkward
rama shoot, throw
ramaDân fast month
Ramîq (Syr.) deep
Ramîq dark (of color)
raml pl. rimâl sand
ramli sandy
Ramm grieve
Ranam (coll.) sheep(s)
Râni pl. *iRniya* aRnîya rich
Ranna sing
raqbi *raqaba* neck
raqîq fine, slender
raqqâS dancer
raqaS dance (v.)
raqS dance (n.)
Rarab go down (sun)
Rarab set (moon, sun)
Rarâm amorousness

Raras plant (v.)
Rarb west
Rarbal sift
Rarbi *Rarba* wish (n.)
Rarîb odd, strange
raRîf (Syr.) pl. irRifi loaf
Rarra glue (v.)
raRRab fî interest (v.)
Rarraq drown
RarRara mouthwash
raRwi *raRwa* foam
râs cape
râs is-sini *râs is-sana* New Year
râs pl. ru'ûs head, point, sharp end, summit, top
RaSab oblige
rasab settle, sink to the bottom
Rasal wash (v., trans.)
rasam draw (with a pencil), paint
râsan directly
Rash'sh cheat, deceive
Rash'sh impose on s.b.
rash'sh sprinkle
rash-H cold (catarrh)
Rashîm pl. Rushm clumsy, stupid
raSîf platform
Rasîl laundry, washing (of clothes)
rasm (Syr.) pl. rusûm duty, tax
rasm pattern (on cloth)

rasmâl (Egypt.) money
rasmi official
Rassal wash (v., trans.)
Rassâla washing machine
raSûl pl. rusul apostle, messenger
RaTa cover, lid
RaTas dive
râtib salary
raTl pl. arTâl pound (weight)
RaTTa cover (v.)
rattab *rattib* arrange, put into order
raTTab refresh
Raushi (Syr.) noise
rauwaH destroy
RawîT (Egypt.) deep
ray opinion; **shû râyak?** *râyak ê?* What is your
            opinion?
Râyi extreme
Râyi *Râya* utmost
Râyib *Râ'ib* absent
râyiq *râ'iq* serene
Râz (Egypt.) gas
Razâli *Razâla* gazelle
razîl pl. arâzîl mean, indecent, low
re'îs (Egypt.) president, principal
rebîb stepson
rebîba stepdaughter
rêdis (coll.) (Egypt.) shrimp(s)

Rêr (Egypt.) else

Rêr in (Syr.) except

Rêr qâdir (Egypt.) unable

resm pl. rusûm (Egypt.) tax, duty

Rêz (Egypt.) rage, annoyance

rîa lung

ribyân educated

RiDa willingness

riDi bi consent to s.th. (v.)

riDi' suck (child at the breast)

Rifi doze, drowse, fall asleep

rigi' (Egypt.) return, give back, turn back

rigl (Egypt.) pl. argul foot, leg

riglêye warmîn (Egypt.) my feet are swollen

rîH (f.) pl. aryâH wind

rîHa pl. rawâyiH *rawâ'iH* smell, fragrance

riHim pity (v.)

rihla flight

riji' (Syr.) return, give back, rn back

riji' *rigi'* to come back, go back

rijif (Syr.) tremble

rijjâl (Syr.) pl. rjâl man

rijl (Syr.) pl. irjul leg, foot

rikâb pl. rikâbât stirrup

rikbi (Syr.) pl. rikbât knee

rikib mount a horse, ride

Rili boil (intrans.)

RiliT fi to make a mistake

Rille *Ralla* crop, produce
Riltân *Raltân* to be mistaken
rimâd ashes
rimâDi (Syr.) gray
rimâya shooting
Rina fortune, wealth
Rina singing
rîqân jaundice
Rirbâl *Rurbâl* sieve
Riri glue (n.)
Ririb desire, want, wish
riRîf (Egypt.) pl. arRifa loaf
Ririq sink (ship)
Ririq to be drowned
Rishsh deceit
rîshi *rîsha* pl. riyâsh feather
rishwi *rashwa* bribe (n.)
rismâ'l (Syr.) money
ritshetta prescription
Riyâb (Egypt.) setting (of the sun)
rizz rice
rôsto roast meat
rSâS *ruSâS* lead (metal)
rub' pl. erbâ' quarter, a fourth part
rub'êmîya (Egypt.) four hundred
rubâT pl. rubâTât lace
rubbama perhaps
rufai'ya' (Egypt.) fine, slender

rufaiy'ya' (Egypt.) lean (adj.)

rufaiya (Egypt.) thin

rugû' (Egypt.) return, coming back (n.)

rûH (f.) pl. irwâH spirit, soul

rûH wara send for s.th.

rûH! Go away! Off!

rûHâni spiritual

rujû (Syr.) return, coming back (n.)

rukba (Egypt.) pl. rukab knee

rukhâm marble

rukhsa permission

rukhSat sewâqa *rokhSit siwâqa* driver's license

rukn pl. arkân corner

rumâDi (Egypt.) gray

Rumia 'alêh (Egypt.) faint (v.)

rummân (coll.) pomegranate(s)

ruq'a pl. ruqa' patch

Rurâb pl. aRribi *aRriba* raven

Rurûb ish-shams sunset

Rushi 'alaih (Syr.) faint (v.)

RuSn (Egypt.) thin branch

rutbi *rutba* rank

ruTib *riTib* damp (adj.)

ruTûbi *ruTûba* dampness, humidity, wet (n.)

ruzz rice

Ryâb (Syr.) setting (of the sun)

s/S

sâ' hold, contain

sâ'a pl. sâ'ât hour, clock, watch

sâ'ad *sâ'id* assist, help

sa'adtak your excellence (m.)

sa'adtik your excellence (f.)

Sa'b 'ala to be hard for s.b.

Sa'b difficult

sa'd happiness

sa'îd happy, lucky

sa'li *sa'la* cough (n.)

sa'al ask; sa'al 'an *sa'al 'ala* ask for

sa'al pl. as'ila question

sâ'il (Egypt.) beggar

sa'iq (Syr.) driver

sab'a seven

sab'în seventy

sab'mîyi (Syr.) seven hundred

sabab pl. isbâb *asbâb* reason, cause

SabaH morning; SabaH il-khair *SabâH il-khêr*
        good morning

sabaH swim

sabânikh (Egypt.) spinach

sabaq precede in time

sabaTa'sh *saba'tâsher* seventeen

sabb curse, swear at s.b.

sabbab cause (v.)

sabbâbi (Syr.) forefinger

sabbat confirm

sâbi' f. sâb'a *sab'a* seventh

Sâbiq former

Sâbiqan formerly

Sabîyi pl. Sabâya, Sbaiyât *Sibâyât* young girl

Sabr patience

Sâbûn soap (n.)

Sabûr patient (adj.)

Sada echo

Sadaf (coll.) shell(s)

Sadaf mother-of-pearl

Sadâqa sincerity

sadd dam; **is-sadd il-'âli** the Aswan High Dam

sadd obstruct

Saddaq 'ala attest, certify

Saddaq believe

Saddiqni *Saddakni* believe me

Sadîq frank

sâdis f. sadsi *sadsa* sixth

Safad mother-of-pearl

sâfar (Syr.) travel (v.)

Safar (Syr.) whistle (v.)

safar departure, journey

safâra embassy

Saff pl. Sufûf line, row, class (in school)

Saff, Saffaf range in a line, line up

Saffâra whistle (n.)

Sâfi clear, net, plain, pure

SafîH (Egypt.) tin
safing, sifing (coll.) (Egypt.) sponge(s)
sâfir (Egypt.) travel (v.)
safîr ambassador
safra travel (n.)
SafSaf willow
sagan (Egypt.) imprison
saggâda (Egypt.) carpet
SaH'Ha health
SaH'HaH improve (trans.)
sâHa square, public space
saHab drag, draw, pull
sahar 'ala watch over (v.)
SaHfa pl. SuHuf page (of a book)
SaHH heal, recover (after sickness)
Sâhi serene
SâHib il-bait *SâHib il-bêt* landlord
SâHib pl. iSHâb, SHâb *aSHâb* friend, owner
SaHîH certainly, correct, genuine, real, true, sound
sâhil coast
sâhil il-baHr seaside
sahil *sahl* light, easy
sâhili coastal
sâHir, saH'Hâr sorcerer
sahl even (adj.)
sahl, sahli pl. suhûl plain, ground level
sahm arrow
SaHn (Syr.) dish
SaHn il-finjân *SaHn il-fingân* saucer

SaHn pl. SuHûn dish (meal), plate

Sahr (Syr.) son-in-law

sahra party, soirée

SaHrâ' pl. SaHâra desert

Sahrîg (Egypt.) cistern

Said *Sêd* hunting

Saidaliya pharmacy; **Saidaliya lailiya** *Saidaliya lêliya* 24-hour pharmacy

saif (Syr.) pl. syûf sword

Saif (Syr.) summer

Saiyad hunt (v.)

saiyib (Egypt.) leave, let alone, let go

saiyid gentleman

sajan (Syr.) imprison

sajjada (Syr.) rug

sajjal (v.) register (v.)

sakan live, dwell

sakat (Syr.) to be silent

sakhawi *sakhawa* liberality

sakhi (Egypt.) liberal

Sakhr pl. Skhûr rock (n.)

sâkin pl. sukkân inhabitant

sâkit quite

sâkit still, silent

sakk (Egypt.) lock (n.)

sakkar (Syr.) lock (v.)

sakkin settle (trans.)

sakkit silence (v.)

sakrân (Egypt.) drunk

Sala pl. Salawât prayer
salab plunder (v.)
salak behave
salâm peace, salutation
salâmi *salâma* health
salaq boil (trans.)
salaTa salad
Salîb pl. Sulbân crucifix
sâlif preceding, previous, prior
SâliH pl. SawâliH interest
sâlim healthy, safe, free from danger, well
Salla pray, say one's prayer
SallaH repair, store
sallam 'ala salute, greet s.b.
sallam give in
sallif, sallaf lend
sallim 'ala greet s.b.; **sallim-li ktîr 'ala jamî'**
          ahl baitak *sallim-li ketîr 'ala gemî'*
          ahle bêtak greet all your family
          from me
sallim submit
salmi peaceful
sama pl. samawât heaven, sky
samaH allow; **ismaH-li** allow me
sâmaH forgive
saman (Syr.) fat (adj.)
samandar salamander
samek *samak* (coll.) fish

samîn fat (of living beings) (adj.)

samkari plumber

samm poison (n.)

samma name (v.)

sammâ‘a receiver (telephone)

Sammad economize

sammam poison (v.)

sammâna (Egypt.) calf (of the leg)

sammi poisonous

samsâr pl. semasra (Syr.) broker

San‘a art, skill, craft, trade

Sanâ‘i pl. Sanâ‘iyi *Sanâ‘iye* artisan

Sanam pl. aSnâm idol

Sandal pl. Sanâdil sandal

sandûq busTa mailbox

Sandûq busTa post office box

Sandûq il-barîd post office box

Sandûq pl. Sanâdîq chest, large box

sann sharpen (v.)

Sanôbar (Egypt.) pine

sâq drive

saqa irrigate

saqâfa culture

saqf (Syr.) ceiling

saqqâTa (Syr.) latch

saqqâTa *suqqâTa* handle (of a door)

Sâr (Syr.) occur

Sâr ‘atm (Syr.) It has grown dark.

Sâr become, happen
Sâr lail *Sâr lêl* It has become night.
Sâr wakhri It is already late.
Saraf spend (money)
saraj (Syr.) saddle (v.)
saraq steal
saraTân cancer
saraTân pl. sarâTîn crab
sarâya castle, palace
sarg (Egypt.) pl. surûg saddle (n.)
sari' quick, fast
sarîf neat
sâriq burglar
sarj (Syr.) pl. srûj saddle (n.)
Sarr (Egypt.) pack (v.)
Sarrâf (Egypt.) money changer
sarrag (Egypt.) saddle (v.)
SarSûr pl. SarâSîr cockroach, cricket
sarûkh pl. sawârîkh rocket
sarwi *sarwa* pl. sarw cypress
saTH roof
saTl bucket
saTr pl. suTûr line (in a book)
Saub (Syr.) side; **fî haS-Saub** on this side; **fî haidâk iS-Saub** on that side; **la haS-Saub** to this side; **rûH la haidâk iS-Saub** go on to the other side
Saub direction

Saufar (Syr.) whistle (v.)

Saum (Syr.) fast, abstinence

Saut (Syr.) sound, voice

sauwa make right, adjust

sauwâq (Eygpt.) driver

Sauwar photograph (v.)

sawa altogether, together

sawa to be worth

sâwama bargain(v.)

sawîyatan commonly

sâyiH pl. suwwâH tourist

sâyil thin (flowing, fluid)

SâyiR *Sâ'iR* gold

sâyis *sâ'is* groom

sayyâra (Syr.) car

sayyârit il-is'âf ambulance

sbânikh (Syr.) spinach

sebtember (Egypt.) September

sêf (Egypt.) pl. siyûf sword

Sêf (Egypt.) summer

sefîna *sefîni* pl. sufun ship, ocean liner

sekretêr (Egypt.) secretary

selli *salla* pl. silâl basket

sellim (Egypt.) pl. selâlîm ladder, stairs

semen (Egypt.) fat (adj.)

serîr (Egypt.) bed

sfinj (coll.) (Syr.) sponge(s)

sha'al (Syr.) burn (intrans.)

sha'b pl. shu'ûb people, nation
sha'îr barley
sha'îr pl. shu'ara poet
sha'r hair
shab'ân satiated (with food or drink)
shabâb (Egypt.) pl. shubbân, shibâb young man
shâbah (Syr.) resemble
shabaki *shabaka* net, network
shabb (Syr.) pl. shubbân, shibâb young man
shabbâbi (Syr.) flute
shadd draw, press, pull
shâf find, look, see
shafa cure, heal (trans.)
shafâqa compassion
shafaqa pity (n.)
shagar (coll.) (Egypt.) tree(s)
shagarat il-Râr (Egypt.) laurel
shaHad *shaHat* beg
shahâda diploma
shâhid (Egypt.) forefinger
shâhid 'ain *shâhid 'ên* eyewitness
shâhid pl. sh'hûd *shuhûd* witness
shahîd pl. shuhadâ martyr
shâHina truck
shaHm (Egypt.) grease
shahr pl. ish'hur, sh'hûr month
shahri monthly
shahwa pl. shahawât passion, desire, passion

shaikh *shêkh* old man
shaikhûkha *shêkhûkha* old age
shaiyâl (Egypt.) carrier, luggage porter
shajâ'a *shagâ'a* courage
shajar (coll.) (Syr.) tree(s)
shaji' *shagi'* bold
shaji' *shagi'* brave, courageous
shajrit il-Râr (Syr.) laurel
shaka (Egypt.) complain
shakar thank (v.)
shakhS pl. ashkhâS person
shakhSi personal
shâkir thankful
shakk doubt (n.)
shakk doubt (v.)
shakkak doubt (v.)
shakmân (Egypt.) exhaust pipe
shakûr thankful
shâkûsh (Syr.) hammer
shakwa, shkâyi *shikâya* complaint
shâl shawl
shalaH undress
shalâl (Egypt.) waterfall
shâm Syria
sham'a candle
shama' wax
shamâm (coll.) (Egypt.) melon(s)
shamandar (coll.) beet(s)

shâmi pl. shwâm Syrian
shamm il-hawa go for a stroll, go for a walk
shamm smell, scent
shams sun
shamsiyi *shamsiya* parasol
shanTa pl. shonaT bag
shaqfit laHm (Syr.) a piece of meat
shaqq crack, split (n. + v.)
shaqqa mafrûsha furnished apartment
shar wickedness
shar'i legal
sharâb pl. sharbât beverage, drink
sharaf honor (n.)
sharâri *sharâra* spark
sharâyit tasjîl *sharâ'it tasgîl* recording-tapes
shâri' pl. shawâri' street
sharîf distinguished, noble
sharîk pl. shuraka partner
sharîr wicked
sharmaT (Egypt.) tear (v.)
sharq east
sharqi eastern, oriental
sharr evil, wickedness
shaRRâla maid
sharT pl. shrûT *shurûT* condition, stipulation;
      bi-sharT in under the condition that
shâsha screen (n.)
shatam (Egypt.) insult (v.)

shatam abuse (v.)
shaTâra diligence
shâTi *shaTT* coast
shâTir clever, diligent, experienced
shaTranj *shaTrang* chess
shatta (Syr.) rain (v.)
shaub (Syr.) warmth
shaub *shôb* heat (n.)
shauki (Syr.) thorn
shauki *shôka* pl. shuwak fork
shauq *shôq* longing
shawa roast meat (v.)
shâwar *shâwir* advise
shây tea
shbâT (Syr.) February
shê (Egypt.) pl. ashya
shedîd hard, rigid; strong, violent
shêk check
shemâl (Egypt.) left
sherîT (Egypt.) pl. ashriTa ribbon
shêTân (Egypt.) pl. sheyâTîn satan, devil
shî (Syr.) pl. ishya thing
shî mubarrid (Syr.) refreshment, drinks
shi'a pl. ashi'a beam of light, beam
shi'r pl. ish'âr poem, poetry
shibi to be satisfied with food, to have one's fill
shibîn godfather
shibshib slipper

shifa cure, recovery (after sickness)

shiffi *shiffa* pl. shifâf *shafâ'if* lip

shiH'Hâd *shaH'Hât* beggar

shiH'HâTa, shaH'HaiTa (Syr.) lightning match

shihâdi *shihâda* pl. shihâdât certificate, testimony

shilH (Syr.) thin branch

shillâl (Syr.) waterfall

shillâl *shallâl* cataract

shirb *shurb* pl. sharbât drink (n.)

shiri, shrâyi *shirâya* purchase (n.)

shirib drink (v.)

shirib dukhân smoke (v.)

shirîT (Syr.) pl. ashriTa ribbon

shirîT Hadîd (Syr.) wire

shirîT *sherîT* band, ribbon

shirki *shirka* company, firm

shirrîb dukhân smoker

shîTân *shêTân* pl. shiyâTîn satan, devil

shiti (Syr.) rain (n.)

shiti *shita* winter

shmâl (Syr.) left

shmâl *shemâl* north

shmâli *shemâli* northern

shmandar (coll.) beet(s)

shôb (Egypt.) warmth

shôfa (Egypt.) look, appearance, aspect

shôka (Egypt.) thorn

shorba soup

shû (Syr.) what

shû bâk? (Syr.) What's the matter with you?

shû biqdir qaddimlak? (Syr.) What can I offer you?

shû fî jdîd? (Syr.) What is the news?

shû ma'nâh?, shû ma'nâto? (Syr.) What does that mean?

shû Sâyir? (Syr.) What is going on?

shu'ûr sensation, feeling

shubbâk pl. shbâbîk window; **iftaH ish-shubbâk!** Open the window!; **sakkir ish-shubbâk** Close the window!; **khalli ish-shubbâk maftûH** Leave the window open!

shubbâk tzâkir *shubbâk tezâkir* ticket window

shûfi? (Syr.) What is going on?

shuHna cargo

shukr thanks

shukran thank you

shumre (Syr.) fennel

shûne (Egypt.) barn

shuRl job

shuRl pl. ishRâl business

shuRl pl. ishRâl, shRâl (the latter Syr. only) work (n.)

shurTa (Syr.) police; **markaz ish-shurTa** police station

shuwaiye shuwaiye! (Egypt.) slowly!

shwai shwai! (Syr.) slowly!

shwaiyi *shuwaiye* a little bit

si'r rate of exchange, set price

sibâHa swimming

sîd gentleman
Sidq sincerity
Sidr breast, chest
Sifa description
Sifa pl. Sifât quality
Sifr zero
sigâra pl. sagâ'ir cigarette
siggil register (v.)
sigill (Egypt.) record, register (v.)
sign (Egypt.) jail, prison
SiH'Ha hygiene
SiH'Hi healthy, sanitary
Sihr (Egypt.) son-in-law
Sihr pl. aShâr brother-in-law
siHr sorcery
sijill (Syr.) record, register (v.)
sijjâdi (Syr.) carpet
sijn (Syr.) jail, prison
sikket il-Hadîd railway
sikki (Syr.) plough (n.)
sikki *sikka* coin
sikkîn, sikkîni *sikkîna* pl. skâkîn *sekâkîn* knife
sikrân (Syr.) drunk
silâH pl. isliHa *asliHa* weapon
silfi *silfa* sister-in-law
silk (Egypt.) wire
silk cable
silsila chain

simi' an hear from
simi' hear, learn
simij (Syr.) awkward
simm poison (n.)
simsâr pl. samasra (Egypt.) broker
simsim sesame
sîna Sinai
Sîni porcelain, china
sini *sana* pl. sinîn, sanawât year; **is-sini, has-sini** *is-sana di* this year; **sint ij-jâyi** *is-sana ig-gâi'a* next year
sinima movie theater
sinn il-fîl ivory
sinn pl. snân *sinân* tooth
sint il-mâdyi, sint il- ma'Dit (Syr.) last year
siqâyi *siqâya* irrigation
sirqa theft
sirr pl. isrâr secret (n.)
Sirrâf (Syr.) money changer
sirri secret (adj.)
Sît reputation
sitâra (Egypt.) curtain
sitt grandmother, lady
siTTa'sh *sittâsher* sixteen
sitti *sitta* six
sittîn sixty
sittmîyi (Syr.) six hundred
SiyâH cry (n.)

siyâHa tourism
siyâHi touristic
Siyâm (Syr.) fast, abstinence
skamli (Syr.) stool
smîk thick
Snaubar (Syr.) pine
Sôfar (Egypt.) whistle (v.)
Sôm (Egypt.) fast, abstinence
Sôt (Egypt.) voice
sû tafâhum misunderstanding
Su'ûbe hardship
Su'ûbi *Su'ûba* difficulty
su'âl pl. is'ili *as'ila* question
sub'emîya (Egypt.) seven hundred
Subâ' (Egypt.) pl. aSâbî' finger
Subbair *Subbêr, Sabbâra* cactus
SubH morning; **iS-SubH** in the morning
Sudfi *Sudfa* chance
Sûf wool; **min Sûf** woolen
Sûfi mystic
sufra dining table
sufragi (Egypt.) waiter
sufraji (Syr.) waiter
sufûf (Syr.) powder
sujuqq *suguqq* (coll.) sausage(s)
sukhn hot
sukhûni *sukhûna* fever
sukkân population
sukkar sugar

sukut (Egypt.) to be silent
sukût silence (n.)
sulaHfât turtle
SulH peace, reconciliation
sullam (Syr.) pl. slâlîm ladder, stairs
sullam mutaHarrik *sillim mutaHarrik* escalator
sulTânîya (Egypt.) dish
sulTâniyi *sulTâniye* bowl
sumk thickness
sûq pl. iswâq market
sûq sauda *sûq sôda* black market
suqf (Egypt.) ceiling
suqqâTa (Egypt.) latch
sûr pl. aswâr rampart, wall (around a town)
sur'a speed (n.)
Sûra pl. Suwar photograph, picture, portrait
surûr joy
sûrya Syria
sûs licorice
sûsta zip
suttemîya (Egypt.) six hundred
suwâri *iswîra* pl. asâwîr bracelet
syâsi *siyâsa* politics

t/T

t'aiyan (Syr.) to be nominated
t'ajjab (Syr.) to be astonished
t'allam (Syr.) learn

t'auwad 'ala *it'awad 'ala* get accustomed to

t'akh'khar (Syr.) to be late

t'ammal (Syr.) hope (v.)

t'assaf 'ala (Syr.) regret (v.)

tâ in order to

Ta"am feed

ta'ab (Syr.) tire (v., trans.)

ta'âfa to be healthy

Ta'âm (Syr.) food

ta'assar stumble

ta'auwuq (Syr.) disability

ta'b *ta'ab* fatigue

ta'bân (Egypt.) tired, weary

ta'bân snake

ta'lab pl. ta'âlib fox

ta'lîm (Egypt.) teaching

Ta'mi *Ta'ma* taste (of s.th.)

ta'rifa tariff

ta'yîn appointment, assignment

ta'zîye (Egypt.) consolation

          muraiyih comfortable

ta'khîra delay (n.)

Tab' edition

taba' follow

Taba' print (v.)

tabâ'ad 'an (Syr.) keep far from

tabaiyan (Syr.) seem

Tabakh cook (v.)

Tabaqa floor, story
Tabaqa social class
tabarTal to receive a bribe
tabashlul (Syr.) embarrassment
tabassam (Syr.) smile (v.)
Tabbâ' printer (profession)
Tâbi' il-barîd pl. Tawâbi' il-barîd postage stamp
tâbi' pl. taba'a partisan, follower
Tâbi' pl. Tawâbi' stamp (n.)
Tabî'a nature
Tabî'i natural
Tabîb asnân dentist
Tabîb pl. aTibba physician
Tabkh, Tabîkh cooked
Tabl drum
tâbût coffin
tadfiya radiator, heating
Tafa extinguish
taff spit (v.)
Taffâya (Egypt.) ashtray
tafsîl pl. tafsîlât detail; **bit-tafsîl** detailed
tafsîli detailed
tafsîr explanation
tagassus (Egypt.) espionage
tâgir (Egypt.) pl. tuggâr merchant
tagriba (Egypt.) experience
tâh (Egypt.) lose one's way
TaH'Han grind

Tah'har circumcise
taham accuse s.b.
TaHan grind
TaHîn (Syr.) flour (n.)
tahrîb contraband
taHt (Egypt.) down, below
taHt il-amr (I am) at your service
taHt under (prep.)
taHtâni (Egypt.) lower, under
TâHûn (f.) TawâHîn mill
taHwîTa (Egypt.) amulet
Taila', Talla' bring out
Tair *Têr* pl. Tiyûr bird
Taiyâra *Tâ'ira* airplane
Taiyib alive
Taiyib good, well
tâj *tâg* pl. tîjân *tîgân* crown
tajâsar (Syr.) dare
tajassus (Syr.) espionage
tâjir (Syr.) pl. tujjâr merchant
takallam talk (v.)
takbîr sûra blow up a photo
takhâlaf (Syr.) disagree
takhîn thick
takhmîn about, near to
takht throne
taksi cab
takyîf air conditioning

Tala' il-ma'âsh (Syr.) retire

Talab application, demand, petition, request

Talab apply, ask, ask for, demand; **biTlub zyâdi**
       betiTlub ziyâde you ask too much

Talab lil-maHkama (Egypt.) summon to court

talabbuk fil-mi'di *talabbuk fil-mi'da* indigestion
       resulting from overeating

talaffuz pronunciation

Talâq divorce (n.)

talâqa (Syr.) meet each other

talât three

talaus pollution

talfan *talfin* telephone (v.)

talg (Egypt.) ice

Talî'a vanguard

Tâlib pl. Tullâb student

tâlit f. tâlti *talta* third

talj (Syr.) ice, snow

tall (Syr.) pl. tlâl hill

tallâga (Egypt.) refrigerator

Tallaq (with acc.) divorce

talmîz pl. talamza, talâmîz pupil

tamâm exactly, quite right

taman (Syr.) price (n.); **kam tamano?** What's
       the price?; **haida taman fâHish** That is
       an excessive price. **mâ 'indak minno
       bi-taman arkhaS?** Don't you have s.th.
       at a cheaper price?

tamar hindi tamarind
Tamâtim (coll.) (Egypt.) tomato(es)
Tamî' (Syr.) greedy
tâmin f. tâmni *tamna* eighth
tamîn precious
tamlîq flattery
tamm finish (v., intrans.)
tamm to be over, to have finished
Tammâ' (Egypt.) greedy
tamman *tammin* estimate (n.)
tammûz (Syr.) July
tamr dried date
tamsîl representation
tanabbu' iT-Taqs weather forecast
tanaffus breathing, respiration
tanaffus Sinâ'i artificial respiration
tanek (Syr.) tin
tangara (Egypt.) pl. tenâgir pot
tanhîda sigh (n.)
tâni (Egypt.) different
tâni f. tânyi *tânye* second
tâni marra *tâni marra* again, once more
tanjara (Syr.) pl. tnâjir pot
Tâq suffer, tolerate
Tâqa strength (to endure s.th.)
taqaddam precede in rank, progress
taqaddum progress (n.)
taqdîm personal introduction

taqi pl. itqya pious
taqîl pl. tiqâl heavy
Tâqiye *Tâqiya* cap
taqrîban around, near to
Taqs weather
taqsîm (Egypt.) division
taqwîm (Syr.) calendar
Târ (v.) fly
Tarabêza (Egypt.) table
Tarad (Egypt.) chase, drive away, dismiss
Taraf pl. aTrâf edge
TaraH subtract
tarak let alone, let go, leave
taraqqi promotion
tarbîya (Egypt.) education
Tard pl. Turûd parcel, package
Tarfa tamarisk
targama (Egypt.) translation
targil (Egypt.) stool
targim (Egypt.) translate
Tari fresh, tender
târîkh date (time)
târîkh history
Tarîq 'âm highway
Tarîq pl. Turuq, Turuqât way road; **biwaddi haT-Tarîq la…?** *biwaddi iT-Tarîq di li…?* Does this ~ lead to…?
Tarîqa way, manner

tarjam (Syr.) translate
tarjimi (Syr.) translation
Tarraz embroider
tartîb (Egypt.) order, arrangement
tartîl hymn (rel.)
tarzi (Egypt.) tailor
taSarruf behavior
taSdîrât exports (n.)
tashannuj *tashannug* cramp
tasHîH (Egypt.) improvement
tâsi' f. *tâs'a* ninth
taslîH (Egypt.) improvement, repair
taslîm submission, handing over
tasliya entertainment
tasliyi, tislâyi consolation
taSrîH declaration
taT'îm vaccination
taTrîz embroidery
Taula backgammon
Tauli (Syr.) table
Tauq *Tôq* necklace
tauqît maHalli local time
tauqît Saifi *tauqît sêfi* summer time
taur *tôr* pl. tîrân bull, ox
tauSîya (Egypt.) order (n.) (of goods, etc.),
         recommendation
Tauwal last long
Tâwa' obey
tâwab (Syr.) yawn

tawâDu' humility

Tawîl middle finger

Tawîl pl. Tuwâl tall, long (adj.)

Tâwûs peacock

Tayarân *Tairân* flight

Tayyâr pilot

tazkaret busTa postcard

teftîsh il-'afsh luggage control

telâta (Egypt.) three

telatâsher (Egypt.) thirteen

telâtîn (Egypt.) thirty

telg (Egypt.) snow

tell (Egypt.) pl. tulûl hill

temantâsher (Egypt.) eighteen

temanya (Egypt.) eight

tembel (Egypt.) lazy

temen (Egypt.) eight

temen (Egypt.) price (n.); **kam temeno**? What's the price?; **di temen fâHish** That is an excessive price. **mâ 'andak shi minno bi-temen arkhaS?** Don't you have s.th. at a cheaper price?

temen id-dukhûl (Egypt.) admission fee

teqîl (Egypt.) burdensome

tezkira (Egypt.) pl. tezâkir ticket

tezkira râyih gâiy (Egypt.) return ticket

tfaDDal (Syr.) please (to a male, speaker offering s.th.); **tfaDDal fût** please enter

tfaDDal (Syr.) to have the kindness

tHâdas (Syr.) chat (v.)

tHammam (Syr.) bathe, take a bath

tHarrak (Syr.) move (v., intrans.)

tHassan (Syr.) improve (intrans.)

ti'bân (Syr.) tired, weary

ti'bân samak (Egypt.) eel

ti'ib tire (v., intrans.)

ti'lîm (Syr.) teaching

Tibb medicine, medical science

Tibbi medical

tifâf, tifâfa (Egypt.) spittle

tiffâH (coll.) apple(s)

Tifl pl. aTfâl small child, infant

tîfûs typhus

tigâra (Egypt.) commerce, trade

tihdîd menace (n.)

tiHtâni (Syr.) lower

tijâra *tigâra* commerce, trade

tijribi (Syr.) experience

tikram! willingly, certainly

tilfân *talfân* blunt

Tili' climb

Tili' come up, land, mount, rise (v., sun, moon)
> **aimta btiTla' ish-shams?** *emta tiTla' ish-shams?* When does the sun rise? **aimta byiTla' il-qamar?** *emta yiTla' il-qamar?* When does the moon rise?

Tili' id-damm (Syr.) it is bleeding

Tili' il-ma'âsh (Egypt.) retire
tilifizyôn television
tilifôn (Egypt.) phone call
tilifôn telephone (n.)
tilifôni by telephone
tilîfûn 'âm pay phone
tillâja (Syr.) refrigerator
timm (Syr.) mouth
timsâH pl. tmâsîH *temâsîH* crocodile
timsâl pl. tamasîl sculpture, statue
tîn (coll.) fig(s)
tîn mud
tiql (Syr.) weight
tiql gravity
tiqlîd rkhîS *taqlîd rikhîS* imitation
tiqsîm (Syr.) division
tir'a canal
tirâs terrace
tirbi (Syr.) tomb
tirbi *turba* cemetery
tirbyi, tirbâyi (Syr.) education
tirtîb (Syr.) order, arrangement
tiRyîr *taRyîr* change, alteration
tis'a nine
tis'în ninety
tis'mîyi (Syr.) nine hundred
tisaTa'sh *tis'atâsher* nineteen
tisHîH (Syr.) improvement

---

tishrîn il-auwal (Syr.) October
tishrîn it-tâni (Syr.) November
tislîH (Syr.) improvement, repair
titâwib (Egypt.) yawn
tiThîr *taThîr* circumcision
tizkri (Syr.) pl. tzâkir ticket
tizkri rauHa wa-rujû' (Syr.) return ticket
tjauwaz (Syr.) marry (intrans.)
tkaffal 'an (Syr.) guarantee (v.)
tkallam (Syr.) speak
tlâti (Syr.) three
tlâtîn (Syr.) thirty
tlâtmîyi (Syr.) three hundred
tlaTTa'sh (Syr.) thirteen
tlazzaq (Syr.) to be stuck
Tlû' ish-shams (Syr.) sunrise
tmakh'khaT (Syr.) blow one's nose
tmânîn *temânîn* eighty
tmanmîyi (Syr.) eight hundred
tmânyi, tmâni (Syr.) eight
tminTa'sh (Syr.) eighteen
tnaddam 'ala (Syr.) repent s.th.
tnah'had (Syr.) sigh (v.)
tnain f. tintain (Syr.) two
Tnâsh (Syr.) twelve
tôrta (Syr.) cake
tqâTal (Syr.) fight
tqîl (Syr.) burdensome
trâb (Syr.) dust, earth, mold, dust, soil

tRassal (Syr.) bathe, take a bath
tRassal (Syr.) wash oneself
tSalaH (Syr.) to be reconciled
tsamma (Syr.) to be nominated
tsamma' (Syr.) listen
tshakka min *itshakka min* complain of
tshakkar (Syr.) thank
Tufaili *Tufêli* parasite
Tûfân deluge
tuhmi *tuhma* pl. tuham accusation, mistrust
Tuhûr circumcision
tukhmi *tukhma* indigestion
tukhn thickness
Tûl 'umri (Egypt.) in my whole life
Tûl length
Tûl throughout
tultemîya (Egypt.) three hundred
Tulû' ish-shams (Egypt.) sunrise
tûm *tôm* garlic
tumm (Syr.) mouth
tumnemîya (Egypt.) eight hundred
tuql (Egypt.) weight
turâb (Egypt.) dust, earth, mold, dust, soil
turbe (Egypt.) tomb
turki pl. atrâk Turkish
turs, tirs shield
turshe *turshi* (coll.) pickles
tus'emîya (Egypt.) nine hundred
tûSyi (Syr.) order (n.) (for goods)

tûSyi (Syr.) recommendation
tuwalitt toilet
twaDDa *itwaDDa* perform religious ablutions
twakkal 'ala (Syr.) trust in
twaqqa! (Syr.) Take care!
tzakkar (Syr.) remember; **mâ bitzakkar ismo** I
    cannot remember his name.

u

û'a! Look out! Watch out! Take care!
u'qud! Sit down!
ûbâr caper
ûDa pl. uwaD (Syr.) room
ûdit sufra (Syr.) dining table
udn (Syr.) pl. dainât ear
ufq *ufuq* horizon
ugra (Egypt.) fare, lease, wages, pay, rent
ugrat busTa (Egypt.) postage
ujâq (Syr.) fireplace
ujra (Syr.) rent, fee
ujret iT-Tarîq (Syr.) fare
ukht pl. akhawât *ukhwât* sister
umm pl. ummhât *ummahât* mother
umma pl. umam nation
ummi illiterate
urgun organ (mus.)
urguwâni (Egypt.) purple (adj.)

urjuwâni (Syr.) purple (adj.)
uRnîyi pl. aRâni song
urubba Europe
usbû'a pl. esâbî' week
usbû'i weekly
uSbur shwaiyi! (Syr.) Wait a little!
uskut! Shut up!
ustâd (Egypt.) pl. asatza professor
ustâz (Syr.) pl. asatza professor

W

wa and
wa'ad (v.) promise
wa'd promise (n.)
wa'z sermon
wa'in (Syr.) although, even if
waafiq suit (v.); **haida mâ bîwâfiqni** *di mâ yifâwiqnîsh* That does not suit me.
waD' situation
waDa' lay, put, set, put, place
wadda lead, send
wadda wara send for
wâdi in-nîl Nile Valley
wâdi pl. widyân valley; **wâdi in-nîl** Nile Valley; **wâdi il-mulûk** Valley of the Kings
wâDiH clear, indisputable, distinct
wafa fidelity

waffaq match (v.)

waffar save, spare, economize

wafr pl. wufurât savings

waga' (Egypt.) pain

wagh (Egypt.) face (n.)

wâgib 'ala (Egypt.) must; **wâgib 'alêk ti'mil di** You
       must do that.

wâHa oasis

waHdânîyi *waHdânîya* loneliness

waHdi *waHda* loneliness

wâHid alone; **waHdi** I alone; **waHdak** you (m.) alone

wâHid f. waHdi *waHda* one

waHîd sole, single

wâhidan wâhidan one by one

waHl mud

waHsh pl. wuHûsh wild animal

waHshi *waHsha* desolation, solitude

waHshi wild (animal)

wain (Syr.) where

wain baddo ykûn? (Syr.) Where may that be?

waja' (Syr.) pain

waja' râs *waga' râs* headache

waja' *waga'* (n.) ache

wâjbi *wâjiba* pl. wâjbât *wâgibât* duty, obligation

wâjib 'ala (Syr.) must; **wâjib 'alaik innak ta'mil
       haida** You must do that.

wâjib *wâgib* due

wâjib *wâgib* duty, obligation

wakaf (Syr.) leak (v.)

wakâle *wikâla* agency

wakf leak (n.)

wakhim nasty, dirty

wakhm dirt

wakhri late

wakîl da'âwi solicitor

wakîl pl. wukala agent

wala (Egypt.) or

wala' (Egypt.) burn (intrans.)

walad pl. ûlâd boy, child

waldi *walda* mother

wali pl. ûliya Muslim saint

wallâh (Egypt.) by God

wallâhi (Syr.) by God

wan-nabi *wan-nebi* by the life of the prophet

waq'a fall (n.)

waqa' (Syr.) happen

waqa' fall (v.)

waqaf (Syr.) stop (v., intrans.)

waqaf 'ala to get inside, into

waqaf stand (v.)

wâqe' (Syr.) fact

wâqi'a *waq'a* pl. waqâyi' *waqâ'i* event

waqqaf arrest (v.)

waqqaf stop (v., trans.)

waqt time

wara after, behind

wara ba'dhon *wara ba'duhum* one after the other

wara min behind (prep.)

wara past (pron. loc.)

waraa- after, behind

waram (Syr.) swell

waram pl. aurâm swelling, tumor

waraq 'ainab *waraq 'ênab* vine leaves

waraq paper

waraq tuwalitt toilet paper

waraqa pl. ûrâq *aurâq* sheet of paper, leaf, label,
           card

ward (coll.) rose(s)

wardi pink

wârim swollen

wâris pl. warâsi heir

warra show (v.); **warrîni** show me

warrad supply (v.)

warsha workshop

wasa'a space

waSaf describe

wasakh dirt

waSal join

wasâyil il-muwâslât *wasâ'il il-muwâslât* means of
           transportation

waSf description; **waSf tafsîli** detailed description

waSf prescription

waSfa recipe

washwash whisper (v.)

waSi guardian
wâsi' wide
waSîyi *waSîya* will, testament
waSl 'ala, waSl 'an receipt
waSl junction
wasl min' il-Haml contraceptive
waSSa order (goods, etc.), recommend
wassakh soil (v.)
wasT (Syr.) middle (n.)
waSt *wuSt* center
wâsTa pl. wasâyiT *wasâ'iT* means (n.)
wasTâni (Syr.) middle (adj.)
wasTâni (Syr.) middle finger
waTan home country, native country
waTani national
wâTi low
wazan (Syr.) weigh (v., trans.)
wazâra, wizâra ministry (governmental); **wazâret il-mâliya** Ministry of Finance; **wazâret id-dâkhiliya** Ministry of the Interior; **wazâret il-'adlîye** *wazâret il-Huqûq* Ministry of Justice; **wazâret il-khârijiya** *wazâret il-khârigiya* Foreign Ministry
wazîr pl. wuzarâ minister
wazn weight (n.)
wazno its weight is …
wazz (coll.) (Syr.) goose (geese)
wen (Egypt.) although, even if

wet ball (v.)

weyâ ... weyâ ... (Egypt.) either ... or ...

weyâmâ ... weyâmâ ... (Egypt.) either ... or ...

wi and

widn (Egypt.) ear pl. ûidân

wiHyâak *waHyâtak* by your life

wiji' *wigi'* (v.) ache; **râsi byûja'ni** *râsi btûga'ni* my
      head aches

wijid *wigid* exist

wikâlit siyâhiya travel agency

wikr nest

wilâyi *wilâya* province

willa (Syr.) or

willa otherwise

win (Egypt.) although

wiqi' (Egypt.) happen

wiqif (Egypt.) stop (v., intrans.)

wirim (Egypt.) swell

wirti *wirâsa* heritage

wisâda pillow

wish (Syr.) front, face (n.)

wishâH scarf

wisikh (Egypt.) soiled (v.)

wiSil arrive, get to

wiSiya (Egypt.) testament, last will

wuDû' *tawaDDi* ablution

wujûd *wugûd* existence

wuqûd fuel

wuqûf 'ala insight into
wusikh (Syr.) soiled (v.)
wusikh *wisikh* dirty
wuSla muhaaya'a adapter
wusT (Egypt.) middle (n.)
wusTâni (Egypt.) middle (adj.)
wusTâni (Egypt.) middle finger
wuSûl arrival

y

yâ 'aini my dear
yâ … yâ … either … or …
yâ dûb (Egypt.) scarcely
yâ khasâra! (Egypt.) What a pity!
yâ laTîf oh God!
yâ or
yâ rabb Oh God!
yâ sîdi Sir
ya'ni namely
ya'ni that is to say, that means
yâbis dry (adj.)
yad pl. iyâdi *ayâdi* hand
yahûdi pl. yahûd Jew, Jewish
yâkhûr (Syr.) stable (n.)
yalla! Now then! Come on!
yâmâ … yâmâ … (Egypt.) either … or …
yamîn (Syr.) oath

yamîn right (adj.); **'al yamîn** on the right hand; **'ala
       îdak il-yamîn** on your right hand

yanâyir (Egypt.) January

yâqa (Egypt.) collar

yâsimîn jasmine

yasîr pl. yusara captive

yatîm pl. îtâm orphan

yaum ij-jum'a (Syr.) Friday

yaum il-aHad, yaum il-Hadd (Syr.) Sunday

yaum il-arba'a (Syr.) Wednesday

yaum il-khamîs (Syr.) Thursday

yaum is-sabt (Syr.) Saturday

yaum it-tlâti (Syr.) Tuesday

yaum ittnain (Syr.) Monday

yaum *yôm* pl. iyâm day

yaumi *yômi* daily

yemîn (Egypt.) oath

yibis (Syr.) dry (v., intrans.)

yigfil (Egypt.) shy

yijfil (Syr.) shy

yimma ... yimma ... (Syr.) either ... or ...

yimma or

yinshâf visible

yôm il-arba'a, l-arba'a (Egypt.) Wednesday

yôm il-etnên, l-etnên (Egypt.) Monday

yôm il-gum'a (Egypt.) Friday

yôm il-Hadd, yôm il-Hadd (Egypt.) Sunday

yôm il-khamîs (Egypt.) Thursday

yôm il-talât (Egypt.) Tuesday
yôm is-sabt (Egypt.) Saturday
yûja' *yûga'* it hurts
yûlie (Egypt.) July
yunâni pl. yunân Greek
yûniye (Egypt.) June

Z

za'farân saffron
za'l temper (anger)
za'lân min (Egypt.) tired of, annoyed with
za'qa shout (n.)
zabâdi (Egypt.) yogurt
zabbâl garbage man
zâbit bôlis police officer
zâbit il-murûr traffic officer
zâbiT pl. zubbâT officer
zaffi (Syr.) wedding procession
zagar (Egypt.) scold s.b.
zâher (Syr.) evident
zâhir clear, indisputable, distinct
zâhiran (Egypt.) evidently
zaHmi *zaHma* crowd
zaHmit il-muwâSalât traffic jam
zahra pl. zhûr *zuhûr* flower
zai (Egypt.) as, like, similar
zai mâ terîd (Egypt.) as you like

zaibaq *zêbaq* mercury
zail (Syr.) appendix (of a book)
zait (Syr.) oil (food)
zait simsim (Syr.) sesame oil
zaitûn *zêtûn* (coll.) olive(s); **zait zaitûn** *zêt zêtûn*
      olive oil
zaitûni *zaitûna* olive tree
zaiyan *zaiyin* adorn, decorate
zajar (Syr.) scold s.b.
zakar mention (v.)
zakhîra (Syr.) ammunition
zâlim cruel
zalRûT (Syr.) pl. zalâRîT shout of joy
zalzali (Syr.) earthquake
zamân (Syr.) time
zamân ktîr *zemân ketîr* a long time
zamân Tawîl *zemân Tawîl* a long time
zamb pl. zunûb fault
zân (Syr.) weigh (v., trans.)
Zann (Egypt.) pl. Zunûn opinion, belief, suspicion
Zann think, suppose, suspect (v.)
zâq taste (v.)
zâqi (Syr.) tasty
zaqq push (v., door)
zâr visit (v.)
zarâ'a agriculture
zarâfi *zarâfa* giraffe
zarf pl. zrûf *zurûf* circumstance

Zarf pl. Zurûf envelope
zarî'a seed
zarîf (Egypt.) kind (adj.)
zarîf nice, pretty, well-mannered
zarRûTa (Egypt.) pl. zarâRît shout of joy
zât self
zâti personal
zauba'a (Syr.) storm, thunderstorm
zauba'a shedîda hurricane
zaujit il-ibn *zôgit il-ibn* daughter-in-law
zauq (Syr.) taste (of s.b.)
zauwaj (Syr.) marry (trans.)
zauwig (Egypt.) marry (trans.)
zâwiyi *zâwya* angle
zâwyi *zâwiya* chapel
zâyid *zâ'id* abundant, excessive
zâyida dûdiya *zâ'ida dôdiya* appendix (anat.)
zbîb (coll.) (Syr.) raisin(s)
zebîb (coll.) (Egypt.) raisin(s)
zeffa (Egypt.) wedding procession
zemân (Egypt.) time
zêt (Egypt.) oil (food)
zêt simsim (Egypt.) sesame oil
zewâg (Egypt.) marriage
zi'il to be vexed
zi'îq shouting
zi'lân min (Syr.) tired of, annoyed with
zi'lân min *za'lân min* bored of

zibâla rubbish, garbage
zibdi *zibde* butter
zikr mention (n.)
ZilHifi *ZilHifa* tortoise
zilzâl (Eygpt.) earthquake
zinjfîl (Egypt.) ginger
zirr *zurâr* pl. zrâr button
ziwâj (Syr.) marriage
ziwâq (Egypt.) make-up
ziyâdi bi *ziyâda bi* one ... too much
ziyâdi biktîr *ziyâda biketîr* far too much
ziyâdi *ziyâda* abundance, too much
ziyâra visit (n.)
zôba'a (Egypt.) storm, thunderstorm
zôq (Egypt.) taste (of s.b.)
zRîr (Syr.) pl. zRâr little, small, young
Zufr pl. aZfâr (Syr.) fingernail
zulm oppression, tyranny
zûm (Syr.) juice
zumurrud emerald
zuqâq dead-end alley
zuqâq pl. zuqâqât lane
zuRaiyar (Egypt.) pl. zuRaiyerîn, zuRâr young,
                small, little

'

'abar cross, pass (v.)

'abd pl. 'abîd slave

'abîT (Egypt.) idiot

'ad again

'ada give

'adad figure, number (n.)

'aDal (coll.) muscle(s)

'adam annihilate

'add bite (of insects)

'add count, enumerate, number

'addâd il-amyâl mileage

'âdi *'âda* pl. 'âdât use, habit

'âdi (adj.) common, usual, ordinary

'âdil fair, frank, just

'adl justice

'aDm pl. 'iDam bone

'ads, 'ades (coll.) lentil(s)

'adu pl. a'âdi enemy

'aDu pl. a'Da limb

'aDw pl. a'Dâ member

'afîf chaste

'afsh luggage; **'afsh zâyid** *'afsh zâ'id* excess
            baggage

'agab (Egypt.) please (v.) **di ktîr bi'gibni ketîr.** That
            pleases me very much.

'agal (Egypt.) hurry (v. or n.)

'agala (Egypt.) bicycle

'agala (Egypt.) pl. **'agel** wheel

'agala ziyâda (Egypt.) spare tire

'agel (Egypt.) haste (n.)

'aggin (Eygpt.) dough

'agîb (Egypt.) wonderful

'agiba (Egypt.) wonder

'âgiz (Egypt.) disabled

'âgiz 'an (Egypt.) incapable of doing s.th.

'agr (Egypt.) unripe

'agûz (Egypt.) old, elderly

'agûza (Egypt.) old woman

'agz (Egypt.) disability

'aib (Syr.) pl. **'iyûb** shame, vice

'âib pl. **'uzzâb** single, unmarried

'ain (Syr.) pl. **'uyûn** eye

'ainab *'ênab* (coll.) grape(s)

'aiyash feed

'aiyyina sample; **'ayyinit qumâsh** a cloth sample

'ajab (Syr.) please (v.); **haida bya'jibni.** That pleases
          me very much.

'ajal (Syr.) haste, hurry (v. or n.)

'ajîb (Syr.) wonderful

'ajîbi (Syr.) miracle, wonder

'ajîn (Syr.) dough

'âjiz 'an (Syr.) incapable

'ajûz (Syr.) old, elderly

'ajûza (Syr.) old woman

'al faur (Syr.) suddenly

'al qiyâs (Eygpt.) regular

'al qyâs (Syr.) regular

'ala on (contracted with the following article) 'ala
    il-kursi = 'al kursi on the chair

'ala against, over

'ala îdak ish-shmâl *'ala îdak esh-shemâl* on the
    left hand

'ala kêfak as you please

'ala khâTrak as you please

'ala l-aqall (Egypt.) at least

'ala malak! (Syr.) slowly!

'ala râsi willingly, certainly

'ala shân (Egypt.) for, in favor of

'ala shân (Egypt.) in order to

'ala shân (Egypt.) in order, that

'ala shân êh (Egypt.) why

'alaiyi *'alêye* I have to do

'âlaj (Syr.) remedy (v.)

'alaj *'alig* cure (v.)

'alak (Syr.) chew

'alam flag

'alâmât murûr traffic signals

'alâmi *'alâma* pl. alâmât sign mark (n.)

'âlami secular

'âli high, loud

'âlig (Egypt.) remedy (v.)

'alîl sick

'âlim pl. 'ulamâ scholar

'âlim wise

'âlit tanDîf kahrabâ'iya vacuum cleaner

'allam (Syr.) teach

'allaq la *'allaq li* feed

'almahl (Syr.) slow

'al-Râlib usually

'am bitshatti (Syr.) It is raining.

'am btitlij id-dinyi (Syr.) It is snowing.

'âm il-auwil *'âm il-auwal* last year

'amal (Egypt.) do

'amal pl. a'mâl action

'amal guhdo (Egypt.) trouble oneself

'amal kalâm (Egypt.) quarrel (v.)

'amâmi (Syr.) pl. 'amâyim turban

'amâr pl. 'amârât building

'amâra fleet

'âmil tilîfûn operator

'amm pl. 'umûmi *a'mâm* uncle (father's brother)

'ammar (Syr.) build

'ammi *'amma* aunt (on the father's side)

'amûd pl. 'awâmid column, pillar

'an gadd (Egypt.) in earnest

'an jadd (Syr.) in earnest

'anaq embrace, hug (v.)

'and (Egypt.) at, near, by

'anid obstinate

'ankabût spider

'anqûd bunch of grapes, etc.

'aqad knot, tie (n.)

'aqîl reasonable

'aql reason, sense, intellect

'aqrab pl. 'aqârib scorpion

'arabaji, 'arbaji *'arbagi* coachman

'arabâyi *'arabiya* carriage

'arabâyi, 'arabîyi *'arabîya* coach

'arabi Arabic; **shû ism haida bil-'arabi?** *ismo ê bil 'arabi?* What is this called in Arabic?

'arabi pl. 'arab Arab

'arabiya (Egypt.) car

'araq perspiration, sweat

'ard (Syr.) breadth

'arD width

'arg (Egypt.) lameness

'arîd broad, large

'arîs pl. 'irsân bridegroom

'arj (Syr.) lameness

'arraf introduce

'ar-râs wil-'ain *'ar-râs wal-'ên* with the greatest pleasure

'arûsa doll

'arûsa pl. 'arâyis *'arâ'is* bride

'aryân (Egypt.) naked

'asal honey

'aSar press (v.)

'aSâyi *'aSâya* pl. 'iSi walking stick

'âsh live

'asha dinner, supper
'ashara (Egypt.) ten
'âshir f. 'ashra tenth
'ashîyi (Syr.) in the evening
'ashra (Syr.) ten
'aSîr (Egypt.) juice
'askari soldier
'asker pl. 'asâkir army
'ata give
'atab (Syr.) reproach (v.)
'atabi *'ataba* threshold
'aTas *'aTTas* sneeze
'atîq pl. 'itiq old, ancient
'aTîyi *'aTa* gift
'aTshân (Egypt.) thirsty
'auwaD 'ala *'auwaD li* indemnify s.b.
'auwaq prevent
'awa bark (v.)
'ayân (Egypt.) ill
'âyli *'êla* pl. 'iyâl family
'âz need, want, wish (v.)
'azâb bother
'azal (Syr.) dismiss
'âzi *'âza* need (n.)
'âzif musician
'azîm considerable, huge, powerful
'azîz dear
'azlaT f. zalTa bald
'azzam exaggerate

'azzar (Syr.) insult (v.)

'azzil (Egypt.) move (house)

'ên (Egypt.) pl. 'uyûn eye

'ibrâni Hebrew

'îd il-fiSiH Easter

'îd il-mîlâd Christmas

'îd mîlâd birthday

'îd, 'aîd pl. i'yâd feast

'ifin putrid

'ijl *'igl* calf (animal)

'ikir dull

'ilâg (Egypt.) remedy (n.)

'ilâj (Syr.) remedy (n.)

'ilba (Egypt.) pl. 'ilab can (n.)

'ilm in-nafs psychology

'ilm pl. 'ulûm science, knowledge

'imd (Syr.) big branch

'imil (Syr.) do, make

'imil juhdo (Syr.) trouble oneself

'imil kalâm (Syr.) quarrel (v.)

'imma (Egypt.) pl. 'imâm turban

'inâd obstinacy

'ind (Syr.) at, near, by, with

'iqd (Syr.) necklace

'irif know, recognize

'iriq perspire; **ana 'irqân ktîr** *ana 'arqân ketîr* I am
      perspiring a lot.

'irq pl. 'urûq vein

'irs (Syr.) wedding

'iryân (Syr.) naked
'ish'sh nest
'ish'sha (Egypt.) hut
'ishb grass
'ishq amorousness
'ishrîn twenty
'itâb reproach(n.)
'itib (Egypt.) reproach (v.)
'itm (Syr.) dark, obscure
'iTr perfume
'iTshân (Syr.) thirsty
'ittâl (Syr.) carrier, luggage porter
'iwaD (Syr.) for, in place of
'iwaD instead
'izza pride, self-esteem
'ubudiya slavery
'ûd harp, lute
'uDw pl. a'Dâ' organ (anat.)
'uDwiya membership
'ukkkâzi *'ukkkâza* pl. 'akâkîz crutch
'ulbi *'ilba* pl. 'ulab *'ilab* box, can
'ullaiqa *'ullêqa* bush
'ulûw height
'umr age (of human beings)
'umr life
'umûmi general, public; **'umûman** in general
'unq neck
'unwân pl. 'anawîn address

'uqab (Egypt.) pl. 'aqîba eagle
'uqd (Egypt.) necklace
'uqdi *'uqda* knot (n.)
'urd (Egypt.) breadth
'urD width
'uSfûr pl. 'asâfîr sparrow
'uTla vacation
'uzr excuse, pretext

ARABIC LANGUAGE TITLES
FROM HIPPOCRENE

DICTIONARIES

**ARABIC-ENGLISH/ENGLISH-ARABIC
STANDARD DICTIONARY**
John Wortabet and Harvey Porter
• **900 pages** • **5½ x 8½** • **ISBN 0-7818-0383-7** • **W**
• **$24.95pb** • **(195)**

**EASTERN ARABIC-ENGLISH/
ENGLISH-EASTERN ARABIC
DICTIONARY AND PHRASEBOOK**
for the Spoken Arabic of Jordan, Lebanon,
Palestine/Israel and Syria
This book provides the traveler to the Eastern Mediter-
ranean with a practical aid for communicating in
Arabic. It is based on the spoken language widely
understood in Jordan, Lebanon, Palestine/Israel and
Syria.
• **142 pages** • **3¾ x 7** • **ISBN 0-7818-0685-2** • **W**
• **$11.95pb** • **(774)**

**MODERN MILITARY DICTIONARY
ENGLISH-ARABIC/ARABIC-ENGLISH**
Maher S. Kayyali
• **250 pages** • **5½ x 8½** • **ISBN 0-7818-0234-1** • **NA**
• **$14.95pb** • **(214)**

ARABIC FOR CHILDREN

THE CHILDREN'S ILLUSTRATED
ARABIC DICTIONARY
English-Arabic/Arabic-English
With this dictionary for Children, Hippocrene offers a delightful antidote to the assumption that difficult languages cannot be taught in a playful way. Featuring 500 Arabic words in their original spelling along with easy-to-use English pronunciation, this dictionary provides an invaluable basis for learning Arabic at an early age.
- **122 pages • 8½ x 11 • ISBN 0-7818-0709-3 • W**
- **\$14.95hc • (796)**

ARABIC LANGUAGE GUIDES

MASTERING ARABIC
Book and Audio Cassettes
Jane Wightwick and Mahmood Gaafar
- **320 pages • 5¼ x 8¼ • ISBN 0-87052-922-6 • USA**
- **\$14.95pb • (501)**
2 CASSETTES: ISBN 0-87052-984-6 • USA
- **\$12.95 • (507)**

SAUDI ARABIC BASIC COURSE
Margaret K. Omar
- **288 pages • 6½ x 8½ • ISBN 0-7818-0257-1 • W**
- **\$14.95pb • (171)**

ARABIC FOR BEGINNERS
Revised Edition
Syed Ali
• **186 pages • 5¼ x 8¼ • ISBN 0-7818-0841-3 • NA**
• **$11.95pb • (229)**

**ARABIC GRAMMAR FOR THE
WRITTEN LANGUAGE**
G.W. Thatcher
• **560 pages • 5¼ x 8¼ • ISBN 0-87052-101-2 • W**
• **$19.95pb • (397)**

BILINGUAL ARABIC-INTEREST BOOKS

ARABIC PROVERBS
Joseph Hanki
First published in Egypt in 1897, this new addition to the Hippocrene bilingual collection of proverbs contains 600 Arabic proverbs written in romanized colloquial Arabic with side-by-side English translations, and where appropriate, explanations of the custom which gave rise to the proverb.
• **144 pages • 6 x 9 • ISBN 0-7818-0631-3 • W**
• **$11.95pb • (711)**

TREASURY OF ARABIC LOVE: POEMS, QUOTATIONS AND PROVERBS IN ARABIC AND ENGLISH
Edited by Farid Bitar
• **128 pages • 5 x 7 • ISBN 7818-0395-0 • W**
• **$11.95hc • (71)**

ARABIC FIRST NAMES
Out of the extremely rich Arab heritage comes this volume of 600 first names with their meaning and historic origins, ranging from names with religious connotations such as *Abdelhamid*—Servant of the Generous to modern names like *Basma*—Smile.
• **100 pages • 5 x 7 • ISBN 0-7818-0688-7 • W**
• **$11.95hc • (777)**

MIDDLE EASTERN COOKBOOKS FROM HIPPOCRENE

EGYPTIAN COOKING
Samia Abdennour
• **199 pages • 5½ x 8½ • 0-7818-0643-7 • NA**
• **$11.95pb • (727)**

TASTES OF NORTH AFRICA
Recipes from Morocco to the Mediterranean
Sarah Woodward
with Food Photography by Gus Filgate
• **160 pages** • **8½ x 9½** • **23 full page color photographs**
• **ISBN 0-7818-0725-5** • **NA** • **$27.50hc** • **(187)**

All prices are subject to change without prior notice. To order
Hippocrene Books, contact your local bookstore, call (718)
454-2366, or write to: Hippocrene Books, 171 Madison Ave.
New York, NY 10016. Please enclose check or money order
adding $5.00 shipping (UPS) for the first book and $.50 for
each additional title.